GENEVIEVE TAYLOR

SEARED

The ultimate guide to barbecuing meat

Photography by Jason Ingram

Hardie Grant

QUADRILLE

INTRODUCTION

Seared is quite simply about cooking GOOD MEAT over GOOD FIRE.

As a committed omnivore I adore vegetables cooked over fire, but there is no denying that meat forms the backbone of good barbecue. Meat and fire were simply made for each other. What I hope to give you here are the skills to make the most of the meat you eat, allowing you to buy better, cook smarter and enjoy it more. There are very many lovely recipes within these pages but importantly, plenty of theory and science too. This is the bit that will really make you a better fire cook. Knowing where on the animal your cut of meat came from and what the muscle function was during its life dictates how and why you should be cooking it the way I suggest. Understanding what fire is and how the energy from heat is transferred from the lit fuel into the food you are cooking allows you to be in control of the process. I see fire as very much a living thing, and as cooks we need to understand it in order to tame and work with it.

Searing is really colouring or browning; think of it as a seasoning in its own right, just as important as the salt you add to your food. With meat it's all about the colour, the crust and the depth of flavour that cooking brings; that happens whether you have a hot fast sizzle, or a long slow smoke. So while we think of 'sear' as a high-intensity process, it can also be a slow and gentle one. What we are witnessing is the Maillard reaction sequence, the cornerstone of all good cooking, more about which will follow shortly.

I often get asked why I cook with fire. Some people will never figure it out, always preferring their kitchen inside, but there is a growing army of people who are becoming addicted to cooking outside and I salute you for embracing a slightly more adventurous way of living. For me, a passion for fire cooking started selfishly, a way to make day-to-day cooking more interesting when my children were young and I felt utterly swamped by domesticity. Now that I'm hooked, it's more about simply being outside, embracing the analogue nature of fire cooking and ditching the digital world for just a little while. And no one can deny that when you get it right, food cooked with fire quite simply tastes amazing.

This book is global in its reach, in part because every single country in the world has a history of cooking with fire. After all, humans' ability to harness, capture and cook over fire is the defining point in our evolution as a species. I have spent a lifetime travelling and gaining inspiration along the way, but I also consider myself rather lucky to be born in the UK. It's part of our culture to be culinary magpies, grabbing inspiration from all over the place in a way that perhaps wouldn't be socially acceptable if you lived somewhere else. Maybe because historically British food was always seen as a touch inferior, somehow we have become adventurous in our tastes. If you live in Italy, for example, for the most part you eat Italian food, every day, every year. In the UK in a single week we can take in culinary delights from all for four corners of the globe. I live in a multicultural city where I have access to a whole tapestry of interesting ingredients – and I appreciate the good fortune of that – but the internet is a wonderful thing and there is nothing in here you shouldn't be able to source online.

Lost in translation

I think it's worth quickly noting the difference between barbecue the noun and barbecue the verb – for the avoidance of any cross-cultural confusion! In the UK the word 'barbecue' is used to describe the action of cooking over fire, the food you serve from the fire, the equipment you cook on and the gathering of people you invite to your garden. A really rather catch-all term then. In the US, 'barbecue' is normally used to describe the food itself, especially among professional fire cooks, and more specifically refers to low and slow cooked meats, smoked for a very long time – like brisket and pulled pork. The equipment used for barbecue (the food!) is called a smoker and generally wood is the fuel. Grilling, on the other hand, mainly uses charcoal and is done on an open grill; the food is generally cooked hot and fast, so steaks, burgers, kebabs and the like. For the purposes of this book, I use the term to describe the equipment I cook on, the act of cooking on it and the food I serve from it.

The Maillard Reaction: the cornerstone of good cooking (and good eating)

Given that this book is all about the sear, the colour, the browning, and that the colouring we see is visible evidence of the Maillard reaction sequence, a brief explanation of what it is seems a sensible place to start.

Maillard was a French chemist who first described the phenomenon in 1912. More than just caramelization, which is simply the burning of sugars, Maillard is a chemical reaction sequence that begins between a simple sugar molecule and a protein, or amino acid, creating an unstable intermediate structure. This then goes on to react again and again and again in a series of simultaneous chain reactions that produce literally hundreds of new flavour molecules. It's no wonder we find browned food irresistible. Maillard reactions are the backbone of good cooking and good eating: things that have undergone its reaction process simply taste of more. Not just limited to meat – the crust on a loaf of bread, the deep toastiness in a pint of beer or a delicious little dram of whisky, the crunchy golden outer of roast potatoes – these are all evidence of Maillard browning reactions. This book is concerned with meat – can anyone deny that meat that has been browned on the surface makes for much better eating than meat that has not?

So, what are the right circumstances for browning? You don't necessarily need high temperatures for Maillard reactions to take place. It takes a minimum of 120°C (250°F), which is pretty low in cooking terms, but you do need time. Maillard reactions get slower as the temperatures get lower. So it happens with low and slow smoking over many hours as well as searing a steak hot and fast. The optimum temperature for visibly quick Maillard is 150–160°C (300–320°F). It is also inhibited by high temperatures; once you hit over 200°C (400°F), what you actually get is mostly caramelization of sugars. It's important to note that these temperatures are the ones at the very surface of the food where the chemical reaction is happening. They are neither the barbecue cooking temperature nor the internal temperature of the food you are cooking.

Driving off moisture promotes browning reactions, which is one of the reasons dry-brining meat is a good thing. Fat also has a role to play – firstly, a thin coating of oil or natural meat fats evens out minor surface irregularities, allowing maximum contact of meat to hot grill surface, and secondly fat and water hate each other with a passion. So a very thin layer of hydrophobic fat on the outside will create a barrier, reducing moisture loss, or water from escaping from within the meat, but if you have dry-brined your meat (see page 21) this is not really an issue as you've denatured the protein bonds and the water can't get squeezed out anyhow.

What is 'GOOD MEAT'?

A key starting point for me in writing this book was the realization that it has never been easier to source good meat and, with a little planning and knowledge, to shun mass-produced plastic-packaged meat from the supermarket. It's absolutely not about meat snobbery but is more an awareness of the hard scientific facts: meat produced on an industrial scale really is no longer sustainable for the health of people or the planet, or indeed the welfare of the animals. Good meat is now straightforward to find online, where you can buy either direct from the farmers or from good butchers, and get it delivered to your door in a flash. There are many excellent places producing and selling meat of exceptional quality, and I have listed some of my favourites at the back of this book.

For me, the definition of 'good meat' is really very simple. It's about allowing the animals we eat to live out their natural lifespan, exhibiting their natural behaviours while eating a natural diet. There are myriad reasons why it is better to avoid mass-produced, chemically laden, intensively reared meat. Without doubt good meat is more expensive, but I think the point is it should be. It's necessary to be reminded of the true value of the animals we eat; they shouldn't ever be a daily commodity. Eat less meat in order to buy better meat is a good mantra to live by. And this book is designed to help you get the cooking right every time so you get more bang for your hard-earned buck.

Meat has had rather a bad rap in recent years. What with cow farts and greenhouse gases, and veganism now being seen as somehow a 'cleaner' way of life, it's easy to believe that meat-eating is the enemy of the planet. I'm not here to diss vegans in any way, but to shout loud about how eating a little good meat can actually be beneficial, rather than harmful, to the environment.

Regenerative agriculture

In recent years there has been a growing movement, termed regenerative agriculture, that uses livestock as a land management tool to improve soil health and biodiversity and to sequester carbon into the ground rather than allowing it to be released into the sky. It's not a new way of farming by any means, but rather takes things back to the old ways and mimics nature's template.

Wild herbivorous animals behave in a very specific way. They gather as a large mob to protect themselves from predators (there's safety in numbers, after all) and then as a gang they move around constantly, mowing the ground short as they go. They don't stay in one place for long. When grazing animals are farmed this way – in groups that intensively graze one piece of land for a short period before being moved on to fresh ground – there are two great benefits. Firstly, their dung enriches the soil beyond belief and populations of dung beetles and other invertebrates explode, which in turn brings in birds, bats and other small mammals that feed on them. Secondly, because the soil is richer, the plant biodiversity increases and more plants grow taller and stronger; they both 'lock' in carbon from the atmosphere and improve water retention in the soil. The short, intense periods of trampling hooves on the grass knocks out the seeds from the grasses, herbs and flowers, which then grow to further enrich the plant life. It's a cycle of land improvement that just gets better and better. Conversely, when grazing animals are farmed in a monoculture on permanent pastures, you see huge decreases in biodiversity and soil health that is usually remedied by adding more and more chemical fertilizers year on year. It becomes a vicious cycle, leading to farmers having to spend more to get the same return from their animals. Both farmers and land get poorer and poorer.

I genuinely believe the future of meat-eating lies in embracing regeneratively farmed pasture-fed animals, and there are lots of farmers out there working this way for beef, pork, lamb and even poultry. There are a lot of resources online if you want to find out more – head to www.pastureforlife.org as a good starting point.

Grain vs pasture-fed

The process of feeding animals grains – most often corn or soy-based feeds – is all about increasing their weight at slaughter and creating the marbling of fat within the meat; you are quite literally fattening them up for the table. Even animals that are labelled as 'grass-fed' are very often given grains to finish them off. The problem with producing vast quantities of grains and soy to feed animals for meat is that you use huge amounts of land in the process, often destroying swathes of wild habitats and consuming vast quantities of resources (fuel, water, chemical fertilizers) to do so. It is this that makes meat-eating 'bad' for the environment.

Farming wholly pasture-fed animals is better for the environment for the reasons outlined above but it's also been proven to be significantly better for our health too – higher levels of omega 3, lower levels of fat, higher levels of vitamins and minerals. A diverse, natural diet for animals simply leads to a more nutritious meat for us.

Meat improves in taste as the animals age, naturally developing more complex flavours with more fat. Similar to the terroir of a wine, where and how they are grown matters. One of my personal favourites is beef from ex-dairy cows that have lived long lives. Not only is the taste insane, rich, complex and fatty, it feels environmentally more sustainable to eat these animals that have had a dual nature to their lives.

What is 'GOOD FIRE'?

For me a love of barbecue and fire cooking is born from a love of being outside, enjoying nature, fresh air and the environment around me. I am just happiest when I'm outside. With this comes a passion for shouting loud and proud about good sustainable fuel – it's such a crucial part of the jigsaw. Your fuel is your number one ingredient in good barbecue and yet too few consider where their fuel came from and just how it was produced. Just like regenerative farming, the harvesting of wood to cook on can be done in an environmentally positive way. It can also be done the wrong way.

Sadly the vast majority of the charcoal we buy is picked up rather impulsively on the way home from work when we realize the weather is looking fine. Chances are that charcoal you grabbed from the garage forecourt or the supermarket will have come from the tropics, the bulk of which is produced in either South America or West Africa and made from tropical hardwood trees, some of which without a shadow of a doubt will have been illegally harvested. I was astonished to learn that the offcuts from illegally harvested wood, the trimmings left over from making a table for example, can often end up being classed as a recyclable product and therefore given a stamp of 'sustainability', fooling the consumer into believing they are somehow making a wise eco-choice.

Not only are the forestry methods dubious, the way the charcoal is made is not the best for the environment either, releasing a lot of gases and dirty particulates into the air, damaging the health of the low-paid workforce as they do so. Then there's the thousands of travel miles, before which much of it will be treated with fire suppressant chemicals to stop it self-igniting on its long journey via container ship. Once it lands on our shores it then gets a hit of fire accelerant chemicals so we can easily light it up. A double whammy of things we don't really want to be cooking on. That story we've long been told about waiting for charcoal to be white and ashy before we cook on it? That's a myth invented for chemically laden charcoal to ensure that any potentially harmful additives are burnt off before our food goes anywhere near the heat. Good charcoal is 95% pure carbon, an inert substance with no smell and no taste that you can light and be cooking on within 5–10 minutes.

In short, I see little point in investing your hard-earned cash on a beautifully aged grass-fed steak from a happy, well cared for cow, only to go and cook it over chemically laden, possibly illegally forested, tropical hardwood charcoal. It makes no sense to me.

So what is good charcoal? Your fuel should be your very first consideration when you are thinking about barbecuing something to eat. Open a bag of charcoal, pull out a piece and give it a big generous sniff. It should smell of nothing, nothing at all. Carbon is completely inert. If it smells of more than zero I would urge you to leave well alone.

It may sound like stating the bleeding obvious, but charcoal is made from trees. You take wood and bake it in an oxygen-starved environment (a process called pyrolysis), driving off practically everything in the wood that isn't carbon. But cutting down trees to make charcoal isn't as bad for the planet as it sounds. Healthy woodlands need managing. When you thin out a woodland, you let light into the forest floor. Nature goes wild for light and in no time at all dormant seeds on the forest floor wake up and new little species of plants grow. They in turn attract insects and other invertebrates that go on to attract birds, bats and other mammals that eat them. This is ecology in action. Woodland management increases biodiversity and that's a really positive thing in terms of the health of our planet. The other thing to point out is that woodlands that are healthy and making money for someone are more likely to stay there for generations to come. In simple economic terms a woodland that pays is a woodland that stays. So by choosing to buy sustainably made charcoal you are having a positive environmental impact.

There are a good number of brilliant British charcoal makers out there who will sell you fuel online and deliver it to your door in a day or so. My personal favourite is Whittle and Flame; not only do they make the most sustainably produced charcoal possible, it also cooks like an absolute dream. Globally, my best advice is to use the internet and search for 'sustainable lumpwood charcoal' and see what comes up. Just as with buying meat, it has never been easier to buy good fuel. You just need to think about it a little before the day you want to cook so there's no need to grab a bag of the rubbish stuff after work.

So what is fire?

Fire is the visible evidence of a chemical reaction called combustion. Think of fire as being trapped in the middle of a triangle, with each side of the triangle essential to keeping the fire alight in the centre. The three sides are fuel, ignition and oxygen. Get them all connected into place and you have yourself a fire. In our case, the fuel is either charcoal or wood to cook on, the ignition is one single match striking a single fire lighter. The oxygen element comes from the way you set out your fuel and how you control the air flow using the vents on your barbecue. Air flow is a vital thing to master – it's a little like playing a game of chicken. You want to reduce the air flow as much as possible to prolong the burn time of your fuel while maintaining the temperature of the fire necessary to cook whatever it is you're trying to cook. More air equals a quicker, hotter fire and less air a slower, cooler fire. The more efficient your barbecue at controlling air flow the more temperature control you have and the less fuel you will burn. So at one end of the spectrum is an open grill with no lid – you have zero control without any air vents, the fire simply burns hot and fast and your fuel will burn up super-quickly. At the other end of the scale is a kamado ceramic oven that, once you shut the vents tight, becomes a sealed unit and gives you maximum air control. Most barbecues fall in between these two extremes and the only way to become a good fire cook is to learn about how the air circulates in your own kit. Which only comes with practice and repetition: the more you do it the better you will become. I am still very much learning every time I light up a fire.

Fire management begins with the physics of heat

Learning how fire and heat works is the single most important thing you need to know about barbecuing. Once you learn how to light, control, adapt and work with the fire it simply becomes a form of cooking like any other. Knowing a little basic physics is the key to understanding why and where to put food on the grill. Don't switch off – even if science isn't your thing, embrace your inner nerd just a moment,

register the value of it in your brain then get on with the cooking without becoming overly obsessed by it.

It's important to remember that heat is a type of energy and that nature always wants to create an equilibrium. So heat energy transfers into cold things, warming them up, trying to equalize the temperature gradient between hot and cold. At the beginning of the cooking process, heat transfers into the outside of your food, exciting the molecules at the surface. They jiggle and bounce around a little, generating more heat that then transfers into the next layer of colder molecules, which become hot and excited and repeat the process. So heat gradually transfers from the outside to the inside. The thinner your meat the more quickly this happens, which is why a big pork joint takes far longer to cook than a single chop.

With fire cooking we are utilizing three kinds of heat:

- **Infrared radiation heat** This is the heat produced from the lit fuel itself, the infrared radiation glowing off the hot surface of your charcoal or wood fire. The closer you are to the source, the hotter the heat. It's the same type of heat energy as the sun gives us. When we turn our face up towards to the sun on a spring day we are soaking up a little infrared heat that warms our skin in a rather lovely way.

- **Conduction heat** The infrared radiation from lit fuel quickly transfers into the cooking surfaces – the grill bars or the cast-iron pan you have placed over the fire. This heat energy is called conduction or contact heat, and is the same type of heat as when we snuggle up to a loved one and feel the heat of their body pressing against our own. Some of their warmth will conduct into your body and some of your warmth will conduct into theirs. It's a sharing kind of heat.

- **Convection heat** The third type of heat energy we are interested in is convection currents – or the circulation of hot air, just like the heat we get from a hairdryer. With cooking, convection heat only really comes into play in a meaningful way when you contain it, so by shutting the lid on your barbecue or by putting a lid on a bubbling pan. For this reason, having the ability to shut a lid when cooking is really rather useful as you can hugely increase the efficiency of the heat your fuel produces, trapping it in, creating a more steamy, moisture-filled cooking environment. You wouldn't dream of trying to bake a cake in your oven while leaving the door open, and it's the same with most sorts of barbecue cooking. A barbecue with a lid also allows you control of the all-important oxygen element in the fire triangle. There are a few rare times when a lid doesn't help you – searing a steak is the key example – head to page 32 for more on that.

Direct vs indirect cooking: the impact of distance

Where you place your food in relation to the three types of heat is important. Food placed on the grill bars directly over the fire will get way more heat energy from both infrared and conduction sources than food placed indirectly off to the side, where the heat source will principally be a little conduction from the grill bars and convection if you shut the lid. The closer the food to the source of the heat, the more heat it gets and the more quickly it cooks.

Learning the difference between DIRECT cooking and INDIRECT cooking is critical to barbecue success. You can then create varying 'heat zones', allowing you to control the heat you are cooking on. I personally think that much – if not most – food is better cooked a little more gently for a little longer. Steak, once again, is the exception to this loose rule.

Why the thermometer on the lid of your barbecue is not totally useful

Good barbecues generally have a thermometer on the lid and they are useful to a point, that is to say they give you an indication of how hot it is inside and whether the temperature is rising or falling. What they measure is the air temperature, or convection heat, at a given point on the inside of the lid. If you were to take an infrared thermometer and use it to scan the temperature in various places you would find wildly differing readings inside. The

thermometer on the lid might say 200°C (400°F), but the lit coals themselves might be something in the region of 400–500°C (750–930°F) or more. The grill bars might also be over 500°C (930°F) directly over the fire, but only if they have had a good amount of time to heat up – shortly after you light the fire they may only be 200°C (400°F) while the grill bars on the opposite side of the barbecue to the fire might only get to a measly 100°C (210°F). All you need to take from this is that you, the cook, have the ability to use these different temperatures to control your cooking. With the recipes here, I do give general guides as to what temperature you should be running your barbecue; they are a good starting point, but don't get too hung up on what the actual reading on the lid is, it's just a part of the bigger thermal picture.

Quantity of fuel

It almost goes without saying, but the more fuel you use the hotter your cooking environment will be. A whole lit chimney of charcoal has the potential to contain twice as much infrared energy as half a lit chimney, so if you want to cook something slowly at a lower temperature, simply using less fuel can be an important first step. Of course, this often means you will need to add fuel during a long, slow cook to keep the fire burning. Another bonus of good pure charcoal is that you can just add it at a lump at a time and keep cooking.

Charcoal vs wood

We burn charcoal because it burns hot and clean with practically no smoke. Charcoal-making evolved in tandem with the Bronze Age as people discovered wood didn't burn hot enough to smelt metal. Charcoal burns two to three times hotter than wood and it's a much more consistent product to cook with. Wood, on the other hand, comes with a lot of variables. Different species have different densities: some burn hotter, some burn more quickly, even different parts of the same tree burn slightly differently, which makes cooking purely with wood exciting, unpredictable and rather addictive. This book is principally concerned with barbecuing, using charcoal as the primary heat source, but many of the recipes can be cooked on an open fire using just wood. However, remember how important a having lid is? With open fire cooking you have less air flow control and no ability to utilize convection heat and so your use of both fuel resources and the energy they give is much less efficient.

Adding smoke with wood

Given that good lump wood charcoal is 95% pure carbon and produces hardly any smoke, if you want to add some 'smokiness' to your food you need to add a little wood into the equation. There is so much choice when it comes to smoking woods, it can be quite bamboozling for the novice. The most important thing? Forget about 'chips' of wood and get chunks. Something a smallish fist size is perfect. Wood chips combust too quickly, so to get any meaningful smoke into your food you would have to keep adding more frequently during the cook. Given that the aim of the game when smoking is to keep your lid down as much as possible, this is far from ideal. You can soak them in water first to prolong combustion (by essentially inhibiting it) but to my mind that creates a mucky, damp, dirty smoke – not smoke I want on my food. Wet smoke also produces more particulate matter that's released into the atmosphere, so it's not great from an environmental perspective. Dry wood burns cleaner. Much better, then, to use two or three bigger bits of wood, arranged on your fire so they give you a little gentle smoke for a good long time. Put one just touching the lit fire, and one or two further away so they catch later on during the cooking time (see page 19 for fire set-ups). A moisture-filled environment helps smoke attach to food, which is why some of the recipes here call for you to add a pan of water to your barbecue at the start of cooking.

When it comes to what sort of wood to choose for smoking with I don't – controversially perhaps, I know some of my fire-friends disagree with me – think there's a huge amount of difference in terms of the actual flavour and taste you get on your food at the end. Sure, different woods have very different smelling smokes, due to the differing densities and organic compounds of various species. You have 'heavier' smokes, like oak, and 'lighter' smokes, like alder or silver birch. Technically I suppose you should grab a heavier smoke for darker meats and a lighter one for white meats, in the way that red wine is for beef and white wine is for fish, but in my world rules are always there for bending. And I prefer red wine. By the time you've rubbed, marinated and dressed your meat I think the smoke is just a little layer in the bigger picture. Sure, if you smoked six plain chicken breasts over six different woods you would be able to tell the difference, but who wants to smoke a plain chicken breast? If you do, you might just be reading the wrong book. The food I enjoy is layered with flavour from spices, herbs, oils and citrus, and those are the recipes you will find within these pages.

I generally grab oak or one of the fruit woods like apple or cherry for most of my smoking, and you won't find me prescribing different woods for different recipes here. I think it's more important to master your cooks with one or two types of wood and learn about the amount of smoke you like, then move on to others. Experiment, taste your food, draw your own conclusions and report back. Often with smoke, less is more and heavily over-smoked foods can be overpowering.

This advice is principally for charcoal-based barbecuing, where you are adding a little hit of wood smoke for smokiness rather than pure wood fire cooking, where the wood is your only fuel. Once again, pure charcoal is virtually all carbon, inert and consistent in its burning. With a wood fire the variables between species are rather intensified.

What kind of charcoal?

I generally burn ash charcoal, not because it imparts any particular flavour to my food but because there is currently a lot of ash around in the European forestry system and as such I feel it's currently the most sustainable choice for me. Ash trees are suffering from a fungal disease called ash dieback and so the foresters are trying to get ahead of it by thinning and taking out these trees before they become rotten and commercially useless.

Just as with different smoking woods, I don't personally believe that it matters too much which species of charcoal you cook on. Some charcoals burn hotter and more quickly, and some are more long-lasting. Back to the game of chicken I mention on page 12, I think it's up to the cook to learn how to balance the heat versus the burn time by controlling the air flow through the fire. In pure taste terms, given the inert nature of carbon, and the fact that good charcoal is 95% pure carbon, the chances of the 5% of other stuff making much difference to flavour are, to my mind, pretty slim. By 'other stuff' I mean the non-combustible mineral content in the wood, plus a little leftover lignin that hasn't fully pyrolyzed in the charcoal-making process.

Charcoal briquettes

Briquettes are made from super-compressed charcoal dust, often with starchy additives to help bind it together, giving you evenly sized pieces of fuel to burn. Briquettes can be an absolute bugger to light but once lit they can burn for hours and hours. For this reason they are often used for long, slow cooking to reduce the number of times you need to top up fuel. But they are invariably made from dubious charcoal sources (see page 10) and so I won't burn them. However, my favourite charcoal makers, Whittle and Flame, have recently started to produce sustainable British 'Whittlebricks' that might just be the answer if you are looking for a long, slow burn. I still prefer lumpwood charcoal for ease of lighting but if I'm going in for the long haul, with brisket or pulled pork for example, I may add a few into the mix.

Barbecue Hardware

There is a vast array of different barbecues out there and, as you might expect, I have many of them in my garden. They all do a pretty similar job and to my mind, learning how to master and control the fire in whatever barbecue you choose to cook on is more important than the actual make and model itself.

At its simplest all you need is a space for your fuel, a grill on which to cook and, ideally, a lid to shut in that all-important convection heat. All the recipes in this book have been tested on a kettle barbecue and if I could only choose one piece of hardware this would be it. Simple and classic in design, and in my view the perfect balance of size, function and affordability.

I am not one for bells and whistles technology and prefer to keep my fire cooking as analogue as possible. That said, ceramic grills – or kamado-style ovens, like the Kamado Joe or Big Green Egg – are great sturdy bits of kit that I do enjoy cooking in. Extremely fuel-efficient, with the ability for very fine-tuned temperature control, they are excellent at trapping moisture in and really excel at low and slow cooking. You can bung in a big joint – pulled pork, lamb shoulder, brisket – and pretty much walk away until it's ready to eat. That's not to say you can't cook any of these things in a kettle barbecue, you just need to be prepared to top up the fuel for longer cooks and really get to grips with air flow to control the temperature.

Another bit of hardware gaining in popularity is the pellet grill, which has a compartment filled with wood pellets that get drip-fed via an auger into a little fire box under the grill bars. The whole thing is driven via a connection to the mains electricity supply so you have a constant whirring of a motor in the background, which I don't personally relish. They too are pretty fuel-efficient and because the thermostat is electronically controlled you have the option to load in your food and pretty much step away until it's done, making things super-easy. Do I always want it easy when I'm fire cooking? Nope. Sure I want a great end result but my love of cooking with solid fuels is also in enjoying being involved in the process of lighting the fire and harnessing and maintaining the heat you have created. I usually want it to be a hands-on process – that's why I like it.

Offset smokers, designed for low and slow smoking, are where the fire, invariably just from wood, is contained in a separate fire box. The hot air and smoke is then channelled up and over the meat, which is placed in a different compartment. I don't own one and am not sure I see the need to in a domestic situation. If I were running a restaurant and needed to turn out multiple briskets every day I would feel differently. Smoking just means adding wood smoke to your food and you can smoke meat in a barbecue but you can't barbecue meat in a smoker. (See also Lost in Translation on page 5.)

How to light a barbecue

The quickest and simplest way to light a barbecue is with a chimney starter, a tall metal cylinder with air holes around the base. Simply pour charcoal into it, remembering that more charcoal will give you more heat, and set a single natural fire lighter underneath. Natural fire lighters are twists of wood shavings dipped in wax and they are by far the best thing you can use. They are really easy to find online and even in larger supermarkets.

Strike a match to provide the source of ignition, and the warmth generated from the fire lighter will draw in oxygen around the base of the chimney, which then whooshes up through the charcoal, causing it to ignite. With good charcoal you can have a chimney lit and ready to use in 5–10 minutes. Do not wait

for the charcoal to be lit fully to the top, just about halfway lit is fine, because with good fuel (see page 10) there is absolutely no need to wait for it to be white and ashy before you start cooking.

For many recipes you will need to top up the fuel during the cooking process to keep the heat constant and steady over a long period of time – unless you are cooking on a really fuel-efficient kamado-style oven or with a wood pellet grill. You have two options. With good-quality charcoal you can just add a lump of two to the lit fire every now and then and keep on cooking. Or, if the fire has burnt down too much for fresh charcoal to catch efficiently, you can light up a little extra fuel in a chimney starter and tip it in over the partly burnt fire.

Fuel set-ups for different sorts of cooking

You can set out your fire in different ways depending on what you are cooking and how long it is going to take. What you never, ever want to do is fill the base of your barbecue with an even layer of lit fuel. This would ruin your ability to create the all-important 'heat zones' and would give you no temperature control whatsoever. Things would just be HOT. So the fuel needs to go in one area while another area is left entirely fuel-free. This gives you direct vs indirect cooking, the absolute linchpin to mastering barbecue cooking.

These are the four different fire set-ups I go to as standard in my kettle barbecue.

- **Half and half** My most used set-up. Lit coals on one half, no fuel on the other. The amount of heat energy is greatest directly over the fire, and falls away in a left to right gradient the further away, or more indirectly, you go. Even if I want to cook purely using a direct heat, I would use this set-up. Being able to slide your food further from the heat just gives you 'wriggle room' when things look to be cooking too hot.
- **Two fires** If I am roasting a chicken or big joint of meat, I usually light two small fires, one to either side of the barbecue, with a good-sized fire-free gap in the centre. This means the food gets a steady, even amount of heat from both sides, meaning you won't need to rotate it mid-cook to make sure both sides get the same amount of heat. It also gives me the ability to set a tray underneath the food to catch the all-important drips and juices that can then be used to make a sauce or gravy. This is also the set-up I use for baking in a barbecue – see the pig cheek lasagne on page 102 – where you want a high-ish convection heat but not so much infrared or conduction heat.
- **Centre fire** If I'm cooking a lot of small things – like chicken wings – I will light a fire in the centre and arrange them in a ring around the perimeter of the barbecue. This way each wing is equidistant to the fire, getting the same amount of heat for a more even cook. I might use this way for sausages too.
- **Minion** This is where you create a bed of unlit charcoal on the base of your barbecue, and light a small area of it in the centre. The fire then gradually spreads outwards from the centre. I only deploy the minion method if I want to go in for the really long haul – with a brisket or pork butt for example (see The Barbecue Big Guns, page 127) – as it's a good way to prolong the burn time of your fuel and just have a little fuel burning at any one time, thus giving you a slow and steady heat. You then need to either use a heat deflector plate to eliminate the infrared heat from the lit fire, which would create a 'hot-spot', or make sure you still have an area of the grill bars for indirect cooking. It can sometimes be a tricky one to master as the coals need to be arranged with just the right amount of air gaps between them. Too big a gap and the lit fuel cannot pass across, too close a gap and it can ignite too quickly. You can definitely cook a brisket using the half and half or two fires set-up, you will just need to add a little fuel fairly regularly to keep the burn steady and even.

My kettle barbecue comes with two charcoal baskets which are super-useful for containing the lit fuel and give me the ability to move the fire around mid-cook if I want to. I just grab them with tongs and push them around. So with the half and half set-up I have them together on one side of my barbecue, and with the two fires set-up I split them up, pushing one to each edge. With the minion method I don't use the baskets. They are really easy and pretty cheap to find online.

If you are using a kamado oven these set-ups become irrelevant because you always start with a full basket of charcoal. You then control the directionality of the fire with heat deflector plates and control the temperature with fine-tuned air vent control.

Meat Structure

Knowing a little about the structure of meat will allow us to work out how best to cook it. Meat is made up of protein, fat and water, with a few other bits and bobs thrown in like minerals, enzymes and vitamins. Water accounts for two-thirds of the weight of meat, whether beef, pork, chicken, lamb, or whatever. The remaining third is split between protein and fat, which varies in proportion depending on the species, and whereabouts the meat came from on the body. The age of the animal and how it was reared also has a significant impact on protein-to-fat ratios.

We'll come to fat later, but the protein element can be further divided up between either muscle tissue or connective tissue. Some parts of the body have more muscle than connective tissues, and vice versa. The balance of muscle to connective tissue has the most significant impact on meat tenderness, best cooking methods and cooking times. Delve into the chapters that follow to learn more about how muscles are different in animals.

Muscles are made up of strands of slim muscle cells bound together in bundles – I like to envisage them like a tightly held bundle of raw spaghetti, long strands that are connected together by protein bonds. With this image in mind I have come to believe that salting, or brining, meat is the single best way to ensure maximum tenderness and flavour. Read on...

Brining is the number one trick to boost meat tenderness

Salt is amazing: a little water-soluble molecule (sodium chloride or NaCl if you're a bit of a science nerd like me) that has the ability to amplify the flavour of everything. Salt makes things taste better, taste of more – your roast pork more porky, your ribeye steak more beefy or your curry more deliciously spicy – but it also has rather more miraculous properties than just enhancing taste.

All meat benefits from the application of salt to increase juiciness and I have got into the habit of salting, or brining, all my meat before I cook it, regardless of the cut or species. You can dry-brine – that is just sprinkle with salt – or you can wet-brine by soaking it in a salty solution. I invariably go for a dry brine; it's quicker, takes up less room in the fridge and uses far less salt. A wet brine adds extra water to meat, whereas dry-brining stops the water that's already there from escaping, so you could argue that wet-brining has a somewhat 'diluting' effect to the meat's own flavour.

With dry-brining, when you sprinkle salt over meat it quickly draws out a little water from the muscle cells, creating a really concentrated salty brine on the surface. Over time this salty brine soaks back into the meat by the process of diffusion. Nature always wants to seek equilibrium – so the more salty outside diffuses into the less salty inside, doing its darnedest to make things equal.

When you salt meat, it physically breaks the protein bonds that hold the muscle cells together in a tight bundle. Back to the spaghetti analogy, over time the tight bundle becomes a much looser bundle. By disrupting the bonds between muscle fibres they cannot physically contract up as much once that meat hits the heat, so less of the water inside gets squeezed out. The result? Juicer meat with the flavour ramped up to the max.

How to dry-brine

Dry-brining is ridiculously easy and quick. Simply sprinkle salt all over the meat, including inside the cavity if you are cooking a whole bird, and briefly rub in. Place the meat onto a rack set over a tray, slide into the fridge, uncovered, and leave undisturbed while the salt does its magic. The rack allows air to circulate and prevents the meat from resting in its own juices. A rough rule of thumb is to use a level tablespoon of flaked sea salt per kilo (2lb) of meat. I try to leave the meat brining for 24 hours as standard, but even a couple of hours is worth doing if you are short of time. Something extra-large, a turkey for example, will happily brine for longer – 72 hours wouldn't hurt. There's no need to wash the salt off after brining. In fact I would encourage you not to as the salt will have slightly dried out the surface and a dry surface results in more effective Maillard reactions.

Marinades and rubs

Marinades also break down and denature the protein bonds between the meat fibres, enhancing tenderness. There are two different ways to go:

- **Acidic marination** This uses citrus juices and vinegars, or lactic acids like yogurt or buttermilk.
- **Enzymatic marination** This uses the proteolytic enzymes found in tropical fruits like pineapple, papaya and kiwi and in the fresh-pressed juices of ginger and turmeric roots.

The reality is that marinades often contain a combination of acidic and enzymatic components, so you might mix lemon juice, yogurt and ginger together as in the spiced yogurt chicken skewers on page 202. They also all contain salt, so you have its magical brining properties going on too.

As well as the tenderizing ingredients you can add flavours via different combinations of herbs and spices. However, the molecules in these are much larger than salt so they simply cannot penetrate more than a few millimetres into the meat at most, no matter how long you marinate for. For this reason marinades are really best saved for smaller cuts with large surface areas – chicken portions, meat diced up for kebabs or thinner steaks or chops. You can also increase surface area by cutting deep slashes into the meat and many recipes here will deploy that tactic.

Marinades often contain a little oil of some sort too and this functions not only to lubricate the surface but also to carry fat-soluble flavours – those from woody herbs, chilli, some spices – deeper into the meat. Once again, though, the flavours are only taken just below the surface.

Rubs are dry – usually a combination of salt and spices and maybe a little sugar – and once again, except for the salt they don't make it very far into the meat so consider them a surface seasoning. Just as with a wet marinade, by cutting deep slashes into the meat or by using smaller cuts with a larger surface area you can increase their impact. Often in these recipes I will call for you to add the rub and leave in the fridge overnight, effectively dry-brining and adding flavour to the meat's surface in one step rather than two. It's just cutting corners, pure and simple, but no matter how long you leave it in the fridge the spices and herbs will just stay on and just below the surface.

As a general rule, avoid adding too much sweetness in a marinade or rub as sugars are prone to burning. Those marinades and rubs that break the sugar rule, like the pork belly burnt ends with tequila and maple syrup on page 146 or cola flanken-cut beef ribs on page 170, are best cooked more gently, using an indirect heat for a longer amount of time so you get more flavour from Maillard browning than burnt-sugar caramelization.

An important note on salt quantities

A tablespoon is not always a tablespoon. I use flaked Maldon sea salt for pretty much everything, a tablespoon of which weighs approximately 10g (⅓oz). A tablespoon of fine salt weighs double, 20g (⅔oz), so if you are using fine salt, halve all my measurements where salt is called for by volume rather than weight. Another point to make is, just like chilli tolerance, salt tolerance is something of a personal thing, so always adapt and adjust to taste.

Fridge-cold meat

I never ever bring meat up to room temperature before cooking. An individual steak or chop would take a good couple of hours to hit room temperature and anything bigger would take considerably longer. And besides, cooking steak from fridge cold promotes better Maillard reactions (see page 6). A joint of meat that's several kilos in weight will take hours and hours to increase to anything like room temperature. It's just a waste of your time and, in food safety terms, not ideal. The reason given for bringing meat to room temperature is that you get less contraction of meat fibres once you start cooking it – so it stays juicer – but because you are (hopefully) dry brining, this becomes irrelevant.

A rather useful guide to internal temperatures

BEAST

BIRD

100°C (212°F)

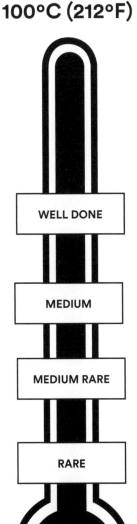

95°C (203°F)
BRISKET
PULLED PORK
PASTRAMI

95°C (203°F)
'PULLED' POULTRY

74°C (165°F)
'safe' temps for
CHICKEN, TURKEY,
MINCED POULTRY

71°C (160°F)
BEEF, LAMB, VENISON,
GOAT, PORK,
BURGERS, SAUSAGES

WELL DONE

71°C (160°F)
DUCK

60°C (140°F)
BEEF, LAMB, VENSION,
GOAT, PORK, BURGERS

MEDIUM

60°C (140°F)
DUCK

56°C (133°F)
BEEF, LAMB, VENSION,
GOAT

MEDIUM RARE

56°C (133°F)
DUCK

52°C (125°F)
BEEF, LAMB, VENSION,
GOAT

RARE

52°C (125°F)
DUCK

Useful Kit

These are a few of my favourite things...

Thermometers

In barbecue we always cook to temperature not time. That is the internal temperature of the food, rather than the barbecue temperature. Time is irrelevant, although you will note I have offered vague ideas of time throughout. In part because cookbook writing etiquette demands it, but more because in terms of you getting a meal on your table it's useful to know if you are heading for a 10-hour cook-a-thon or a quick midweek grill. Do (please, please, I beg you) take them with a pinch of salt. Every fire I light is a little different from the one I lit before, and I'm a professional, I light fires every day. If you are somewhat newer to the art of fire cooking this variable may be exacerbated. Fuel, atmospheric humidity, wind direction, precipitation, these things all change to make fires a touch unpredictable. That's not to say it's hard, you just need to be a little more flexible than with your convection fan oven with its timer button. Learn the basics of fire and heat and embrace the challenge, and have plenty of snacks on hand for when things take longer than you expect.

With temperature firmly in mind, the most useful (I think essential) bit of kit you can invest in for cooking meat on the barbecue is a temperature probe. I wouldn't dream of firing up my barbecue to cook meat without my Thermapen tucked in a pocket (the exception is ribs – see page 164).

Ideally you need two – most important is a standard probe for most things and then, optionally, a wired probe that you leave in the meat. The wired one means you can observe the cook from afar without opening the lid of the barbecue – really useful for bigger joints and long, slow cooks when you've stabilized the barbecue heat just so and opening it up to check will just slow down the cooking. I guess it gives you x-ray eyes to what's going on under the lid. If the barbecue temperature is holding steady and the temperature of your meat is rising, things are heading in the right direction and you don't need to keep checking.

Tongs, spatulas, gloves

Long-handled spatulas and tongs for grabbing and turning your food are essential, as are a set of sturdy heatproof gloves. Leather welder's mitts are the best at protecting your hands and lower arms from the fierce heat but I do wish they made them in smaller sizes. Surely there must be female welders out there?!

Pots, pans, trays

Taking pans to your fire increases the variety of things you can cook. Throughout this book the recipes call for you to grab a tray to catch drippings and make a gravy, or a frying pan (skillet) to toast spices or make a sauce. Pretty much anything goes when it comes to choosing what sort and I usually just grab whatever cooking kit I have to hand in the kitchen – enamel tins, stainless steel saucepans, spun steel frying pans. It doesn't need to be sold as 'barbecue friendly' – just make sure it has no plastic or wooden handles so it's fireproof, and I wouldn't advise using non-stick surfaces.

Vegetable grilling trays

These are really useful. They are simply metal trays perforated with lots of holes, allowing you to cook smaller things that might fall through the grill bars while still letting the smoke through to add flavour.

Chapa or plancha

A heavy-duty flat metal sheet that you set on your grill bars and use to cook on – great for the lamb smash burgers on page 86 – and also brill for cooking non meaty things like frying eggs or making pancakes. You can easily substitute a large, flat frying pan (skillet) – something heavy is best so you get lots of good conduction heat going on.

Cloche

A metal dome with a handle that you can use on an open grill to trap in a bit of very useful convection heat, or you can sit it over a chapa when cooking small burgers, to create a steamy heat to help melt the cheese. You can improvise a cloche with a large metal mixing bowl or even a dome of foil.

Pestle and mortar and a spice mill

I use both almost daily. The pestle and mortar for small quantities of spices and for when the spice is just the beginnings of a rub, so you grind the spice then add the sugar, garlic, herbs or whatever and pound to a paste. A spice mill is more convenient for bigger quantities of spices, or for grinding up whole toasted chillies or cinnamon sticks, for example.
As far as I'm concerned spice is a keystone in good cooking; be generous, use them often and experiment. The majority of spices are better stored whole in airtight jars, then toasted to order with each recipe to wake up their flavours before grinding. Ready-ground spices lose their aroma very quickly.

Beast

Regardless of species, all mammals (or beasts) have the same set of muscles performing principally the same set of mechanical functions. If we know the work the muscles have done during their life, we can pretty easily work out how best to treat them during cooking. The rule of thumb is that the more work muscles do, the longer we have to cook them to render them tender. Quite simply:

More work = you cook low and slow
Less work = you cook hot and fast

The beasts we eat – be they cows, pigs, sheep or others – spend most of their lives grazing and foraging. That is, moving around on all four legs with their heads moving almost constantly up and down. The muscles at the front end do way more work than those at the back end. Shoulder, neck and chest muscles need to be strong and well developed enough to move and support the bulk of the animal's weight. They contain loads of connective tissues to help pull and push various muscles in opposition, instigating and sustaining motion. The cuts of meat from the front end of any beast all benefit from slow cooking. Pork butts (actually shoulder, see page 31) and ham hocks, beef chuck (also shoulder) and shin, or lamb shoulders and shanks all benefit from gentle and lengthy cooking. Muscles from the underside, the belly and ribs, also need slow cooking as there is much fat and connective tissue between with rib bones and layers of intercostal muscles. However, in cows there are nuggets of tenderness to be found in bavette, onglet and skirt steaks.

The muscles back end of the animal are also involved in constant motion but are not so weight-bearing and the individual muscles tend to be larger. So you get bigger, leaner cuts of meat with less tough connective tissue that can therefore be cooked more quickly, like rump steak. With lamb and pork, steaks cut from around the rump end are also lean and fairly tender.

The tail, right at the back, is very often swishing from side to side – think of a cow's tail, it just never stops. So with the beasts which have tails worth eating, oxtail principally, you have a vast array of connective tissue between individual vertebrae and so therefore you need to cook very slowly indeed to make it unctuous and delicious.

The muscles that run along the spine do very little physical work of pushing and pulling; these muscles are more tender with far less connective tissue and therefore they can be cooked quickly and eaten rare. These are the 'prime cuts', centred around the longissimus dorsi muscle of any mammal. In cows, the fillet is the most tender (and, I would argue, often the least flavourful), followed by sirloin and ribeye and their associated bone-in cuts of tomahawk, T-bone and porterhouse. In pigs, it's tenderloin and ribeye steaks, and in lamb the rather pricey rack.

Myoglobin is the protein that makes meat red; it serves to store oxygen within the muscle cells that then provides the energy for motion. The darker the meat the more myoglobin. Beef is deep red as cows have more myoglobin in their muscle cells; lamb and pork have slightly less. Age plays a part too. Veal, the meat from young cows, is considerably paler than fully mature beef cattle. We tend to eat both lamb and pork at a younger age than beef so that meat is a little paler. Size matters as well, so a small rabbit has a lot less myoglobin than a massive cow. The situation is a little different in birds and we'll come to that later.

Fat is Flavour!

Fat is a truly wonderful thing, enhancing both the flavour and texture of the meat we eat. Animals have two types of fat. Intramuscular fat forms in layers in between individual muscles – think of the layer of fat on a pork chop or a sirloin steak; intramuscular fat, known as marbling, forms in thin ribbons within the muscles themselves – ribeye steak is often beautifully marbled. An extreme example of marbling is the distinct waves of fat found within wagyu steak from cows that are genetically pre-dispositioned to carry more fat.

Fat is the energy store of an animal so the older it is the more fat will have been laid down within the body. Fat levels can be boosted by feed regimes and traditionally animals have often been 'fattened' up just before slaughter.

Extremely fat-rich meat, such as duck, some cuts of lamb or sausages, can cause the dreaded 'flare-ups', where the fire gets a bit out of control with melting fat dripping down and quite literally adding fuel to the fire and causing flames to rise. The best thing to do is cook fattier meats more indirectly, further from the fire so they cook more gently. Sometimes, though, you really want a high heat – when searing a steak for example – so you just need to work with the flare, moving food to over the heat to sear, to away from the heat for a short while to let the flare-up die down, then back over the heat again. If the flare-up gets extreme the best solution is to remove the food altogether and let it die down completely before starting again.

Ageing Meat

The ageing process is the period between slaughter and cooking and it varies considerably between different species and different cuts. All beasts get hung initially as whole carcasses, then they are butchered into large cuts that get further aged, usually on the bone and with a good layer of protective fat. Dry-ageing rooms are very finely tuned environments to provide just the right conditions to allow enzymes within the meat work to soften and break it down a little, tenderizing it without letting it spoil.

Beef gets aged longest and sees the most benefits in tenderness. Pork and lamb are generally eaten at a younger age and so are more tender to start with but that's not to say they don't improve in taste with a little ageing. Birds – especially darker meat, like duck or pheasant – also get aged, or 'hung'.

Economics, as ever, plays a role here – the longer you hang, the more water is lost and therefore the animal becomes up to 15–20% lighter with less saleable weight. Aged meat also develops a dry outer layer that needs to be trimmed off before cooking, further reducing the weight. So the longer you dry-age, the more expensive the meat becomes. After about 28 days of ageing beef the meat has become about as tender as it will become. So ageing beyond that – to 40, 60, 80 or more days – is about adding depth of flavour, increasing the nuttiness, the 'funkiness' of the meat.

'Wet-ageing', when meat is butchered in saleable-size portions and vac-packed into bags, was developed to prevent weight loss, increase profitability and speed up the traditional dry-ageing process. The 'wet' bit comes from the meat sitting in its own juices. You can add some tenderness by wet-ageing; the enzymes will still do their job, but you don't get more flavour.

Some cuts don't get dry aged at all and are sold as fresh because they are lean and tender with less protective fat – hanger steak is a good example – although the carcass would have been initially hung before butchery, adding a little tenderness that way.

BEAST CUTS

This is not an exhuastive list of cuts of meat by any means, but here I've laid out the cuts that I have used in this book with the alternative names that I know for them:

BEEF

1. Round
Rump steak / Round steak
Picanha / Top rump

2. Sirloin
Rump tail / Tri-tip
Top sirloin
Bottom sirloin

3. Tenderloin
Fillet / Fillet mignon
Beef tenderloin

4. Short Loin
T-Bone
Porterhouse
Sirloin / Strip steak
New York strip

5. Rib
Ribeye / Entrecôte
Tomahawk / Bone-in ribeye /
    Cote de boeuf
Rib roast / Ribeye roast

6. Chuck
Chuck steak
Shoulder
Flat iron steak / Top blade
Minced (ground) steak

7. Head
Ox cheeks

8. Flank
Bavette / Flank steak

9. Plate
Hanger / Onglet
Short ribs / English cut short ribs
    / Jacob's ladder
Flanken short ribs / Cross-cut
    short ribs
Skirt steak

10. Brisket
Whole brisket / Packer cut
Point half
Flat half

11. Shank
Shin / Shank
Osso buco / Cross-cut shin

12. Oxtail

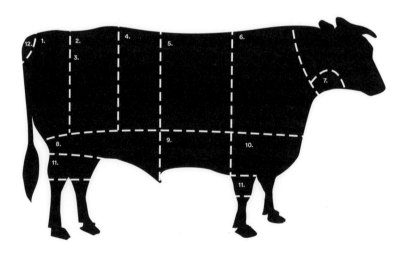

PORK

1. Leg
Gammon steaks
Leg steaks
Ham

2. Belly / Side
Belly slices
Spare ribs / St Louis cut ribs
Pork belly

3. Loin
Baby back ribs
Tenderloin / Fillet
Ribeye steaks
Loin steaks
Pork chops

4. Shoulder
Pork butt / Boston butt
Shoulder joint / Picnic shoulder
Minced (ground) pork

5. Head
Cheeks / Pork jowl

6. Hock
Gammon hock / Pork foot

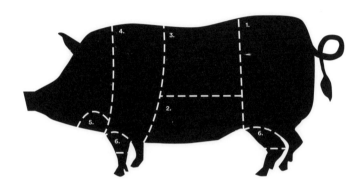

LAMB

1. Neck
Neck fillet / Lamb ribeye

2. Shoulder
Shoulder
Minced (ground) lamb

3. Middle
Lamb rack
Lamb chops
Barnsley chops
Loin chops / Lamb t-bone

4. Leg
Leg steaks
Whole leg

5. Breast
Breast ribs / Belly ribs
Belly
Minced (ground) lamb
Lamb spare ribs / Denver ribs

6. Shank

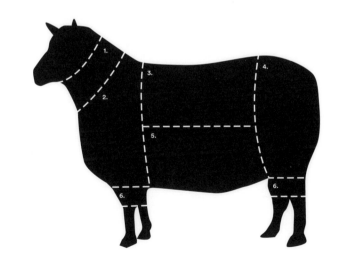

Chapter 1: Steak – the epitome of SEAR!

Steak – good steak – is quite possibly the pinnacle of a carnivore's food-dreams. Certainly nothing sums up the idea of 'sear' better and a perfectly cooked steak is one of life's great pleasures. Traditionally the best, or prime, cuts come from along the back of the cow – the sirloin, ribeye and fillet – and these are the most tender as they've done the least manual labour. Correspondingly they are also the most expensive. Are they my favourite? Nope, but you will need to read on for that reveal.

With steak you have nowhere to hide and I think the quality and the provenance of the meat is critical – cooked properly and served simply, you will have a meal to remember. Steak should never be considered as everyday eating but rather a rare treat, perfect for a celebratory meal and worth forking out for the best you can afford. Head to the back of the book for a list of places where you can buy excellent meat.

There are two principal ways to cook a steak – most commonly to start hot and finish low, or start low and finish hot (otherwise known as the almighty reverse sear technique) and in the following pages I cover the detail of how and why you would do one and not the other. But before we get to the nitty gritty of cooking there are a few critical things it's worth underlining in red, some of which have already been covered in earlier pages. These are the founding principles of good steak cooking and, I think, important enough to warrant repetition. Also, worth pointing out the obvious, please treat my recipes as your own. If you fancy the fillet with romesco, why on earth not? Or the tri-tip with porcini and garlic butter, go for it! Or maybe the hanger, minus the chip butty? I just hope to give you the tools to cook steaks as well as they can be cooked. The accompaniments, as far as I'm concerned, are totally interchangeable.

The definition of a steak is simply a flat piece of meat, so even though I start with beef (it's what we instantly think of), all animals have 'steaks'. You'll find recipes for gammon, pork and lamb steaks here too.

Dry-brining, or salting: do it every time

Just do it. It makes scientific sense, it makes taste bud sense, and once you get into the habit of doing it, it takes up practically no time at all (see page 21).

Fat is flavour

Fat offers us more than lubrication, it brings so much flavour to the party and is to be actively encouraged. Some steaks, like sirloin, have a strip of outer fat down one side and others, like ribeye, have more intramuscular marbling within the meat itself, as well as a generous nugget of intramuscular fat in the centre. And some, like fillet, hanger or skirt are often fairly lean and therefore often benefit from fat added by way of a butter- or olive oil-based sauce. See page 28 for more on fat, but generally the deeper yellow the fat the more aged the cow is. A grass-fed ex-dairy cow that is six or seven years old may have fat that is practically buttercup yellow thanks to a long life lived grazing naturally outside. That's the kind of life I'd like to live if I were a cow.

Cutting across the grain

Remembering back to the spaghetti-as-meat fibre analogy on page 20, imagine your now-cooked bundle of meat fibres. Cut it with the grain, i.e following the line of the meat fibres, and what you put in your mouth is a long spaghetti-like strand of meat. Pretty tough to chew on. If you cut across the grain you are mechanically shortening the meat fibres into a collection of little short pieces, so like chopped up spaghetti. So while you have done nothing in real terms to make that meat tender (in the way salt brine or a marinade would) what you are doing is increasing the perception of tenderness when the meat hits your mouth – your knife has essentially started off the chewing process. Sometimes it's easier to spot which way the grain is running prior to cooking your meat, so try and get into the habit of just sizing it up before it hits the grill.

Remember fridge-cold meat gives you the chance of the best Maillard reactions!

I never bring meat up to room temperature, as discussed on page 22. With steak, fridge-cold is especially beneficial. Quite simply, the colder the steak, the more time you have to develop the glorious, deep brown crust that is the Maillard reaction sequence in evidence. With a room-temperature steak, the energy transfer from the hot grill to the interior of the meat will happen faster, so you have less time to work on the crust before the inside overcooks. In fact, with a thin steak – say 1–1.5cm (½–¾in) – I would even dare to say it might be best to cook from frozen. With a steak that thin you haven't a hope in hell of browning before overcooking the inside. Much easier, though, to cook a thicker steak for sharing in the first place. You give yourself more time to get it right. And if you are reverse searing a chunky old steak, say over a kilo in weight, then you still don't need to bring it to room temperature as that happens during the low and slow part of the cook.

Forget perfect grill bars

While we may have been led to believe that perfect grill bar marks on our steak are the end goal, if evidence of the Maillard reactions is shown by browning on the surface, it almost goes without saying that grill marks are 100% not the aim here. You are only allowing the browning reaction to happen where the marks are, all the unmarked bits don't get the insane flavour boost Maillard gives you. The more browning, the more flavour and an evenly browned crusty outer is the goal rather than the neat parallel lines mirroring your grill bars.

Bone in or out?

I guess a big bone-in steak looks kind of sexy in a caveman way, but the presence of the bone actually makes life harder for yourself. Maximum browning (I feel like a stuck record here) is the name of the game and the bone quite simply gets in the way of maximum contact of meat to grill surface. There's simply no way the bone will actually impart any of its tasty goodness into the meat the way it would if you were slow braising in a liquid. That said, sometimes just sometimes, style over substance wins out, which is why you'll find brief advice on cooking a tomahawk, porterhouse or T-bone on page 45.

Constant turning is key

The best way to achieve the even browning I keep banging on about is to keep moving your meat around the grill bars, turning it, rotating it, flipping it almost constantly – every 30 seconds or so. Essentially when you put a cold steak on hot grill bars, the grill bars will lose heat and the steak will gain heat, so after 30 seconds or so, lift the steak, turn it over and slap it down on a fresh bit of grill where it is still hot. Leave it in the same place for too long and you, once again, minimize your chances of maximum browning. When searing hot and fast always cook with the lid up. You want to take away the convection heat a lid gives you and just have very directional bottom heat (that is, the infrared heat from the coals and radiation/conduction heat from the grill bars). If you added convection heat into the mix, chances are you would overcook your steak before getting enough browning on the surface.

Dirty steak

With the physics of fire and heat energy in mind, now is the time to hold my hand up high and say I don't really get with the idea of cooking 'dirty' when it comes to steak so you won't find any recipes for that in my book. To explain, cooking dirty is when you lay your steak directly onto the hot charcoal, thus bypassing the grill bars entirely. It looks pretty cool, again kind of caveman-esque (am I implying here that meat cooking can be all a bit macho?! No comment your honour...) but I don't personally believe it's the best way to cook steak. Going back to the idea of the 'fire triangle' (see page 12) – oxygen is one of an essential trio of things for a successful and hot fire, the others being fuel and ignition. Slap a big cold steak onto a bed of hot glowing coals and what you do is shut off the oxygen and pretty much instantly you put that bit of fire out, or at least slow down combustion hugely. So, while you might not intuitively think so, cooking dirty is a fairly gentle way of cooking and, as I hope you've already cottoned on to, what you actually want when cooking steak is a good hot sear to get maximum Maillard reactions.

Always cook to temperature not time, and definitely don't poke!

A meat thermometer has never been more important (see page 24). It simply takes the guess work away, and if you've forked out on an expensive bit of steak, why risk overcooking it? There's a nonsensical and outdated bit of steak cooking advice known as the 'poke' or 'prod' test, whereby you compare the feel of your steak to the feel of fleshy pad of your palm when you pinch together thumb and different fingers. Supposedly thumb pinched to index finger feels like rare, while thumb pinched to pinky is well done. What utter nonsense. Are the muscles in my hands likely to be several magnitudes different when compared to a six-foot six rugby player? Yes they are. And a fillet steak will 'prod' in an entirely different way to ribeye. Say no more. Get a thermometer.

The all-important rest?

I remain fairly ambivalent about resting meat, that is leaving it off the heat for a while before you tuck in. The idea is that the meat 'reabsorbs' its own juices, making it more succulent to eat. While this is true to a certain, fairly minimal, extent, I think there are a couple of good reasons not to bother. Firstly, meat carries on cooking once it's off the heat because the heat on the surface keeps travelling inwards to the centre, trying the reach that state of equilibrium. It will possibly rise by another 8, 10 or more degrees or so, depending on the ambient air temperature, which means you need to get it off the heat before your probe says it's done. But if it's a cold, damp day, the carryover cooking will be less than if it's an absolute belter of a summer's day. So you need to factor in that variable. Variables in time vs temperature don't make for the best eating. Better to cook it to how you want to eat it and get on with eating it as soon as it's ready. Which is kind of my second point: my kids rarely have the patience to sit around waiting while meat rests. There are, of course, exceptions to my anti-resting theory – brisket and pulled pork (see pages 131 and 137) being prime examples as the rest creates the right eating texture – but with other low and slow cooking the rest is happening while it's actually cooking.

HANGER, MY DESERT ISLAND STEAK, AND TWO THINGS TO DO WITH IT

If I could only buy, cook and eat one steak in the world it would be a hanger steak – also known as onglet (pronounced with a hard T!) or thick skirt. Cooked right (that is pretty rare, certainly no more than medium-rare) it has the same tenderness as fillet but masses more flavour. I love it for its insane beefiness, deep minerality and open-grained texture. A slightly difficult muscle to categorize – think of it as the diaphragm's supporting muscle – positioned near the kidneys, it is effectively classed as offal as it is pulled out of the animal with the 'pluck' (or the organs). Untrimmed, they are around 800g–1kg (1lb 12oz–2lb 4oz) in weight, obviously depending on the size of the cow. For both these hanger recipes you can substitute skirt or bavette as they cook in a very similar way – that is hot and fast.

Steak and chips butty, mustard mayo, watercress

It perhaps feels a little brave-slash-foolish to start my ode to meat over fire with something so simple as a steak butty, but I surely can't be alone in thinking this might just be my perfect last supper? A double carb hit from bread and chips, double heat hit from mustard and watercress, with my favourite steak in the world slapped squarely in between. Oh, yes please. Oh, and yes, you can cook frozen oven chips on the barbecue! Read on…

In an ideal world, dry-brine your steak the day before you cook it. Simply sprinkle the salt over and place on a rack set over a tray and slide into the fridge. Even if you do this for a couple of hours or so it will benefit taste and tenderness (see page 21).

When you are ready to cook, fire up your barbecue ready for high temperature direct and indirect grilling, piling a whole chimney of lit coals to one side of the grill (see page 17).

Once the barbecue is hot, scatter the frozen chips onto a grilling tray or sheet of foil. Set onto the grill bars away from the fire so that they cook over a high but indirect heat. Shut the lid of the barbecue and cook for around 20 minutes, turning and tossing about a few times until crisp in parts and just a touch soggy in others. Yes, here I think a little soggy can be a good thing so you get that good 'squish' when you bite.

Stir together the mayonnaise, both mustards and a generous grind of pepper. Set aside.

Serves 2 as a feast, or 4 as a snack

400–500g (14–18oz) hanger steak
1 tbsp flaked sea salt
300g (10½oz) frozen oven chips –
    I like skinny French fries
3 tbsp mayonnaise
1 tbsp wholegrain mustard
1–2 tsp English mustard
1 ciabatta loaf
olive oil, for drizzling
a good handful of watercress
freshly ground black pepper

Continued overleaf…

Open up the ciabatta lengthways to give you two long pieces and drizzle a little oil over the cut sides. Grill for a couple of minutes to warm and lightly toast. Then rest on top of the cooked fries to keep warm off the heat while you cook the steak.

Drizzle a little oil all over the steak and set on the grill bars directly over the fire. Cook, turning frequently with the lid up, until grilled to perfection – use your meat probe here. If you are not resting your steak (see page 34), take it to 52°C (125°F) for rare or 56°C (132°F) for medium-rare. If you want to rest, go a few degrees less to allow for carryover cooking.

Scatter the watercress in the base of the ciabatta and top with the fries, sprinkling a little extra salt over them. Slice the steak across the grain into 1cm (½in) strips and add on top of the fries, adding any juices that have seeped from the meat. Finish by dolloping on the mustard mayo and topping with the other piece of ciabatta. Give it a firm squish down to meld everything together and slice in half to give you two very generous portions, or into quarters for four if there is more to follow. Tuck in without delay!

Cambodian hanger steak salad

This is inspired by Lok Lak, a Cambodian steak salad with a peppery lime dressing. If you get the marinading done the day before this is a super-quick supper. The soy marinade not only tenderizes the meat but adds bags of umami flavours.

The day before you want to cook, marinate the steak. Take a dish that will fit the steak snugly and pour in the soy, oyster and fish sauces and the sesame oil and stir to mix. Add the steak and toss about to mix. Cover and slide into the fridge to marinate for 24 hours, turning it over a few times if you can.

The next day, get everything lined up so when you start cooking the steak you can just concentrate on that. Add the butter, garlic and lime leaves to a small fireproof pan and have ready to take to the barbecue. Boil the eggs to your liking – soft, hard or in between – then peel and slice in half.

Make the dressing by whisking together the lime juice, fish sauce, sugar and peppercorns. Season with salt to taste and set aside.

Spread out the lettuce leaves – either on one serving platter or divide over two individual plates – and top with the onion, tomato and cucumber. Add the egg halves.

When you are ready to cook, fire up the barbecue ready for direct grilling, leaving a space under the grill bars fire-free so you have room to manoeuvre the steak if things are getting a little hot (see page 19 for more on set-ups).

Lift the steak from the marinade onto the grill bars above the fire. Set the pan with the butter alongside, slightly off the heat so it can gently melt. Turn and rotate the steak frequently, every 30 seconds or so until it's cooked to your liking, 52°C (125°F) for rare, 56°C (132°F) for medium-rare, basting any leftover marinade on as you turn. Remove from the heat, along with the pan of melted butter. Cut the steak across the grain into thick slices, dropping them into the melted butter as you go. Toss to mix then pile onto the prepared salad. Drizzle over the dressing and serve straight away.

Serves 2

3 tbsp soy sauce
2 tbsp oyster sauce
1 tbsp fish sauce
1 tbsp sesame oil
400–500g (14–18oz) hanger steak
50g (2oz) butter
3 garlic cloves, crushed
4 lime leaves (fresh or frozen), finely chopped
2 eggs
1 soft lettuce, leaves separated and washed
1 red onion, very thinly sliced
3 large vine tomatoes, sliced
½ cucumber, thinly sliced

For the dressing
juice of 2 limes
1 tbsp fish sauce
1 tbsp caster (superfine) sugar
1 tbsp black peppercorns, crushed
salt, to taste

Continued overleaf...

Other favourite thinner steaks (2cm/¾in or less) for quick, hot and fast cooking

- Skirt – a delicious open-textured full flavoured steak, this is the animal's diaphragm muscle, cut from the plate, or forequarter belly of the cow. Be sure to cut across the grain for tenderness (see page 33).

- Bavette (flank or goose skirt) – around 2cm (¾in) thick, cut from the lower abdominal on the sirloin primal, so the back quarter, bavette has a similar open-grained texture to skirt and is full of flavour, best cooked rare to medium-rare and cut across the grain.

- Feather blade – cut from the chuck (shoulder), this is a really tender and well marbled steak, although there is a line of connective tissue running down the middle, looking like the central rib on a feather. Sometimes this is removed, giving you two separate steaks, and then it becomes known as the flat iron.

Rump tail or tri-tip, plus three steak sauces

Rump tail or tri-tip is a triangular cut from the bottom tip of the sirloin, so you get two per cow, one either side. It's a tender and tasty cut cooked hot and fast, but do take a careful look at your meat before you cook it – although it's one single muscle, the grain actually runs in two different directions. To ensure that all-important cutting across the grain, you need to slice it in one direction to the point where the grain changes, about in the middle, then turn through 90 degrees and slice it in the other direction. Also, because of its triangular shape, the thin end does have a tendency to be done before the fat end.

Begin by dry-brining the steak – simply sprinkle the salt all over and place on a rack set over a tray. Slide into the fridge for 24 hours if you have time.

Decide on your sauce and get that ready. If you are making romesco, go ahead and fire up the barbecue first as you need it to grill the peppers; for the other two sauces, begin inside. Either way, when you are ready to cook, fire up your barbecue ready for direct grilling but leaving half of your grill coal-free so you can manoeuvre if things are getting too hot.

To make the walnut and tarragon pesto, tip the walnuts into a small fireproof frying pan (skillet) and toast over a medium heat for a couple of minutes. Add to a food processor along with the tarragon, garlic, olive oil and white wine vinegar and blend to a smooth paste. Season to taste with salt and freshly ground black pepper and scoop into a bowl. Set aside.

For the romesco sauce, set the red peppers onto the grill bars directly over the fire. Grill for around 20 minutes, rotating regularly until they are soft and lightly charred. Remove from the heat and put in a bowl. Cover and allow to cool for a few minutes, then peel and slice in half, removing the seeds and stems. Add to the bowl of a food processor. Toast the almonds in a dry frying pan (skillet) over a medium heat for a couple of minutes until they are golden. You can do this on the barbecue by setting the pan slightly off the fire, or on the hob inside. Add to the food processor, along with the bread, olive oil, garlic and smoked paprika. Blitz until smooth, adding just enough cold water to make a smooth paste. Season with a little vinegar and salt and black pepper to taste, then scoop into a bowl and set aside.

Serves 4

1kg (2lb 4oz) rump tail
1 tbsp flaked sea salt
a little olive oil
flaked sea salt and freshly ground
    black pepper

For the walnut and tarragon pesto

100g (3½oz) walnuts
a good bunch of fresh tarragon
    (15g/½oz), leaves and fine
    stalks roughly chopped
1 garlic clove, chopped
100ml (3½fl oz) extra virgin olive
    oil
2 tbsp white wine vinegar

For the romesco sauce

2 large red peppers
50g (2oz) whole blanched
    almonds
1 slice of slightly stale sourdough
    bread, torn into chunks
5 tbsp olive oil
3 garlic cloves, crushed
½ tsp smoked paprika
1–2 tsp sherry vinegar, to taste

Continued overleaf...

For the chimichurri, add the garlic to a pestle and mortar and crush. Add the parsley, oregano and chillies and pound together. Stir through the olive oil, lemon juice and sugar to taste and season with a little salt and pepper. Scoop into a bowl and set aside.

When you are ready to cook your steak, make sure your grill is really good and hot, adding extra charcoal to the fire if necessary if you've been grilling the peppers for romesco. Drizzle a little oil over the rump tail and rest on the grill bars directly over the fire, turning every 30 seconds or so, to build up a good crust all over. Using a meat probe, check the temperature of the meat at the thickest point – 52°C (125°F) for rare, 56°C (132°F) for medium-rare. If the thin end is overcooking but the thick end isn't ready, rotate the steak so the thinner end stays further from the fire each time you turn.

Set the steak onto a board and carve into thick slices before eating with your chosen sauce. If you want to rest the steak before carving, be sure to remove it a few degrees below eating temperature to allow for carryover cooking.

For the chimichurri sauce
3 garlic cloves, chopped
a large bunch (about 100g/3½oz) of flat-leaf parsley, larger stalks discarded, chopped
2 tbsp fresh oregano leaves
2 long red chillies, chopped
100ml (3½fl oz) olive oil
juice of ½–1 lemon, to taste
a pinch of caster (superfine) sugar

A simple, but perfect, boneless steak for two – ribeye, sirloin or rump

If I wasn't cooking a hanger steak – my personal favourite – then I would always, always cook a thick – 3–4cm (1¼–1½in) – steak for sharing, allowing about 600g (1lb 5oz) for two people. I just prefer to cook one steak to share; it's easier to nail the internal temperature vs crust conundrum, i.e. max sear on the outside, minimal chance of overcooking the inside. And I like the spirit of generosity it's served in; a sharing dish always feels like a more friendly way of eating, offering an edible gift to those I love.

First, which cut to choose? As always, these things are a matter of personal preference. Working from the front to the back of the cow:

- Ribeye – cut from the upper rib area of the cow, comprising mostly the longissimus dorsi muscle and a little section of spinalis muscle. These muscles are not particularly hard-working and more supportive along the spine so are good and tender. It's the exact same muscles as a standing rib roast, just cut as a steak. Ribeye has a lot of natural intramuscular marbling, making this a supremely juicy, flavoursome steak. Even if you like steak rare, and I do, this is a cut to take a little higher in temperature – you want to give it some time for the juicy nugget of fat in the centre to render out a little. I think a medium cook, or just slightly under, is your best bet. See the reverse sear temperature chart on page 44.

- Sirloin (or strip steak) – this is also cut from the longissimus dorsi muscle and therefore considered a tender 'prime' cut, coming from further down the back but before the rump. This muscle runs from shoulder to hip. Less intramuscular fat than a ribeye and usually has a strip of fat on the top edge.

- Rump – cut from the other end of the back, the cow's bum – or rump – is a collection of five different muscles. Rump steak is a cross section of these muscles. It's an area of the cow that works fairly hard and is naturally on the lean side. So there's not a lot of fat but the meat itself is good and flavourful if a little tougher than either ribeye or sirloin. Locate the grain before cooking and be sure to cut against it to eat.

Why reverse sear?

I always cook fat sharing steaks using a brilliantly failsafe technique called reverse sear. The weight of steak is irrelevant as you are cooking to temperature and so this technique is identical whether you are cooking a 600g (1lb 5oz) steak for two or a 1.2kg (2lb 10oz) steak for four.

With the reverse sear technique you flip the traditional way of cooking steak on its head, so instead of searing hot and fast, then moving to a cooler spot to finish cooking, you start very cool and finish very, very hot indeed. The result is a steak cooked to equal perfection from the outside to the centre, with a glorious deep brown crust all over.

Heat energy from the fire of your barbecue excites the molecules on the outside of the steak and those molecules transfer the heat into the centre of the meat. By starting your cook very slowly that heat transfer happens evenly, so your steak will be the exact same temperature on the outside as it is in the middle. Call it the fire cook's equivalent of sous vide, if you like. The danger with starting high and finishing cooler is that you overdo the outside while trying to get the inside done as you like it, so the outside layer of a steak can be dry and overcooked. Reverse sear gives you, the cook, the chance for gentle equilibrium from top to bottom, resulting in a juicer steak with a better crust. It's worth pointing again out that reverse sear only works with a thicker steak, ideally 3–4cm (1¼–1½in) or more.

Continued overleaf...

How to reverse sear

Begin by dry-brining your steak of choice. Please do it, it really makes the biggest difference (see page 21). Simply sprinkle flaked sea salt over both sides of the steak, place on a rack set over a tray and slide into the fridge for 24 hours if possible. The rack allows the air to circulate so the steak doesn't swim in its own juices. Allow a tablespoon or so of flaked sea salt per kilo of meat, although salt is a personal thing so adjust to taste (see page 22).

When you are ready to cook, fire up your barbecue ready for slow indirect cooking, aiming for a temperature of around 120–130°C (250–265°F). You can add a little smoking wood to the fire if you like, but I wouldn't overdo the smoke as you want to the steak to shine here.

Set the steak, always straight from the fridge, onto the grill bars far from the fire, and shut the lid. If you have a wired temperature probe (so very useful, see page 24) insert it deep into the centre of the steak before shutting the lid. If you only have a regular meat probe that's fine too, you'll just need to keep checking it. Either way, using very gentle convection heat, take the steak up to a temperature 10°C (18°F) below the temperature you want to eat it at (see right). No need to turn or rotate, just let it very gently do its thing. It will look dry and unappetizing at this point, never fear. The drying of the surface is going to work in your favour, allowing for the crust to build up during the sear.

Once you have your temperature, remove the steak to a plate. The aim of the game now is to get the barbecue really good and hot, so get those coals glowing red. I generally start another little chimney of charcoal, or half a chimney if you're using a full-size chimney (see page 17) and get the bottom air vent open really wide. Don't worry about the top vents as you sear with the lid up.

When your fire is hot, get the steak directly on the hot grill bars over the fire. Sear it hot and fast, flipping every 30 seconds or so with the lid up. Every time you turn, try to place it back on a different bit of the grill bars (see page 19). Once the steak has a deep, mahogany brown crust on both sides and has reached your desired eating temperature, get it off and tuck in.

> **Steak temperatures**
> 52°C (125°F) for rare, so take it to 42°C (107°F) before removing
>
> 56°C (132°F) for medium-rare, so take it to 46°C (115°F) before removing
>
> 60°C (140°F) for medium, so take it to 50°C (122°F) before removing

Three favourite flavoured butters for steak

Ridiculously easy: simply mix up the softened butter with plenty of salt and pepper and your chosen seasonings. Scoop onto a sheet of baking paper and roll up into a cylinder. Slide into the fridge to firm up for an hour before slicing and using. Will keep for a week in the fridge if you want to get ahead and will freeze, really well wrapped, for 3 months.

100g (3½oz) butter, softened
flaked sea salt and freshly ground black pepper

porcini and garlic

25g (1oz) dried porcini, soaked in boiling water for 10 minutes, then finely chopped
2 garlic cloves, crushed

wasabi and chive

2 tsp wasabi paste
a small bunch of chives, finely snipped

Parmesan and smoked paprika

10g (⅓oz) freshly grated Parmesan
2 tsp hot smoked paprika

Bone-in steaks

The bone in a big bone-in steak is not necessarily your friend (see page 33), even if it looks good; I personally cook them very rarely indeed. That said, if you are cooking these bone-in steaks treat them exactly the same as bone-out steaks – get a big one and reverse sear it as opposite.

- Cote de Boeuf – this is a ribeye steak that includes the rib bone, from the fore rib, so essentially it's a single rib portion of a standing rib roast. When the rib bone is left long, you have yourself a tomahawk steak. Same amount of meat, same cut, you just get more bone.

- T-bone and Porterhouse – with a T-bone you get the sirloin steak on one side of the spinal bone and a fillet steak on the other. While you might think you're getting a good deal with two types of steak, they are actually pretty tricky to cook because the sirloin takes longer than the fillet. Deploy the reverse sear technique but make sure the sirloin is the side facing the fire so the fillet is furthest from the heat. A Porterhouse could be described as 'posh T-bone', because the fillet section is bigger as it comes from further up the cow.

- Bone-in sirloin – this is just a sirloin steak with its attached spinal bone, so a T-bone minus the fillet section.

Picanha piri piri, grilled veg

The picanha is also known as the rump cap as it's cut from the top section of the rump, with a thick strip of fat running all along the top surface. The fat makes it a tricky cut to cook as it's prone to flare-ups. I like to treat this as a two-part cook – essentially a reverse sear – so you cook it super low and slow at first to bring it to a constant temperature and start to render the fat, then sear it off to develop a beautiful browning. Slicing it into steaks and threading it horseshoe-like onto skewers before the hot and fast sear is traditional in Brazil, where it's a hugely popular cut.

The day before you want to cook, dry-brine the steak (page 21). Cut deep slashes through the fat in a diamond pattern; this will help the fat render. Sprinkle plenty of salt over the steak and rub in. Place on a rack set over a tray then slide it into the fridge, uncovered, and leave overnight.

To make the piri piri sauce, simply put all the ingredients and a little salt and pepper into a mini food processor and blitz until smooth. You can also use a stick blender in a deep jug. The sauce will keep for at least 3 days in the fridge.

Fire up your barbecue ready for gentle indirect grilling.

Lay the steak, fat side up, as far from the fire as you can, and cook until the internal temperature reaches 40°C (104°F); this may take an hour or so. A wired temperature probe is a useful bit of kit here as you won't need to keep opening up the lid to check. Remove the picanha to a board and cut into 2cm (¾in) thick steaks *with* the grain (see page 23). You should get about 6–8 steaks. Curl each steak into a horseshoe shape, with the fat on the outside edge, and pierce two metal skewers through to secure. You should be able to line up 2 or 3 pieces on one double skewer. Cutting *with* the grain here is important as then, once you have your individual seared steaks, you can cut *across* the grain to eat.

Get your barbecue pumping hot, but still with an indirect set-up. Drizzle oil over the courgettes (zucchini), peppers and spring onions (scallions) and season with salt and pepper. Grill until lightly charred and just cooked, then set aside to keep warm.

Sear the steaks hot and fast for a few minutes directly over the fire, brushing with piri piri sauce as you cook. Keep turning the skewers so they brown evenly. Remove from the grill when they reach your desired internal temperature – 52°C (125°F) for rare, 56°C (132°F) for medium-rare, a little higher for medium.

To serve, pile the vegetables on a platter and top with the steaks. Serve the rest of the piri piri alongside.

Serves 4

1–1.3kg (2lb 4oz–2lb 14oz) picanha
2–3 courgettes (zucchini), quartered lengthways
3 long red peppers, cut in half lengthways
a bunch of spring onions (scallions)
a little olive oil
flaked salt and freshly ground black pepper

For the piri piri sauce

60g (2½oz) mixed red chillies, roughly chopped, seeds left in for more heat or removed for less
6 garlic cloves
3 fresh bay leaves, tough central stem removed
a small bunch of flat-leaf parsley, leaves and stalks roughly chopped
100ml (3½fl oz) olive oil
juice of 1 lemon
½ tsp smoked paprika
a pinch of caster (superfine) sugar

Fillet with dill béarnaise, charred asparagus

How do I feel about fillet steak? As a general rule I'd say it's a (rather expensive) case of style over substance... sure, it's very, very tender, but for that you sacrifice flavour. Then, one truly glorious day, beef-master Olly Woolnough of Meatmatters fed me a fillet from an ex-dairy cow that he'd dry-aged for 14 days. Game. Changer. A piece of fillet full of rich ribbons of fat marbling through it. Both tender and ludicrously tasty. If I couldn't get a fillet this good, I would probably use hanger/onglet instead. Fraction of the cost, way more flavour.

Béarnaise, that classic steak sauce, can ring fear in even the most experienced cooks, but the only thing you need to know is don't let it get too hot then it won't split. I made this over the barbecue, moving the pan on and off the heat to keep the temperature nice and steady. I love to encourage people to just think of a charcoal fire as your heat source, just like you would a hob, but (of course) you can make this inside if you prefer.

Begin by dry-brining the steak – simply sprinkle the salt all over and place on a rack set over a tray. Slide into the fridge for 24 hours if you have time, but even a couple of hours would be good.

Fire up your barbecue ready for direct grilling, but piling the coals to one side so you can cook the béarnaise slightly away from the heat.

Take a small fireproof pan, pour in the vinegar and set over the heat. Add the shallot, garlic, dill stems (reserve the fronds) and peppercorns. Bring up to the boil and simmer gently for a few minutes until the liquid has reduced to a tablespoon. Strain into a small bowl and set aside. Wash the pan and add a couple of centimetres (an inch) of water, setting back onto your grill, this time away from the fire so it warms gently. Put the egg yolks into a heatproof glass or ceramic bowl and sit over the saucepan, making sure the base is well away from the water or it'll get too hot. Add the mustard and, using a balloon whisk, mix it through over a low heat until it starts to thicken a little. Pour in the vinegar reduction and whisk until smooth. Start to add the butter a couple of cubes at a time, whisking as it melts. Keep adding and whisking in the butter until you are left with a smooth, glossy sauce the consistency of double (heavy) cream. Finely chop the dill fronds and stir through. Add a little salt and pepper to taste and remove from the heat, keeping the bowl over the pan of hot water to keep warm while you cook the steak and asparagus.

Serves 2, easily doubled up for more

400g (14oz) fillet steak, in one piece (ideally cut from the fat end)
2 tsp flaked sea salt
olive oil, for drizzling
a bunch of asparagus, trimmed
flaked sea salt and freshly ground black pepper

For the béarnaise
4 tbsp white wine vinegar
1 shallot, finely chopped
1 garlic clove, chopped
a handful of dill, stems and fronds
a few black peppercorns
2 egg yolks
1 heaped tsp English mustard
100g (3½oz) butter, diced into 1cm (½in) cubes

Make sure your fire is good and hot, adding a little more fuel if necessary, but (as always) keeping the fuel to one side, so you have room to manoeuvre your food should things get too hot (see page 19).

Drizzle a little oil all over the steak and rest the steak directly over the fire. Cook over a really hot heat, keeping the lid up and turning every 30 seconds or so until you reach your desired internal temperature – 52°C (125°F) for rare, 56°C (132°F) for medium-rare.

Drizzle a little oil over the asparagus and set onto the grill over the fire. Cook for just a few minutes until lightly charred all over, turning frequently. If you're pretty nifty with the tongs it's possible to cook the steak and asparagus at the same time, constantly turning both. If you are a little less confident, cook the steak first, take the temperature a little lower, and rest for a few minutes while you grill the asparagus. Serve the steak and asparagus with the béarnaise.

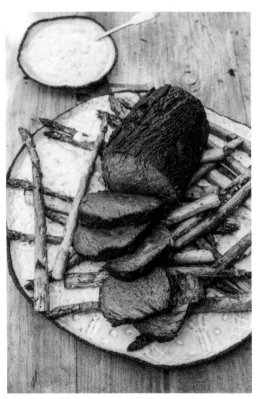

Sticky caraway gammon, potato salad

Seared hot and fast and finished in a pan of sticky spiced sauce, this is one of my favourite ways to eat ham. Gammon steaks, cut from cured pork leg, can sometimes be harder to find from high-welfare butchers and farmers. A simple solution is to buy a gammon joint and slice your own steaks. Freezing the joint for a couple of hours before cutting will help your slices be nice and even, a sharp knife is essential too.

Begin with the potato salad, as it will sit quite nicely for a while, and once you get the steaks on the cooking is all pretty speedy.

Tip the potatoes into a saucepan and cover well with cold water. Shake in a little salt and set over a high heat. Bring to the boil and simmer until just tender, around 15 minutes depending on the size. Drain well, tip into a bowl and leave to cool to room temperature.

In a small bowl, stir together the mayonnaise, crème fraîche and mustard and a good seasoning of salt and pepper. Pour over the potatoes and stir through to mix. Add the spring onions (scallions) and tomatoes and fold through lightly. Spoon into a serving bowl and set aside. Just before you eat, scatter the beetroot (beets) over the top. You can also stir it through for a rather vibrant pink salad, if you prefer.

When you are ready to cook, fire up your barbecue ready for direct and indirect grilling, using about three-quarters of a chimney full of charcoal.

Take a fireproof frying pan (skillet) and add the butter, honey, mustard, caraway seeds, chives and good grind of black pepper. Set on the grill bars on the opposite side to the fire so it can gently melt together.

Drizzle just a little oil over the gammon and lay onto the grill bars, directly over the fire, and sear over a high heat for about 5 minutes, or until you have a minimum temperature of 62°C (143°F) if you are using a probe. As with any steak, flipping regularly, every 30 seconds or so, will give you the best results in terms of browning and therefore taste.

Once the steaks are done, add them to the pan of sauce and slide the pan over the direct heat. Use tongs to toss the steaks about for a couple of minutes to glaze and caramelize them. Serve hot from the grill with the potato salad alongside.

Serves 4

50g (2oz) butter
2 tbsp honey
2 tbsp wholegrain mustard
2 tsp caraway seeds, roughly
    crushed in a pestle and mortar
a handful of chives, snipped
4 gammon steaks, about 1cm
    (½in) thick or 200–225g
    (7–8oz) each
a drizzle of olive oil
freshly ground black pepper

For the potato salad
750g (1lb 10oz) new potatoes,
    halved
2 tbsp mayonnaise
2 tbsp crème fraîche
1 tsp English mustard
½ bunch of spring onions
    (scallions), thinly sliced
4 ripe vine tomatoes, chopped
250g (9oz) cooked beetroot
    (beets), finely diced
flaked sea salt and freshly ground
    black pepper

Ribeye pork steaks, creamy mushroom sauce

Pork steaks are a rich, dare I say fatty meat, but remember, fat is flavour. For this reason they take so well to bright zingy Asian flavours but I think, sometimes, you really desire something doubly unctuous and decadent. Fat layering on beautiful fat, if you like, occasionally ticks a whole lot of comfort boxes for me. While I doubt I would eat this on a warm summer's day in the middle of 'barbecue season' it's something rather wonderful to cook on a chilly spring or autumn night, and taken inside to the snug warmth of your home.

Dry-brine the pork steaks by sprinkling with salt all over and resting on a rack set over a tray. Slide in the fridge and leave, uncovered, for 24 hours if you have time.

When you are ready to cook, fire up your barbecue ready for indirect and direct grilling.

Put the dried mushrooms in a bowl and pour over just enough boiling water to cover. Set aside to soak until soft, then strain over a bowl, reserving the soaking liquid. Chop the mushrooms finely and add back to the liquid.

Add the oil and butter to a fireproof frying pan (skillet) and set directly over the fire to melt. Add the fresh mushrooms and fry until soft, stirring a few times. Add the garlic and fry for a few minutes, then pour in the wine, along with the chopped dried mushrooms and their soaking liquid. Leave to bubble until reduced almost completely, then add the cream, tarragon and seasoning. Heat the cream through, then cover and set aside.

At the same time you begin the sauce, rest the pork steaks on the opposite side of the fire so they can cook gently – you are reverse searing them (see page 43). Cook until the internal temperature is 50°C (122°F) – around about 30–40 minutes, depending on the heat you have and how thick your steaks are.

Remove the steaks to a tray and, if necessary, add a little more fuel to the fire to get it pumping hot. Set the pan of sauce on the grill bars, this time away from the fire so it can warm a little. Then sear the steaks over a really high heat, keeping the lid up, and flipping them every 30 seconds or so to build up a really good, browned crust on the outside. Keep cooking until you have reached your desired temperature – from 63°C (145°F) for medium to 71°C (160°F) for well done.

Serve with the sauce spooned over. In the spirit of total comfort, I would eat this with mash and something green.

Serves 4

4 pork ribeye steaks (you could also use shoulder or leg steaks), about 300g (10½oz) each
1 good tbsp flaked sea salt
10g (⅓oz) dried mushrooms (e.g. porcini, ceps)
1 tbsp olive oil
25g (1oz) butter
300g (10½oz) chestnut mushrooms, sliced
2 garlic cloves, crushed
175ml (¾ cup) white wine
300ml (1¼ cups) double (heavy) cream
20g (¾oz) fresh tarragon, leaves picked and chopped
flaked sea salt and freshly ground black pepper

Pork tenderloin, pistachio crust, grilled spring veg

A light and bright recipe for spring – just add a few new potatoes if you want an extra carb hit. Tenderloin is the equivalent to beef fillet steak – a long, slim muscle running along the side of the spine that does very little hard graft so it's super-tender. It usually has a layer of silver skin to one side, a thin layer of tough connective tissue that won't melt and soften during a quick cook so you need to remove it. Slide a sharp knife just under the surface and slice it away, working with the grain and leaving as much meat as possible.

Sprinkle salt all over the tenderloin and place it on a rack set over a tray. Slide into the fridge to dry-brine for 12–24 hours.

The next day, get your prep done: add the butter, honey, garlic and thyme to a small fireproof saucepan. Add the pistachios and mustard powder to a small food processor and blitz up to fine crumbs (or crush in a pestle and mortar). Tip into a fireproof roasting tin that's big enough to hold the pork fillet. Trim the woody ends from the asparagus and top and tail the beans. Spread out on a plate, drizzle with a little olive oil and season with salt and pepper. Make the dressing by whisking together the olive oil with the mustard and honey, then whisk in the lemon juice and season with a little salt and pepper.

When ready to cook, fire up your barbecue with the coals to one side so you can cook directly and indirectly. Once the fire is hot set the pan with the butter and honey to one side of the fire and allow it to melt. Lay the pork onto the grill bars above the fire and brush all over with a little of the melted butter. Keep basting while you sear the pork hot and fast, turning it every 30 seconds to build up a caramelized surface – you are aiming for maximum Maillard.

Lift the seared pork into the tin with the pistachio crumbs and roll it around, pressing the nuts to surface as best you can. Some will fall off; never mind, the tin will keep them safe. Slide the tin onto the grill bars away from the fire and shut the lid of the barbecue. Leave to finish cooking through indirectly until the pork reaches an internal of temperature of 63°C (145°F) for medium, 71°C (160°F) for well done.

Once the pork is nearly ready, drizzle a little oil over the asparagus and beans and grill for a few minutes until just tender. Rest them perpendicular to the grill bars so they don't fall through, or grab a veg grilling tray if you have one. Transfer to a serving platter and and pour over the dressing. Lift the pork to a board and slice, then rest on top of the vegetables. Scoop up any fallen nuts from the tin and on the chopping board and sprinkle them over to top.

Serves 4

650g (1lb 7oz) pork tenderloin, trimmed
1 tbsp flaked sea salt
50g (2oz) butter
3 tbsp honey
2 garlic cloves, crushed
a few sprigs of thyme, leaves picked
150g (5½oz) shelled pistachios
2 tbsp English mustard powder
500g (1lb 2oz) asparagus
250g (9oz) green beans
1 tbsp olive oil
flaked sea salt and freshly ground black pepper

For the dressing

75ml (⅓ cup) extra virgin olive oil
2 tbsp wholegrain mustard
2 tbsp honey
juice of 1 lemon

Smoky lamb leg steaks, red pepper relish

Like the shoulder end of a lamb, the back legs are constantly working, but the muscles are comparatively lean with less intramuscular marbling. This means that leg steaks are more suited to hot and fast cooking otherwise they can dry out. As always, a little dry-brining is a great thing for upping tenderness, although being a relatively thin cut you can get away with a few hours if you're short of time.

Sprinkle the salt all over the lamb steaks and place on a rack set over a tray. Slide into the fridge, uncovered, and leave to dry-brine for up to 24 hours.

The next day, set a small frying pan (skillet) over a medium heat on the hob and tip in the cumin seeds, toasting for a minute or two until fragrant. Tip into a pestle and mortar and roughly crush. Add the smoked paprika, garlic and oil and pound together to make paste. Take this spicy oil to the barbecue with a silicone brush for basting.

Fire up the barbecue ready for direct and indirect grilling.

For the pepper relish, set a sturdy fireproof frying pan near the fire but not directly over it. Pour in the olive oil, add the onions and peppers and cook for about 45 minutes until really soft and lightly charred. You will need to keep an eye on them, stirring and rotating the pan so they cook evenly. Once soft, add the sherry vinegar, honey, garlic and smoked paprika and season with a little salt and pepper. Stir together and slide over a higher heat for 10 minutes or so to allow the vinegar to evaporate and concentrate. Stir through the parsley and then slide to the opposite side, away from the fire, so it keeps warm while you cook the steaks.

Lift the lamb onto the grill bars over the fire and brush over a little of the spiced oil. Keep brushing and flipping every 30 seconds or so until the lamb is at your preferred eating temperature, so 52°C (125°F) for rare, 60°C (140°F) for medium. If the oil is causing flare-ups, and it very well may, just slide the meat a little further away from the fire for a few seconds before moving back.

Slice the lamb, then serve with a spoon of relish on top, and plenty of crusty bread to mop the juices. A big green salad wouldn't go amiss.

Serves 4

4 lamb legs steaks, about
   200–250g (7–9oz) each
1 tbsp flaked sea salt
2 tbsp cumin seeds
1 tbsp smoked paprika
2 garlic cloves, chopped
4 tbsp olive oil
bread and salad, to serve

For the red pepper relish

4 tbsp olive oil
2 large red onions, thinly sliced
2 large red peppers, thinly sliced
2 tbsp sherry vinegar
1 tbsp honey
2 garlic cloves, sliced
1 tsp smoked paprika
a handful of flat-leaf parsley,
   chopped
flaked sea salt and freshly ground
   black pepper

TWO QUICK MIDWEEK CHOPS

You can't beat a quick chop on the grill. Both these recipes need a little forethought for the brining process – wet for the pork chops, dry for the lamb chops – but once you've got that out of the way the actual cooking takes minutes.

Treacle-brined pork, coriander sauce, burnt apricots

A very simple brine of salt with a little treacle and brown sugar that adds both a touch of sweetness and colour. Out of season, a can of apricots in juice makes an excellent substitute to fresh apricots.

Begin by making the brine. Pour 250ml (1 cup) boiling water into a heatproof jug. Add the salt, sugar and treacle, stirring well until dissolved. Top up with cold water to give you 500ml (2 cups) of brine. Set aside to go completely cold.

Prepare the pork chops by cutting a few slashes through the strip of fat on each, cutting down to the meat but not into it. This will help the fat render on grilling. Put the chops into a freezer bag hung in a bowl and pour the cold brine over. Tie the bag up tight, squeezing out the air, and slide into the fridge for 24 hours.

The next day, make the sauce by adding the oil, lime zest and juice, coriander (cilantro) and garlic to a bowl. Whisk together well and season to taste with honey, salt and pepper. (Alternatively, blitz all the ingredients in a mini food processor.) Set aside.

Fire up your grill ready for direct cooking, piling the coals to one side.

Drizzle a little oil over the cut halves of the apricots. Drain the chops, discarding the brine, and pat dry with paper towels. Drizzle over a little oil and take to the grill.

Lay the chops on the grill bars directly over the fire. Cook, turning every 30 seconds or so for maximum sear and cooking until they reach your desired temperature – 63°C (145°F) for medium to 71°C (160°F) for well done. At the same time, grill the apricots directly over the fire for a few minutes each side until lightly charred.

Serve the chops with the apricots on top and drizzle over plenty of the sauce.

Serves 4

50g (2oz) flaked sea salt
2 tbsp brown sugar
3 tbsp treacle
4 pork chops, about 350–400g
    (12–14oz) each
6 ripe apricots, cut in half, stone
    removed
a little olive oil, for drizzling

For the coriander sauce

100ml (3½fl oz) extra virgin olive
    oil
zest and juice of 1 lime
a good handful of coriander
    (cilantro), leaves and stalks,
    finely chopped
1 garlic clove, crushed
1–2 tsp honey, to taste
flaked sea salt and freshly ground
    black pepper, to taste

Barnsley lamb chops, salsa verde

A Barnsley chop is a slice cut through the saddle of the lamb, effectively a double lamb loin chop, cut through the chine bone, which is nestled in the centre. Treat like any thin steak, that is cook hot and fast and keep on flipping as you cook for maximum Maillard reactions. A little dry-brining always helps with tenderness but as these chops are fairly slim, you can get away with less time – 12 hours would be good, even a couple of hours helps.

Dry-brine the chops 12 hours or so before cooking. Simply sprinkle the salt all over, put on a rack set over a tray and slide into the fridge, uncovered, for up to 24 hours.

For the salsa verde, add the roughly torn herbs to a food processor, along with the garlic, mustard, anchovies, capers, cornichons (small gherkins) and lemon juice. Pulse until coarsely ground then, with the motor running, pour in the olive oil. Season to taste with sugar, salt and pepper. Scoop into a bowl and set aside. You could also make by hand for a slightly coarser result, just finely chop all the elements and stir together in a bowl.

Fire up your barbecue ready for direct grilling, piling the coals to one side so you have room to manoeuvre the food to a cooler spot if things are getting a little hot.

Drizzle a little oil on the chops and rest on the grill bars directly over the fire. Keep grilling and flipping over every 30 seconds or so until they are cooked to your liking. Use a temperature probe, taking them to 52°C (125°F) for rare, 56°C (132°F) for medium-rare and 60°C (140°F) for medium. I never bother to rest lamb chops, they are quite a thin cut and I don't want to eat them cool. But if you do want to rest them, take them off the grill a few degrees below these temperatures to allow for a bit of carryover cooking.

Serve with a little salsa verde dolloped on top and the rest alongside.

Serves 4

4 Barnsley chops, about 250g
   (9oz) each
1 tbsp flaked sea salt
a drizzle of olive oil

For the salsa verde
a generous bunch of flat-leaf
   parsley, roughly torn
a small bunch of mint, roughly
   torn
a small bunch of chives, roughly
   torn
1 garlic clove, roughly chopped
1 tbsp Dijon mustard
30g (1oz) anchovies in olive oil
2 tbsp capers
4 cornichons (small gherkins)
juice of 1 lemon
150ml (2/3 cup) extra virgin olive
   oil
1–2 tsp caster (superfine) sugar
flaked sea salt and freshly ground
   black pepper

Chapter 2: Other Fast Cooks – kebabs, stuffed, wrapped and rolled things

Steaks are not the only hot and fast cooking you can do on your grill. These recipes take, generally, quick-cooking cuts and cook them, er, quickly. There are a couple that break the rules, namely the Korean pork belly, where you cut slow-cooking belly sliver-thin so it cooks super-fast, and the lamb neck sosaties that seems tender anyhow, principally because you slice it across the grain and give it a really long marinade.

Speeding up cooking times by making the cuts smaller, in the kebab recipes for example, also has the advantage of increasing the surface area. Remember, more surface area equals more bang for your buck in flavour terms when it comes to rubs and marinades.

Stuffed rolled bavette, tomatoes and balsamic

I would classify bavette, or flank, as one of my top three steak cuts, the perfect balance between flavour and tenderness. Here a whole bavette is treated more like a roasting joint, stuffed full of tasty things and rolled up porchetta-style. Then you slice it through to cut across the all-important grain to give you succulent slices. For me, with an abundance of gloriously sweet ripe tomatoes, this is high summer eating at its absolute best.

'Butterfly' out the steak, opening it up into a thinner layer and effectively doubling its size. Lay the steak on a board and press the flat of your hand firmly onto it to apply downward pressure. Use a really sharp knife to make a horizontal cut through the middle, using short slicing strokes like you are filleting a fish. Stop when you are a couple of centimetres from the other side and open it out like a book into a large flat rectangle.

Turn the steak so the grain of meat runs horizontally from left to right – this will ensure that you slice across the grain when you come to serve. Lay the slices of prosciutto onto the steak, covering it as much as you can, then dot the 'nduja over the top. Sprinkle with the Parmesan, basil leaves and capers and finish with a generous grind of pepper.

Starting from the side nearest you, roll it up tight into a long cylinder. Take the lengths of string and tie at regular intervals to secure the roll tight. Sprinkle salt over the outside and rest on a rack over a tray. Slide in the fridge for 2–24 hours.

When you are ready to cook, fire up your barbecue with two strips of fire down either side (see page 19). Leave the vents wide open. You want a good hot barbecue of around 220–240°C (430–465°F) with an indirect heat down the centre.

Rest the bavette on the grill bars, seam side down, in the centre of the barbecue and shut the lid. Cook indirectly for around 30 minutes, or until a probe reaches about 40°C (104°F) in the centre. Then use tongs to slide the roll directly over the fire and sear over a high heat, turning every few minutes for a further 15 minutes. For a medium-rare steak roll, lift it off the grill when the centre reaches 56°C (130°F).

Scatter the tomatoes over a serving platter and sprinkle on the basil. Drizzle generously with balsamic and olive oil and season with a little salt and pepper. Rest the roll on the centre of the platter and carve into slices.

Serves 4–6

1kg (2lb 4oz) bavette steak
80g (3oz) prosciutto
60g (2½oz) 'nduja
60g (2½oz) Parmesan, freshly grated
a bunch of basil, leaves torn (about 30g/1oz)
2 tbsp capers
1 tbsp olive oil
flaked sea salt and freshly ground black pepper

For the tomato salad

750g (1lb 10oz) really ripe mixed tomatoes, sliced
a bunch of basil, leaves torn
3–4 tbsp best quality balsamic vinegar
3–4 tbsp extra virgin olive oil

You also need 8–10 x 25cm (10in) lengths of butcher's string

OTHER FAST COOKS

Pork belly, gochugang sauce, pickled salad

This is designed as something of a do-it-yourself recipe, using a little tabletop grill, with the sauce and the leaves in bowls alongside. Then you and your table companions can grill little bits of meat yourselves, roll up and eat and then grill some more. Relaxed sharing barbecue at its best (plenty of cold beers optional). You need to cut the pork belly into rather thin slices which is much easier if it's partly frozen. So if you have time, slide it into the freezer for a couple of hours before starting. Also, because the rashers of meat are thin, they have a large surface area, meaning it only needs a short marinating time; an hour or two is plenty.

A perforated grilling tray (also known as a vegetable grilling tray, see page 25) is a good idea to cook the pork on so the pieces don't fall through the grill bars and into the fire, while letting a little smoky goodness bathe the meat as it sizzles. If you don't have one you can improvise by taking a double layer of foil and poking scissors through to make holes all over.

Rest the semi-frozen meat on a board and use a really sharp knife to cut across the grain into thin slices – around 4–5mm (¼in) is ideal – dropping them into a bowl as you go. Add the sesame oil, garlic and plenty of salt and pepper. Stir to mix, then cover and leave to marinate for an hour or two.

Meanwhile, cut the spring onions (scallions) and carrots into fine julienne and toss in a bowl. Add the toasted sesame seeds, soy sauce, rice wine vinegar, sesame oil, gochugaru flakes and sugar and stir together to mix. Slide into the fridge to chill a little.

To make the sauce, pour the soy sauce into a small saucepan and set over a low heat on the hob. Stir through the garlic, gochugang paste, miso and brown sugar and warm gently for a few minutes until you have a thick sauce. Pour into a bowl and set aside to cool.

When you are ready to cook, fire up your grill ready for direct grilling. When it's hot, set your grilling tray (or foil) over the fire and add a few bits of pork, grilling really hot and fast until it's crispy around the edges. Pile a few pieces of pork into a lettuce leaf, top with a little salad and a good dollop of gochugang sauce, roll up and eat. Then begin again...

Serves about 6

1kg (2lb 4oz) boneless, rindless
    pork belly, semi-frozen for
    easy slicing
2 tbsp sesame oil
3 garlic cloves, crushed
flaked sea salt and freshly ground
    black pepper

For the pickled salad
a bunch of spring onions
    (scallions)
2 carrots
2 tbsp sesame seeds, toasted
2 tbsp soy sauce
2 tbsp rice wine vinegar
2 tbsp sesame oil
1 tbsp gochugaru pepper flakes
2 tsp dark brown sugar

For the gochugang sauce
150ml (⅔ cup) soy sauce
3 garlic cloves, crushed
2 tbsp gochugang paste
2 tbsp miso
3 tbsp brown sugar

To serve
2 soft round lettuces, leaves
    picked, washed and dried

Lamb rack, hazelnut and thyme crumbs

A lamb rack is the equivalent of a beef rib roast – so a prime cut featuring super-tender meat from back muscles that don't do a lot of physical work. Just like a beef rib roast, lamb rack is a pretty spendy cut so save for a treat and give it simple treatment to let the meat shine. This recipe also works really well with kid-goat racks if you can get hold of them. Because they are slightly larger, they will take a little longer to cook – as always just cook to temperature not time.

The day before you want to cook, dry-brine the lamb racks by sprinkling the salt all over them and resting them on a rack set over a tray. Slide into the fridge, uncovered, and leave for up to 24 hours.

Tip the hazelnuts into the middle of a clean tea towel and fold up the edges to totally enclose. Use a rolling pin to bash with some vigour to crush them up. Transfer to a bowl, and stir through the breadcrumbs, thyme leaves and a little salt and pepper. Set aside, ready to take to the barbecue.

When you are ready to cook, fire up the barbecue for direct and indirect grilling. You want a good high heat so use a full chimney of charcoal (see page 17).

Add the butter and olive oil to a small fireproof frying pan (skillet) and set over the direct heat to melt. Stir through the garlic and cook for a minute or two before adding the seasoned hazelnut and breadcrumb mixture. Cook over the fire for a few minutes, stirring regularly, until the crumbs are golden and crispy, then remove from the heat and set aside.

Rest the lamb racks, bone side down first, directly over the fire and sear over a really high heat for 2–3 minutes on each side until well browned. Remove to a roasting tin, resting bone side down, and use the back of a spoon to spread the mustard all over the top. Sprinkle over the crispy crumbs, pressing them firmly onto the mustard and set the tin on the barbecue away from the fire so they can finish cooking over an indirect heat. Shut the barbecue lid and cook until a probe reading takes it to 52°C (125°F) for rare, 56°C (132°F) for medium-rare, 60°C (140°F) for medium – as always this will take as long as it takes, perhaps 15–20 minutes or so.

Remove the roasting tin and slice into individual ribs to serve. As usual if you would like to rest the meat a little, take it a few degrees below the temperatures above.

Serves 4

2 lamb racks
1 tbsp flaked sea salt
2–3 tbsp Dijon mustard

For the crumbs
50g (2oz) hazelnuts
50g (2oz/½ cup) fresh
    breadcrumbs
4 sprigs of fresh thyme, leaves
    picked
50g (2oz) butter
1 tbsp olive oil
1 garlic clove, crushed
flaked sea salt and freshly ground
    black pepper

THE VEAL STORY

Veal, or young beef meat, still has a very real image problem stemming from the eighties when the appalling welfare issues surrounding the use of 'veal crates' was big news. Today, using crates as a way of closely confining young cows has been totally banned in Europe and in many states of the US. With high-welfare veal (sometimes known as rose veal because of the pink colour of the meat) the young cows are allowed to live a natural life of drinking milk and grazing outside. They are killed for the table at around 8–10 months old, which incidentally is the same age that the lamb we eat is killed. The veal industry is based around male dairy calves that would otherwise be killed and disposed of at birth as they are obviously no use to the dairy industry. So eating ethically reared veal is a good sustainable meat choice. In fact I would go as far as to say that if you are consumer of cow dairy products you have something of a moral obligation to support the growth of the veal industry.

Veal escalope and aubergine skewers, caper spaghetti

While veal escalopes themselves can be cooked in a flash, in this recipe they get wrapped around grilled aubergine (eggplant), sliced and skewered. Kind of a barbecue equivalent of the Italian classic saltimbocca, I guess. A bit labour-intensive, not tricky, but perhaps just a touch fiddly. Perhaps consider it a love meal for two, something to make while sharing a little wine, catching up, laughing, listening to music. All my favourite things. Sometimes cooking is more than just getting a meal on the table.

If the escalopes are any greater than a centimetre thick, thin them out a little by laying them a piece at a time between two sheets of baking paper and gently bashing them out a bit with a rolling pin. Sprinkle salt on both sides and spread out on a rack over a tray while you light the barbecue and grill the aubergine (eggplant). Veal is super-tender so the steaks do not need more than a quick brine with salt.

Fire up your barbecue ready for direct grilling, piling the coals to one side so you have a direct heat-free space to manoeuvre food to should things be getting too hot.

Cook the spaghetti according to the packet instructions, drain well and drizzle a little oil over while it's still in the colander and give it a shake to coat the strands so they don't stick together. Set aside.

Spread the aubergine slices out on a roasting tray and drizzle over the olive oil. Season with salt and pepper. Grill over a direct heat until lightly charred and soft. If they are catching too quickly, slide them a little further from the heat source so they can properly soften all the way through. Not much eats more

Serves 2, generously

For the skewers

4 veal escalopes, 400g (14oz) total weight
1 tsp flaked sea salt
1 aubergine (eggplant), cut lengthways into 5mm (¼in) slices
2 tbsp olive oil
a handful of sage leaves
50g (2oz) freshly grated Parmesan

For the spaghetti

150g (5½oz) spaghetti
1 tsp olive oil
50g (2oz) butter
1 garlic clove, sliced

Continued overleaf...

disappointingly than an al dente aubergine! Remove from the grill and arrange the aubergine slices on top of the meat so they cover it completely, cutting the slices if necessary to make them fit neatly. Scatter over the sage leaves and around a third of the Parmesan. Roll up really tight, then slice through into generous 1–1.5cm (½–¾in) discs; you should get around four per escalope. Turn a disc so it's flat and insert a skewer through the centre, so it looks like a pin wheel. Repeat with the other discs to give you four skewers with four-five wheels of veal escalope on each.

Set a large fireproof pan directly over the fire and add the butter. Once it's melted add the garlic and fry for a minute or so, then tip in the breadcrumbs and fry over the heat until they crisp up. Add the capers, chilli flakes and the cooked spaghetti, tossing together to warm the spaghetti through. Slide the pan away from the heat to keep warm while you cook the skewers.

Rest the skewers on the grill bars directly over the fire and grill for a couple of minutes on one side to get a little colour to the meat. Turn over and sprinkle a little Parmesan over the grilled side. Keep grilling, turning and sprinkling Parmesan for around 10–12 minutes until the skewers are a deep golden brown all over.

To serve, pile the spaghetti onto warmed plates and top with the skewers.

50g (2oz/½ cup) fresh
    breadcrumbs
2 tbsp capers, roughly
    chopped
1–2 tsp chilli flakes
flaked sea salt and
    freshly ground
    black pepper

You also need 4 metal
    skewers

TWO EASY WAYS WITH PORK LEG

Pork leg is a lean cut compared to shoulder and can become dry with long cooking, so it's ideally suited for quick cooks like these kebabs. Increasing the surface area of meat, by slicing or dicing, is a brilliant way to maximize the effectiveness of a marinade. As discussed on page 22, marinades only ever penetrate a few millimetres in, so quite simply more surface area = more flavour.

Lemony pork kebabs, feta and pepper sauce

Inspired by Greek holiday eating, all bright skies and twinkly seas, these skewers might just transport you deliciously far from your own back yard.

Mix together the lemon zest and juice, olive oil, garlic and thyme. Season with salt and pepper, then add the diced pork and stir well to coat. Cover and refrigerate for 12–24 hours.

When you are ready to cook, fire up the barbecue for direct and indirect grilling.

Rest the whole peppers for the sauce directly over the fire and char the skins all over until blackened, turning regularly. Transfer to a bowl and cover with a plate, then leave for a few minutes; the steam will help loosen the skins. Peel the skin and discard it, along with the seeds and stem. Drop into a food processor, along with the feta, chilli flakes and olive oil. Add a little salt and pepper then whizz to a purée. Scoop into a bowl and set aside.

Thread the pork onto skewers, alternating it with pieces of pepper. Rest on the grill bars, slightly away from the fire so they cook over a medium heat (see page 19 for fire management and controlling the heat over a horizontal plane) and cook on all sides for 15–20 minutes. Use a meat probe to check the temperature, taking care the tip doesn't touch the metal skewer or you will get a false reading. Pork is safe to eat at 63°C (145°F) for medium or take it up to 71°C (160°F) for well done.

Serve with the feta and red pepper sauce alongside.

Makes 6–8 kebabs

zest and juice of 2 lemons
4 tbsp olive oil
2 garlic cloves, crushed
a good few sprigs of thyme,
    roughly chopped
1.2kg (2lb 10oz) pork leg, diced
    into 3–4cm (1¼in–1½in) cubes
2 red peppers, diced into 4cm
    (1½in) pieces
flaked sea salt and freshly ground
    black pepper

For the feta and red pepper sauce

2 red peppers
200g (7oz) feta
½–1 tsp chilli flakes
3 tbsp olive oil

You also need 6–8 metal skewers

Balsamic pork kebabs, pesto dressing

Vinegar is a wonderful acidic tenderizer (see page 21) but the slight sweetness to this marinade means the kebabs can burn over too high a heat, so be prepared to cook slightly away from the fire for a little longer.

Mix together the balsamic vinegar, olive oil, brown sugar, garlic and smoked paprika in a bowl. Season with salt and pepper, add the pork and toss together to coat. Cover and refrigerate for 12–24 hours.

To make the pesto, tip the pine nuts into a small frying pan (skillet) and set over a medium heat. Toast for a couple of minutes until golden, then tip into a food processor. Add the basil, Parmesan, olive oil, lemon juice and garlic along with a little salt and pepper. Blitz to a purée then scoop into a bowl. I always think pesto tastes best when freshly made, but you can make a few hours ahead if you prefer. You can also make by hand by chopping everything and pounding to a paste in a pestle and mortar.

When you are ready to cook, fire up the barbecue ready for direct and indirect grilling.

Thread the pork onto metal skewers, alternating it with the spring onion (scallion). Cook as on page 71, taking care to keep the kebabs a little away from the fierce infrared heat directly over the fire.

Serve the kebabs with the pesto dressing on the side.

Makes 8 kebabs

4 tbsp balsamic vinegar
3 tbsp olive oil
1 tbsp brown sugar
3 garlic cloves, crushed
1 tsp smoked paprika
1.2kg (2lb 10oz) pork leg, diced
    into 3–4cm (1¼in–1½in) cubes
a bunch of spring onions
    (scallions), cut into 4cm
    (1½in) lengths
flaked sea salt and freshly ground
    black pepper

For the pesto

50g (2oz) pine nuts
30g (1oz) basil, leaves and stems,
    roughly torn
40g (1½oz) Parmesan, grated
    (shredded)
6 tbsp olive oil
juice of ½ lemon
1 garlic clove, crushed

You also need 8 metal skewers

THREE RED MEAT KEBABS

Tandoori venison kebabs

Venison haunch is really lean and prone to drying out so the yogurt-based marinade here is designed to tenderize and relax the meat fibres to keep things as juicy as possible (see page 21 on the magic of marinades). Achiote paste, made from the ground seeds of the annatto tree, adds a glorious red hue to the meat. It's easy to find online and is used in two other recipes in the book (see page 234 and 260). Kashmiri chillies are mild and brightly coloured, so if you substitute a different chilli, reduce the quantity unless you want it mind-blowingly hot!

Set a small frying pan (skillet) over a medium heat and tip in the achiote, chillies, cumin and fenugreek seeds. Toast for a couple of minutes then transfer to spice mill and grind to a power. Pour into a bowl and stir through the yogurt, ginger, garlic and salt to make a paste. Add the venison and mix thoroughly so all the pieces are coated. Cover and slide into the fridge for 24 hours.

The next day, fire up the barbecue ready for direct cooking, piling half a chimney of coals to one side of the barbecue so you can slide the kebabs off the heat if they are cooking too fast.

Thread the venison onto the skewers, alternating it with the red pepper and slivers of onion. Grill directly over the fire for about 15 minutes, turning regularly. Yogurt marinades can burn so be prepared to slide them further from the heat if they are catching too fast.

Rest on a serving plate, scatter over the coriander (cilantro), then zest and squeeze over the lime.

Makes 8

50g (2oz) achiote paste, very finely chopped
5g (¼oz) Kashmiri chillies, roughly torn
1 tbsp cumin seeds
2 tsp fenugreek seeds
150g (5½oz/¾ cup) Greek yogurt
50g (2oz) fresh root ginger, grated
3 garlic cloves, crushed
1 tsp salt
750g (1lb 10oz) venison haunch steaks, cut into 2–3cm (1in) cubes
2 red peppers, cut into 2–3cm pieces
1 small red onion, cut into 6–8 wedges, and slivers pulled apart

To serve
a little coriander (cilantro), chopped
zest and juice of 1 lime

You also need 8 metal skewers

Steak, spring onion and ginger skewers chilli peanut oil

I love using bavette (also known as flank) steak for kebabs: sliced across the grain and ribboned onto sticks it cooks quickly and stays tender. You could substitute it for hanger (onglet) too. It also stands up to a good long marinade for maximum flavour – 48 hours wouldn't hurt – and the chilli oil gets better after a couple of days, so start early if you can. Then the cooking is a breeze. Served with steamed rice and something green like stir-fried asparagus or broccoli, this is insanely good and fast.

Rest the steak on a board and use a large sharp knife to cut into 1cm (½in) strips, making sure you cut across the grain (see page 23). Toss into a bowl and add the spring onions (scallions), ginger, soy sauce, five-spice and a generous grind of black pepper. Toss to mix, cover and refrigerate for 24–48 hours.

At the same time make the chilli oil as it improves after a day or so. Pour the oil into a small heavy-based saucepan and set over a low heat on the hob. Add the peanuts, chilli flakes, garlic, shallots and salt and simmer really gently for a good 30 minutes until the chilli is crispy and the peanuts, garlic and shallot are golden. Leave to cool in the pan before transferring to a screw-top jar or a bowl with a lid. Once cold, slide into the fridge where it will keep for a good month, although I guarantee it won't last that long.

When you are ready to cook, thread up the meat onto the skewers, ribboning the slices a few times on the sticks, and alternating them with pieces of spring onion.

Fire up your barbecue ready for direct grilling – the skewers cook quickly, so you shouldn't need to use too much fuel, just half a chimney or so, if you are using the best quality charcoal.

Sear the skewers over a high direct heat for 5–7 minutes with the lid open, turning regularly. Cooking with the lid open means you are only using direct radiant heat from the charcoal plus conduction heat from the grill bars, so you have a good chance of a getting a lovely caramelized sear on the meat before it overcooks.

Serve straight away with the crispy chilli oil alongside.

Makes 8

800g (1lb 12oz) quick-cooking
   steak – bavette (flank), skirt
   or hanger (onglet) is ideal
a bunch of spring onions
   (scallions), cut into 3–4cm
   (1¼–1½in) lengths
50g (2oz) fresh root ginger,
   grated
4 tbsp soy sauce
½–1 tsp Chinese five-spice
   (to taste; it's quite a strong
   spice blend)
freshly ground black pepper

For the chilli peanut oil

250ml (1 cup) vegetable oil
50g (2oz) salted peanuts,
   chopped
50g (2oz) dried chilli flakes
4 garlic cloves, sliced
1 banana shallot, finely chopped
2 tsp flaked sea salt

You also need 8 metal skewers

Lamb and apricot sosaties

With all that bending down to graze, lamb neck muscles are super hard-working and full of connective tissue. In theory this should mean they are best suited to low and slow cooking but actually it is one of my favourite cuts for slicing across the grain and cooking hot and fast, like in these tasty South African kebabs. A good long marinade and/or dry brine is really useful and I have left the meat to marinate for up to 72 hours with only positive effects. Although the fact that the marinade is cooked and the use of apricot jam might feel a little weird, you are creating something similar to a spicy chutney that the lamb then soaks in. Trust me, it's delicious.

Set a small saucepan over a medium heat and add the cumin and coriander seeds and cardamom pods. Toast for a couple of minutes until they smell fragrant, then tip into a pestle and mortar and roughly grind.

Pour the oil into the pan, add the onion, bay leaves and salt and cook very gently for 15-20 minutes until softened. Add the garlic, crushed spices, turmeric and cinnamon and cook for another minute. Spoon in the jam and add the vinegar, along with a good grind of black pepper. Cook for a few minutes until the jam has melted and you have a sticky sauce. Pour into a bowl and set aside to cool completely.

Once the marinade is cold, add the lamb and stir thoroughly to coat each piece. Cover and slide into the fridge for at least 24 hours – longer wouldn't hurt at all.

When you are ready to cook, fire up your barbecue ready for direct grilling, leaving a good area of the grill surface with no coals under so you can slide the skewers off the direct heat if they are cooking too fast. The sugary jam can make them prone to catching.

Thread the lamb onto skewers, alternating with the slivers of onion and apricots. Lay the skewers on the grill bars over the fire and cook for 8-10 minutes in total – until the lamb is cooked and the apricots are lightly charred.

Serve hot from the grill.

Makes 8, serving 4 or so

900g (2lb) lamb neck fillet,
cut into 1cm (½in) discs
1 small red onion, cut into
6-8 wedges, and slivers
pulled apart
200g (7oz) dried apricots

For the marinade

2 tsp cumin seeds
2 tsp coriander seeds
4 cardamom pods
2 tbsp olive oil
1 small red onion, finely chopped
3 bay leaves, chopped
1 tsp salt
2 garlic cloves, crushed
1 tsp ground turmeric
1 tsp ground cinnamon
5 tbsp apricot jam
5 tbsp red wine vinegar
freshly ground black pepper

You also need 8 metal skewers

Chapter 3: Sausages and Burgers – slow cuts, cooked faster

With sausages and burgers you are effectively taking the tough hard-working parts of the animal – most often the shoulder or belly cuts – and, by mincing it up fine, turning it into something you can, in theory, cook quickly. Although this is not always necessarily the best way – the Texas hot links recipe, with its 2½ hours of intensely smoked awesomeness, is a good case in point.

While you can buy perfectly good mince (ground meat) from both reputable butchers and direct from the farmers, mincing your own is surprisingly satisfying. I think there's something good about knowing your meat is coming from one animal, just as it would be if you were roasting a joint. You also get to choose the exact cuts of meat you want to mince and you can control the fat level; remember, fat is flavour and you want to aim for a good 20–30% fat. You can combine different meats together, as in the hot links recipe overleaf, and add seasonings as you mince so everything gets blended to your specification. And believe me, it's rather fun – an excellent wet weather day activity.

When you are making your own mince for sausages or burgers it's essential everything stays as cold as possible. You are increasing the surface area of the meat as you grind it, and that therefore increases the potential for harmful pathogens to colonize. Start with very cold meat, ideally partly frozen, and freeze all the moving parts of the machine that contact the meat too, so the auger, cutting blade and grinding discs. Work as quickly as you can and get it in the fridge between stages.

SAUSAGES

Making sausages is quite the process: you need a meat grinder (you can get attachments for food mixers) and ideally a separate dedicated sausage-filling machine. Grinders often have attachments for filling but they are not the best tool for the job (as I discovered to my cost); it's quite hard, but not impossible, to control the flow of the filling and reduce air gaps. Air gaps make for a baggy sausage, and one that's prone to bursting on cooking. Two pairs of hands are also useful.

There is only room for a couple of my favourite sausage recipes in this book but be warned, you may get hooked on the process. You'll find a lot of good resources online if you want to take your sausage journey onwards.

Texas hot links

I adore Texas hot links, or 'hot guts' as they are also known – spicy, succulent and super-smoky. As usual, very cold meat is important in sausage-making so don't skip the freezing step and make sure everything is squeaky clean when you begin. Fat is a really important ingredient to ensure juicy snags – ideally you want a 20–30% fat content, so don't trim up the fat on the meat before you grind it. It will add bags of flavour and succulence.

Tip the peppercorns into a pestle and mortar and grind. You want a mix of fine and coarse ground pepper so don't overdo it. Add the salt, sugar, mustard, smoked paprika and cayenne, if using, and stir together until mixed.

Put the pork and beef cubes in a bowl, sprinkling over the spice powder, garlic and sage and tossing about thoroughly so they are evenly coated. Spread out over one or two trays in a single layer. Freeze for an hour until the outside is just starting to freeze a little but the inside is still soft. Put the mincer tube, grinding blade and discs – I used a large 7mm (¼in) disc followed by a 4mm (⅛ in) medium disc for mincing – in the freezer at the same time.

Remove the meat and mincer equipment from the freezer and fit the mincer with the larger sized disc. Grind up the semi-frozen meat, letting it fall from the machine onto a clean tray. Pour the cold beer (or water) over the mince and use your hands (ideally with gloves on, it will be very cold, not to mention spicy!) to really mash the liquid in; you want the mix to feel good and sticky.

Fix the medium grinding plate to the mincer and regrind the meat, this time letting it land in a bowl. Store in the fridge while you wash down the equipment and clean up ready for filling.

To fill the sausages, set up your sausage stuffer or convert your mincer with a stuffing attachment. Load the machine with the cold sausage mixture. You want to fit a stuffing nozzle appropriate to the size of the hog casing – generally 30mm (1¼in) hog casings need a 20mm (¾in) nozzle. Lightly grease the nozzle with a few drops of vegetable oil to help load the casings on smoothly. Drain the soaked casings in a sieve (strainer) and rinse under a cold tap. Find one end of the casing and feed it onto the nozzle – this is perhaps the trickiest part of the whole process, so be patient! Set a wet tray under the nozzle to catch the sausages as they land – the water just helps them slide along easily as they are made so you will avoid a sausage pile-up!

Makes 6–8 ring sausages

1 tbsp black peppercorns
25g (1oz) flaked sea salt
1 tbsp caster (superfine) sugar
1 tbsp English mustard powder
2 tsp hot smoked paprika
1–2 tsp cayenne pepper (optional, for extra heat)
1kg (2lb 4oz) pork butt (shoulder), diced into 4cm (1½in) cubes
500g (1lb 2oz) beef chuck (also shoulder), diced into 4cm (1½in) cubes
3 garlic cloves, crushed
3 sprigs of fresh sage, leaves finely chopped
200ml (generous ¾ cup) ice-cold beer (or water)
vegetable oil, for greasing

You also need about 3m (3yd) of hog casings, soaked overnight in cold water

With the sausage mixture loaded into the machine and the casing in place, start to fill the casing, going slowly at first and trying to maintain an even pressure so the links will be an even thickness. This may take a bit of practice, but remember that even slightly wonky links will taste great.

Once you have a long length of sausage it's time to form the links. Use your thumb and forefinger to pinch in and twist. For hot links, I like to keep them long, about 30cm (12in) then curl them into a classic horseshoe shape – tying the two ends together with a little butcher's string. But you can keep them short and straight if you prefer.

Once you've made all your sausages, rest them on a wire rack set over a tray and put in the fridge, uncovered, for 24 hours for the skins to dry out. This will help prevent the skins splitting on cooking and also allows plenty of time for the spicy flavours to marinate the meat.

To cook the sausages, fire up your barbecue ready for indirect grilling. You want a steady low temperature of 130°C (265°F). Add a good 2–3 lumps of smoking wood to the fire. Set the links on the opposite side of the grill to the fire so they are as far away as possible and smoke for 2½ hours. Halfway through, turn the links over and add more charcoal and wood to the fire to keep it steady.

I think these hot links are best eaten straight off the grill, where the skin will have a good 'snap' to it and the meat will be at its most juicy and succulent. They do reheat well, though; simply slice up and fry quickly. They also freeze well for up to 3 months, cooked or uncooked.

Merguez and quick veg tagine

I like to make my own harissa paste for these intensely spiced North African lamb sausages – it's just infinitely fresher and punchier. This recipe makes more than you need for the merguez, but it goes brilliantly with lots of things. It freezes really well too, so if you're not going to use it up in a week or two, freeze it to keep it fresh. However, if it's all a step too far, just substitute for ready-made, adding an extra couple of teaspoons of freshly ground cumin to your sausage mix. I made a quick tagine to eat with my merguez, using up a little more of the homemade harissa. If you fancy trying this, begin it 30 minutes before you start to cook the sausages.

This recipe makes about 20 sausages – allow about 3 or so per person, then freeze the rest, well wrapped, for up to 3 months.

Grill the pepper until the skin is blackened all over. Do this on a barbecue if you already have one lit, or use tongs to hold it over a gas flame on your hob. Put into a bowl and cover with a plate to seal in the steam and loosen the skin. Once cool enough to handle, peel and deseed, then roughly chop and put in a food processor. Add the rest of the harissa ingredients and blitz to a purée. Scoop into a tub and refrigerate to chill. You can make the harissa ahead of time; it'll keep in the fridge for a week or so.

Dice the lamb into 4–5cm (1½–2in) pieces and spread out on a baking sheet. Spoon over the harissa, and sprinkle on the ground spices and salt. Using gloved hands, mix thoroughly to make sure each piece of meat is evenly coated. Set this tray in the freezer for an hour so the meat is partially frozen. At the same time, set the moving parts of your meat grinder in the freezer to get super-chilled.

Feed the meat through your mincer using a medium grinding disc. Once minced, pour over the ice-cold water and use gloved hands to really work it in until you have a sticky paste. Feed this back through the mincer one more time. Scoop into a bowl and refrigerate while you clean down and set up your sausage stuffer.

Drain the soaked lamb casings and stuff your sausages using the instructions for the Texas hot links on page 80. Spread out the links on a rack set over a tray and dry out in the fridge overnight.

When you are ready to cook, fire up your barbecue with the charcoal to one side.

Makes about 20 sausages

For the harissa paste
1 large red pepper
200g (7oz) medium-hot fresh red chillies, deseeded if you prefer less heat
4 garlic cloves
6 tbsp extra virgin olive oil
2 tbsp smoked paprika
1 tbsp caraway seeds, toasted and ground
1 tbsp cumin seeds, toasted and ground
1 tbsp tomato purée (paste)
1 tbsp red wine vinegar
1 tsp sea salt

For the merguez
1kg (2lb 4oz) fatty lamb – I used boned lamb breast, you could use shoulder too
6 tbsp harissa paste
1 tbsp coriander seeds, toasted and ground
1 tsp ground cinnamon
1 tsp freshly ground black pepper
20g (¾oz) flaked sea salt
200ml (generous ¾ cup) ice-cold water

Continued overleaf…

If you are making the tagine, bring a pan of salted water to the boil and blanch the carrots for 5 minutes, then drain and drizzle in a little olive oil. Grill over the fire for a few minutes until lightly charred all over. Slide off the heat.

Heat the rest of the olive oil in a heatproof pan set over the fire (I used a terracotta casserole dish with a lid) and add the onions. Fry for 20 minutes until just beginning to soften, then add the harissa and tomatoes, stirring well and cooking for another 10 minutes or so until the tomatoes start to break down. Add the grilled carrots and broccoli and half the coriander (cilantro) and season well with salt and pepper. Pour over enough boiling water to just cover the vegetables and cover the pan with a lid or piece of foil. Leave to simmer directly over the fire while you cook the merguez. Sprinkle over the rest of the coriander just before serving.

Grill the sausages for about 20 minutes slightly indirectly so they cook over a medium heat (see page 19 for more on temperature control). They are quite fatty so be prepared to move them around and further from the fire if they are cooking too quickly.

For the tagine (serves 4)
6 carrots, quartered lengthways
3 tbsp olive oil
2 onions, sliced
3 tbsp harissa paste
250g (9oz) cherry tomatoes, halved
1 large head of broccoli, florets and stem sliced
a good handful of coriander (cilantro), chopped
flaked sea salt and freshly ground black pepper
plenty of buttered couscous, to serve

You also need 4m (4½yd) lamb casings, soaked for an hour in warm water and rinsed

Pork and chorizo burger, sherry onions, manchego

I like to cook these burgers on a chapa or hot plate (see page 25) to make sure I don't lose any of the little nuggets of chorizo or melting cheese to the fire. As with beef mince, it's pretty easy to source good pork mince but if you fancy making your own, go for the shoulder cut.

Tip the pork mince (ground pork) into a bowl and add the diced chorizo, garlic, parsley, smoked paprika and a generous seasoning of salt and pepper. Use your hands to mix together well. Shape into 4 even-sized balls, pushing the chorizo bits in as much as possible – they may try to escape! Flatten out to around 1cm (½in) thick. At this point you can refrigerate for a few hours if you want to get ahead.

To make the onions, take a large deep saucepan and set over a low heat on the hob. Pour in the olive oil and add the butter. Once the butter has melted, add the onions and a little salt and pepper and cook really gently for at least 30 minutes, stirring every now and then. Pour in the sherry and allow to bubble away and reduce for another 15 minutes or so. You could, of course, cook them on your barbecue but as they have a much longer cooking time than the burgers, I tend to get them ready inside ahead of time.

When you are ready to cook the burgers, fire up your barbecue ready for direct grilling and set a chapa over the fire to heat up. You can also cook in a fireproof frying pan (skillet) if you like. Either way, once it's really hot, add the burgers, pressing down with a fish slice so you get good contact with the hot surface. Cook for a couple of minutes then flip over and grill the other side for a minute before turning again once more. Top with the manchego and a good spoonful of onions, then shut the lid and cook for another couple of minutes. If you have a cloche (see page 25) this is a good time to use it – it will help the cheese to melt.

To serve, toast the buns a little, then add a handful of rocket (arugula) to each. Add a burger, scraping up any little bits of chorizo and melted cheese that are on the chapa (they are flavour gold dust!) and top with the ciabatta lid, squishing it shut.

Makes 4

500g (1lb 2oz) pork mince (ground pork)
250g (9oz) fresh chorizo, skinned and finely diced
2 garlic cloves, crushed
a loose handful of flat-leaf parsley, chopped
1 tsp smoked paprika
1 tbsp olive oil
25g (1oz) butter
2 large onions, sliced
75ml (⅓ cup) sherry (I love dry Oloroso for its rich nutty flavour)
175g (6oz) manchego, sliced
flaked sea salt and freshly ground black pepper

To serve
ciabatta buns
rocket (arugula)

Minty lamb smash burgers, feta and beetroot relish

I made these with freshly minced lamb shoulder, but good-quality ready-minced lamb would be perfectly fine. I like to make these quite spicy but adjust to your preference.

Tip the lamb mince (ground lamb) into a bowl and sprinkle in the mint and spices to taste. Mix together lightly with your hands. Divide the mixture into 4 even-sized pieces, rolling each into a nice compact ball. Set aside on a plate.

To make the relish, finely chop the beetroot (beets) and tip into a bowl. Stir the spring onions (scallions) through the beetroot, along with the mint, olive oil, vinegar and sugar. Season to taste with salt and pepper. Set aside.

Fire up your barbecue ready for direct grilling. Set a chapa or flat plate onto the grill bars directly oven the fire to get really hot (see page 25).

Take a ball of mince and add it to the chapa, then use a fish slice to quickly smash it down flat so it is about 1cm (½in) thick. Repeat with the other balls of mince, then sprinkle a little salt and pepper over each. After a minute, flip the burgers over and sprinkle some seasoning on the other side, then top with the feta and a spoon of beetroot relish. Have your cloche (or metal bowl) at the ready, then sprinkle a good couple of tablespoons of water onto the chapa around the burgers, quickly cover with the cloche and cook for another couple of minutes. The steam will help to melt the cheese.

To serve, place a little lettuce in the base of each bun. Use a fish slice to slide the burgers onto the bases, scraping up any loose crispy bits of cheese as you go, then top with the lid and tuck in.

Serves 4

600g (1lb 5oz) lamb mince (ground lamb)
a good handful of fresh mint leaves, chopped
1–2 tsp cumin seeds, toasted and roughly crushed
1–2 tsp chilli powder or flakes
200g (7oz) feta, crumbled
flaked sea salt and freshly ground black pepper

For the beetroot relish

1 pack ready-cooked beetroot (beets)
3 spring onions (scallions), finely chopped
a good handful of fresh mint leaves, chopped
1 tbsp olive oil
1 tbsp red wine vinegar
a pinch of caster (superfine) sugar

To serve

4 brioche buns, sliced and toasted
a handful of crisp lettuce leaves

You also need a chapa, plancha or hot plate (see page 25) and a cloche or large metal bowl

Spiced beef and halloumi burgers, saffron yogurt

These spiced burgers are a touch delicate and can be prone to falling apart. Cooking on a squeaky-clean grill helps, so once your barbecue is hot, give the grill bars a really good scrub with a wire brush. You could also grill them on a chapa or hot plate or vegetable grilling tray (see page 25) if you have one.

I have a really great Turkish shop near me, which is where I found the date syrup, which is lovely and treacly. Have a hunt for it online if you fancy using it or substitute with the more easily found pomegranate molasses. It's pretty easy to buy great beef mince, but if you do fancy making your own, beef chuck is the cut I'd go for.

Tip the beef and grated halloumi into a bowl and add the date syrup, garlic and herbs. Set a small frying pan (skillet) over a medium heat on the hob and add the pine nuts, toasting for a couple of minutes until golden. Tip about two-thirds of them into the bowl, reserving the rest in a small dish for garnishing. Add the cumin seeds to the pan and toast for a minute, then roughly crush in a pestle and mortar and add to the burger mix, along with the cinnamon and a good seasoning of salt and pepper.

Mix together really well using clean hands then divide into 8 even-sized balls. Rest on a plate and set aside while you get everything else organized. You can make these up to 24 hours before cooking and chill in the fridge if you want to get ahead.

Put the sliced onion in a small bowl and pour over the vinegar. Stir through the sugar and salt and set aside for 30 minutes or so until they have softened a little in the pickling liquid.

Sprinkle the saffron into a small heatproof bowl or jug and pour oven a tablespoon of boiling water. Set aside to soak for 10–15 minutes. Add the yogurt, garlic and season to taste with salt and pepper, stirring well to mix. Once the onions have finished pickling, drain the pickling vinegar into the yogurt, reserving the onions, and stir through. Taste to see if it's sharp enough – add a splash more vinegar if you fancy.

Makes 8 mini burgers, serving 4–6

500g (1lb 2oz) beef mince (ground beef), ideally 20% fat
225g (8oz) halloumi, grated
2 tbsp date syrup (or use pomegranate molasses)
1 garlic clove, crushed
a good handful (about 35g/1½oz) of fresh herbs, chopped – I used dill, parsley, coriander (cilantro)
75g (3oz) pine nuts
2 tsp cumin seeds
½ tsp ground cinnamon
flaked sea salt and freshly ground black pepper

For the pickled onions
1 red onion, sliced
2 tbsp sherry vinegar
2 tsp caster (superfine) sugar (or to taste)
a pinch of flaked sea salt

Continued overleaf...

When you are ready to cook, fire up your grill ready for direct cooking (but, as always, leaving an area of the barbecue without fire so you have room to move if things are getting a little hot, see page 19). Once it's hot, give the grill bars a really good scrub clean with a wire brush.

Lay the burgers on the grill, directly over the fire, and cook for around 4 minutes each side, using a fish slice to turn. Slide slightly away from the fire if they look to be catching too quickly.

To serve, scatter a little salad over your flatbread and top with one or two burgers. Drizzle over some saffron yogurt and spoon on some pickled onions. Top with the reserved pine nuts and a few extra herbs. Roll up and tuck in.

For the saffron yogurt
a pinch of saffron
150g (5½oz/¾ cup) Greek yogurt
1 garlic clove, crushed

To serve
green salad
warmed flatbreads (or pitta
    breads)
a few extra herbs

Thai red curry with pork meatballs, green beans

Grilling the meatballs and green beans before adding to the curry sauce adds bags of flavour to this fragrant curry. If you're really strapped for time, feel free to sub in ready-made Thai curry paste, red or green, although fresh paste will have a lot more oomph.

To make the curry paste, tip the peppercorns and cumin and coriander seeds into a small frying pan (skillet) and toast for a minute or two until fragrant. Grind using a pestle and mortar.

Add the chillies to a heatproof bowl and pour over enough boiling water to cover. Set aside for around 30 minutes to soften. Remove, reserving the soaking water, and roughly chop. Add to a deep jug, along with the shallots, coriander (cilantro) stems, ginger, garlic, lemongrass, lime leaves, ground spices, shrimp paste and salt. Pour in a few tablespoons of the reserved water and use a stick blender to whizz to a paste, adding more water as necessary. You can also make the paste in a mini food processor or with a pestle and mortar and a bit of elbow grease.

Pour the oil into a frying pan and set over a medium heat. Add the curry paste and stir-fry for 5 minutes until a deep rich colour. Remove and cool completely.

To make the meatballs, put the pork mince (ground pork) in a bowl and add 2 tablespoons of the cold curry paste, along with half the chopped coriander. Mix together really well and shape into walnut-sized balls. At this point you can refrigerate the meatballs for up to 24 hours if you want to get ahead.

When you are ready to cook, fire up the barbecue ready for direct and indirect gilling.

Add the remaining curry paste, coconut milk and fish sauce to a deep fireproof frying pan and set over the grill bars directly over the fire. Bring up to the boil and simmer for a few minutes before sliding away from the heat to keep cooking indirectly.

Drizzle a little oil over the meatballs and rest on the grill bars directly over the fire. Grill for a few minutes each side until they have a nice bit of colour to them, then lift and drop them into the curry sauce.

Serves 4

500g (1lb 2oz) pork mince (ground pork)
a good handful of coriander (cilantro) leaves, chopped
400ml coconut milk
2 tbsp fish sauce
300g green beans, topped and tailed
1 tbsp vegetable oil
juice of 1 lime
steamed rice, to serve

For the curry paste

1 tsp white (or black) peppercorns
1 tsp cumin seeds
1 tsp coriander seeds
8 dried red chillies
2 banana shallots, roughly chopped
a handful of coriander (cilantro) stems, roughly chopped
30g (1oz) fresh root ginger, roughly chopped
4 fat garlic cloves, roughly chopped
1 lemongrass stalk, roughly chopped
4 kaffir lime leaves, central rib removed and roughly chopped
1 tsp shrimp paste (or use 2 tbsp fish sauce)
1 tsp flaked sea salt
1 tbsp vegetable oil

Continued overleaf...

Drizzle a little more oil over the green beans and rest on the grill bars at 90 degrees to the bars to stop them falling through to the fire. If you have a vegetable grilling basket this is the perfect time to use it (see page 25). Grill the beans for a couple of minutes each side to char them a little then drop them into the curry sauce. Once all the beans are in the pan, slide it over the fire and leave to bubble away for around 10 minutes or so until the beans are just tender and the sauce a little thickened. Just before serving, stir through the lime juice and the other half of the coriander.

Serve with steamed rice.

Herby veal meatballs, lemon yogurt

This is an exercise in using fresh, summery herbs in abundance. I like to make them as mini tapas-sized meatballs, perfect for dunking in the lemony yogurt dip, but you could line up the balls on four metal skewers for a main course.

I talk about the ethics of veal on page 68 so won't repeat myself here, other than to reiterate that if you are a consumer of dairy products, you would do well to seek out well-reared veal. The two industries go hand in hand.

Tip the veal mince (ground veal) into a bowl and add the herbs, garlic and salt and pepper. Use clean hands to massage everything together really well until the mixture is sticky. This will help it stick to the skewers. Divide into walnut-sized pieces – you should get around 22–24 even pieces. Shape into little ovals and line up on a plate or tray then chill in the fridge for an hour or so – longer wouldn't hurt.

Spoon the yogurt into a small bowl and stir through the lemon zest and juice, garlic and a little salt and pepper. Chill in the fridge.

When you are ready to cook, fire up your barbecue ready for direct grilling, as usual setting up the fire on half the barbecue to give yourself control of the heat.

Rest the meatballs on the grill bars over the fire and cook for a few minutes on each side. They can be a little sticky, so make sure your grill bars are clean before you start – once they are hot give them a vigorous scrub with a wire brush. If you have a vegetable grilling tray (see page 25), it can be a good thing to use here to help with potential sticking.

Once cooked, transfer to a serving plate or board and nestle the bowl of lemon yogurt alongside.

Makes 22–24 tapas-sized meatballs

For the meatballs
500g (1lb 2oz) veal mince (ground veal)
100g (3½oz) chopped mixed herbs – dill, parsley, chives, coriander
2 garlic cloves, crushed
flaked sea salt and freshly ground black pepper

For the lemon yogurt
150g (5½oz/¾ cup) Greek yogurt
zest and juice of 1 lemon
1 garlic clove, crushed

Chapter 4: Smoke+Braise – the best of both worlds

If I could only cook meat in one way for evermore, I think the 'smoke plus braise' method would be it – a deep rich bathe in some sweet smoke followed by a long wallow in a bath of stock, wine or beer. Quite simply, you get the best of both worlds, the intensity of flavour from the added smoke and the guaranteed succulence from braising tougher, cheaper cuts like shoulders and shanks. And I would take cheaper cuts over expensive ones any day of the week.

In theory, once you're done with the smoking part of all these recipes you could transfer the whole operation to your kitchen – using the hob to soften veg, followed by the oven to complete the cooking. Unless the weather is absolutely revolting, I tend to stick outside for the duration. Once you're braising and the lids on it's almost entirely hands-off and easy.

I know I like to bang on about using a meat probe to get your meat cooked to perfection, but in the case of smoking and braising it becomes somewhat irrelevant. The internal temperature of the meat during the smoke phase isn't important because you use the braising period to cook it to tenderness. So the goal in the beginning is to hit it with as much smoke as possible. After 3–5 hours the meat will have taken on as much smoke as it can – once the outer surface is cooked it will no longer absorb smoke effectively.

Dry-brining is less important in this chapter because the braising stage guarantees tenderness but I usually do it nevertheless for the flavour-enhancing properties.

Smoked lamb shank vindaloo

Smoking meat is not traditional for a vindaloo, but pre-cooking it and then adding it to the curry sauce base is common in restaurants, saving time and adding layers of flavours, so smoking the shanks here seemed like an excellent place to begin.

Just a little chilli warning: this recipes uses 10g (⅓oz) Kashmiri chillies – which is a good handful – as they offer a lot of deep red colour but not a vast quantity of heat. If you can't get Kashmiri chilli, adjust the quantity down to taste.

Set a small dry frying pan (skillet) over a medium heat and add the cinnamon, peppercorns, cumin, cloves, cardamom and chillies. Toast for a minute or two until you can smell a deep spiciness wafting up from the pan, then tip into a spice mill and grind to a powder. Put into a bowl and add the salt, ginger, garlic and vinegar, stirring well to mix.

Put the lamb shanks into a bowl so they can sit, cut side down, fairly snugly together. Spoon half the marinade over the lamb shanks, rubbing it really well into the cracks and crevices, especially on the cut surfaces. Cover and slide into the fridge to marinate for, ideally, 24 hours. Refrigerate the other half of the marinade too, ready for the braise.

When you are ready to cook, fire up your barbecue ready for indirect grilling, adding 2–3 lumps of smoking wood to the fire. Set a drip tray under where the shanks will sit (on the opposite side of the grill to the fire) and pour in 500ml (2 cups) water. The water will create steam, which will help the smoke adhere to the shanks, plus the drips from the lamb will flavour up the water, which you use in the braising step.

Set the shanks on their side onto the grill bars over the drip tray and close the lid. Shut the vents to moderate the temperature to around 140°C (280°F). Smoke for 3 hours (because shanks are relatively small in terms of cut they smoke a little faster than the bigger joints in this chapter), turning them over halfway through cooking.

Serves 2 generously, or more if you're combining with several other dishes as a curry feast

6cm (2½in) cinnamon stick, crumbled
1 tbsp black peppercorns
1 tbsp cumin seeds
1 tsp cloves
8 cardamom pods
10g (⅓oz) dried Kashmiri chillies, roughly chopped
2 tsp flaked sea salt
50g (2oz) fresh root ginger, grated
4 garlic cloves, crushed
100ml (3½fl oz) malt vinegar
2 lamb shanks, about 450g (1lb) each
1 tbsp vegetable oil
25g (1oz) butter
3 red onions, sliced
400g (14oz) vine tomatoes, chopped
6–8 green chillies, sliced in half lengthways
1 tbsp brown sugar

Continued overleaf...

Once smoked, remove to a plate and then carefully remove and set aside the drip pan. Open up the vents on your barbecue a little and allow the temperature to creep up to around 160–180°C (320–350°F), topping up with fuel if necessary.

Set a fireproof casserole dish (a Dutch oven or terracotta pot with a lid is ideal) onto the grill bars, slightly offset to the fire so you can cook over a medium heat. Pour in the vegetable oil and add the butter, allowing it to melt, then add the reserved marinade, frying it over a medium heat for 5 minutes. Add the onions and fry for another 10 minutes before adding the tomatoes, chillies and sugar, stirring well to mix.

Add the smoked shanks and the liquid in the drip tray, tossing about to coat the shanks in the liquid. Pour in a little more water if necessary – you want the shanks to be half-submerged in liquid. Cover with a lid or snug-fitting piece of foil and shut the lid of your barbecue. Cook for another 2½–3 hours, or until the shanks are super-tender and falling off the bone. Remove the lid for the last 30 minutes or so to reduce the sauce a little.

Keralan spiced beef and aubergine

Bavette, or flank steak, is a cut you can take to tenderness two ways – either rare, or cook low and slow. Anything approaching a middle ground results in tough and chewy meat. Here you use a high heat to sear and brown both steak and aubergines (eggplants), then you gently braise in a deliciously spicy curry sauce. Adding a little wood to the fire at the searing stage – or indeed cooking the whole thing over a purely wood fire – will add a glorious hit of smoke to the finished dish.

Start this recipe the day before you want to eat, by dry-brining the steak for 24 hours, but even 2–4 hours would be good. Sprinkle 1 tablespoon of flaked sea salt over the steak, rubbing in well on both sides, then rest the on a rack set over a baking sheet. Slide into the fridge, uncovered, and leave to dry-brine.

Set a small frying pan (skillet) over a medium heat on the hob and add the coriander, fennel, cloves, cinnamon, cardamom and star anise. Toast for a minute or two until you can smell the fragrance wafting up from the pan, then tip into to a spice mill with the chilli powder and whizz to a powder. You can also use a pestle and mortar for a slightly coarser powder.

When you are ready to cook your curry, fire up the barbecue ready for direct and indirect grilling, lighting a full chimney of charcoal. Add a couple of chunks of smoking wood to the fire to give the steak a smoky hint.

Drizzle a little olive oil over the aubergine (eggplant) wedges and season with a little salt. Set on the grill bars, directly over the fire, and grill for a few minutes on each side so they take on a little colour on the outside. Slide off the heat away from the fire so they can continue to soften indirectly while you sear the steak.

Drizzle a little oil over the steak and set it directly over the fire, searing over a high heat until it's beautifully browned, flipping it every 30 seconds or so to get maximum colour (see page 43). Remove to a plate and allow to cool a little before cutting across the grain into finger-thick slices. Remove the cooked aubergine too, and allow to cool a little before dicing into 4–5cm (1½–2in) chunks. Set aside.

Set a deep fireproof frying pan directly over the fire and pour in a generous tablespoon of oil. Add the garlic, ginger and turmeric, stir-frying over the heat for a few minutes before adding the spice powder and tomatoes. Cook for another few minutes until the tomatoes start to collapse.

Serves 4–6

1kg (2lb 4oz) bavette steak (or you could use skirt or onglet/hanger)
1 tbsp coriander seeds
2 tsp fennel seeds
½ tsp cloves
3cm (1¼in) cinnamon stick, crumbled
5 cardamom pods
1 star anise
1–2 tsp chilli powder, to taste
3 tbsp vegetable oil
2 medium aubergines (eggplants), about 600g (1lb 5oz), sliced into wedges lengthways
3 fat garlic cloves, crushed
50g (2oz) fresh root ginger, grated
30g (1oz) fresh turmeric, grated (or 1 heaped tsp dried)
4 large vine tomatoes, about 400g (14oz), chopped
400ml (1¾ cups) water or stock
3 sprigs of fresh curry leaves
flaked sea salt and freshly ground black pepper
naan breads or rice, to serve

Slide the sliced beef and aubergines into the pan and pour
in the water or stock, stirring well to mix. Bring up to the boil,
slide the pan a little off the direct heat and shut the lid of the
barbecue. Leave to simmer until the sauce has thickened and
the beef is really tender, about 45 minutes depending on the
heat. Stir through the curry leaves about 15 minutes before the
end of cooking.

Serve with plenty of rice or naan bread to mop up the sauce.

Smoked pig cheek, cannellini and spinach lasagne

I adore pig cheeks, tough little nuggets of muscle that turn soft and intensely flavourful over time. There are, obviously, only two cheek muscles per pig, each one weighing in a measly 100g (3½oz) or so – compare that to the weight of the whole pig, which may be 80kg (175lb) or so and I consider them to be a rare treat. Here they get combined with cannellini beans to make them go further. Whether you are cooking indoors or out, lasagne is always a labour of love, but as a once in a while comfort dish I'm not sure it can really be beaten.

Fire up your barbecue ready for indirect cooking, aiming to get a nice steady, low temperature of around 130–140°C (260–280°F), adding a couple of chunks of smoking wood.

Sprinkle a teaspoon of salt all over the pork and rest on the grill bars away from the fire. Shut the lid and leave to smoke for a couple of hours. Remove to a plate and set aside.

Open up the vents on the grill, allowing the temperature to creep up to around 150°C (300°F). You may need to add a little more fuel. Set a fireproof casserole onto the grill bars over the fire, pour in the oil and add the onion. Shut the lid and allow to soften and caramelize for a good 30 minutes, stirring once or twice. Add the garlic, tomatoes, wine, water or stock, and season with plenty of pepper and a little salt, stirring well to mix. Add the smoked pork cheeks, pushing them under the surface, then cover with a tight-fitting lid, sliding the casserole slightly off the direct fire. Shut the barbecue lid and leave to braise for 2 hours, or until the meat is really tender. Check once or twice to make sure there is enough liquid, adding a splash more water if it looks to be getting a little dry.

Remove the casserole from the barbecue, shutting the lid to keep in the heat. Use two forks to tease apart the pork into little bite-sized strands – this should be easy if the meat has cooked for long enough. Stir through the cannellini beans and tip the spinach on top. Re-cover with the lid, and set back onto the barbecue, again slightly offset from the fire, and shut the lid. Cook for another 20 minutes or so until the spinach has wilted.

While the braise is in the final stages of cooking, make the béchamel. Set a large saucepan on the hob over a medium heat and add the butter. Once it's melted, stir through the flour to form a smooth paste. Pour in the milk, whisking constantly as the sauce thickens, and allow to bubble away over the heat for 5 minutes to cook the flour. Add the cream, tarragon and

Serves 4

For the ragù
600g (1lb 5oz) pork cheeks
    (6 cheeks)
2 tbsp olive oil
1 onion, chopped
3 garlic cloves, crushed
750g (1lb 10oz) ripe vine
    tomatoes, chopped
200ml (generous ¾ cup) red
    wine, plus 100ml (3½fl oz)
    water or stock
400g (14oz) can cannellini beans,
    drained
200g (7oz) baby leaf spinach,
    washed and shaken dry
about 8 sheets of dried lasagne
    (or more or less depending
    on the shape of your dish)
flaked sea salt and freshly ground
    black pepper

For the béchamel sauce
50g (2oz) butter
50g (2oz) plain (all-purpose) flour
450ml (scant 2 cups) milk
100ml (3½fl oz) double (heavy)
    cream (or extra milk)
a small bunch of tarragon (about
    20g/¾oz), leaves chopped
75g (3oz) Parmesan, plus a really
    good dusting for the top

Parmesan and season to taste with salt and pepper. Remove from the heat and set aside.

Once the pork is ready, it's (finally) time to build up your lasagne. You now have a choice to make – I invariably cook mine on the barbecue because it's hot anyway and it's actually very straightforward to bake in a barbecue. You need it to be hot, but for the heat to be indirect – you'll be using convection heat (see page 12). I normally deploy to a two-fire setup (see page 19). Aim for a temperature of around 200°C (400°F), opening up the vents wide and adding a little more fuel as necessary. You can, of course, do it in your oven inside, in which case go for a temperature of 180°C (350°F) in a fan oven.

Build the lasagne in a deep heatproof dish – something square or rectangular is obviously going to work best because of the shape of the pasta sheets. Start with a layer of ragù, followed by a layer of pasta, then add a layer of béchamel, followed by another layer of pasta. Finish with a really good dusting of Parmesan.

Bake, either in your barbecue or your oven, until crisp on top and bubbling away beautifully. This will take 45 minutes–1 hour depending on the heat you have.

Ox cheeks with fennel, red wine and balsamic

If you think about the life of a cow, with their constant chewing day in, day out, it's hardly surprising to learn that the cheeks are one of the most hard-working muscles in the whole body. They are also fairly lean too so they need very long, slow cooking to tenderize and soften to a melting texture. Which makes them the perfect candidate for the smoke+braise treatment. The quantity of meat sounds a lot but you get a fair amount of shrinkage. Any leftovers freeze very well, or try using them in one of the leftover ideas from page 251.

This is just the sort of unctuous rich dish that might convert you to the joys of winter barbecuing! Served with mash or buttery polenta and a big bowl of greens, this is comfort food in the extreme.

The day before you want to cook, dry brine the ox cheeks by rubbing 1½ tablespoons of flaked sea salt all over. Place on a rack set over a tray and slide, uncovered, into the fridge for 24 hours.

The following day, fire up your barbecue ready for low and slow smoking (see page 19). For this, I light two small fires, one either side of the barbecue, adding a lump of smoking wood to each fire and shutting the vents almost fully to stabilize the temperature at around 130–140°C (260–280°F).

Drizzle a tablespoon or so of oil over the ox cheeks and lay them onto the grill bars, between the two fires, nestling them snugly together. Shut the lid and leave to smoke for 2 hours.

Once the ox cheeks have been smoking for a couple of hours, drizzle over a little olive oil and rest them on the grill bars directly over the fire. Grill for 15–20 minutes, turning regularly, until they are nicely browned all over. Remove to a plate. At the same time, place the onion wedges on the grill until nicely charred.

Pour the rest of the olive oil into a large fireproof casserole dish and set it onto the barbecue over the fire. Add the garlic and fennel seeds, and some salt and pepper, and stir over the heat for a few minutes. Then add the charred onions and ox cheeks and pour in the wine, balsamic vinegar and sugar, tossing everything about. Slide the casserole off the direct heat. Take a large sheet of baking paper and scrunch it up under a running tap, unfold and shake off the excess water. Press this damp sheet onto the surface of the braise – this will help keep everything steamy and cooking evenly – then cover with a lid. Shut the lid of the barbecue and braise gently until the meat is fork tender, around 3½ hours, turning the cheeks over a couple of times during cooking so that both sides get equally submerged in the liquid.

Sprinkle with the parsley just before serving.

Serves 4–6

approx. 1.7kg (3lb 12oz) ox cheeks
    (4 cheeks)
4 tbsp olive oil
6 red onions, peeled and cut
    through the root into wedges
4 garlic cloves, crushed
1 heaped tbsp fennel seeds,
    toasted and roughly crushed
500ml (2 cups) red wine
250ml (1 cup) balsamic vinegar
1 tbsp brown sugar
flaked sea salt and freshly ground
    black pepper
a little chopped flat-leaf parsley,
    to garnish

Beef chuck chilli

Chuck is cut from the shoulder; tough, fatty and with plenty of connective tissues between the muscles it's therefore the ideal candidate for a long slow smoke followed by a long slow braise. Masa harina, here used to thicken the chilli, is cornmeal flour, the same ingredient that corn tacos are made from. You could indeed shove any leftovers of this chilli into tacos in the same ways as the birria tacos on page 260 and it also freezes really well. I've listed a few ideas for garnishes below and I suggest you don't be shy. I would no doubt have them all, lots of little bits of this and that sprinkled on top really make this dish.

The day before you want to cook, dry-brine the meat. Sprinkle the salt all over, rubbing in, and place on a rack set over a tray. Slide into the fridge and leave, uncovered, for 24 hours.

Fire up your barbecue to run at around 130–140°C (260–280°F); when it's hot and the temperature is stable, add 2–3 lumps of smoking wood. Depending on your cooking set-up you may need to top up the fuel during the cook.

Just before you start the beef, set the ancho chillies in a pan directly over the fire to toast for a few minutes; they will start to smell deep and chocolatey when they are ready. Take inside, cover in boiling water and leave to soak for a generous hour. Then blitz up to a purée and set aside.

Rest the beef on the grill bars far from the fire, shut the lid and smoke indirectly for 5 hours, checking once or twice and rotating to make sure it's cooking evenly. Remove and leave to cool for a while so you can handle it, then dice up to about 3–4cm (1¼–1¼in) cubes. Don't worry too much about cutting out the fat or collagen seams, they will render down deliciously on braising.

Once the beef is off and cooling, tip all the veg – the onions, tomatoes, chillies – onto the grill bars, directly over the fire. Cook until caramelized and softening, turning regularly so they cook evenly. Remove to a tray as they are cooked; the chillies will cook quickest followed by the tomatoes, with the onions taking the longest. Allow to cool a little, then chop everything up roughly.

Makes loads, feeding about 8

2kg (4½lb) beef chuck, in one piece
2 tbsp flaked sea salt
2–3 (25g/1oz) dried ancho chillies
2 large onions, quartered through the root
8 large tomatoes, halved
6 fresh green chillies (I used serrano)
2 tbsp olive oil
4 garlic cloves, crushed
1 tbsp cumin seeds, toasted and crushed
1–2 tsp chipotle chilli, to taste
2 tbsp masa harina
approx. 1 litre (4 cups) beef stock or water
40g (1½oz) best quality dark chocolate

Optional garnishes, to serve
grated Cheddar or Monterey Jack
sliced spring onions (scallions)
pickled jalapeños
crumbled tortilla chips
chopped coriander (cilantro)
sour cream

Take a fireproof casserole – a Dutch oven is ideal – and set it over the fire to heat up. Pour in the olive oil and add the garlic, frying for a couple of minutes. Add the cumin and chipotle, followed by the puréed ancho paste and the smoked diced beef, stirring well to mix. Sprinkle in the masa harina, stirring well to coat the meat. Then add all the vegetables and enough beef stock or water to just cover, about a litre (4 cups). Cover with a lid or piece of foil.

Shut the lid of your barbecue and leave for about 3–4 or so hours, or until the meat is really tender. About an hour before the end, add the chocolate and stir to melt, then continue cooking. Remove the lid towards the end of cooking to thicken up the sauce to your liking.

Serve bubbling hot with plenty of rice to soak up the sauce and whatever garnishes float your boat.

Smoked oxtail and pit beans

Smoked oxtail adds a glorious layer of complexity to these barbecued baked beans. Oxtail is a wonderful, flavour-packed and unctuous cut provided you give it enough time and gentle heat to yield its full potential. The constant swishing of a cow's tail means it's packed full of super-hard-working little muscles and connective tissue, meaning low and slow is your only option for tenderness.

The day before you cook, dry-brine the oxtail by sprinkling a tablespoon of salt all over and rubbing lightly in. Rest on a rack set over a tray and slide into the fridge, uncovered, overnight.

At the same time, tip the beans into a large bowl and cover generously with cold water. Set aside to soak overnight. The following day, drain and add to a large saucepan, cover in cold water and set on the hob. Bring up to the boil and simmer steadily until just tender – about an hour depending on the age of the beans. Drain well and set aside.

Fire up your barbecue ready for indirect grilling and add 2–3 lumps of smoking wood. Shut the barbecue vents down to moderate the temperature to around 130–140°C (260–280°F).

Take the oxtail pieces and rest onto the grill bars away from the fire. Shut the lid and leave to smoke gently for 3 hours, turning over halfway through. Remove to a plate and set aside.

Set a fireproof casserole over the fire, pour in the oil and add the onion. Shut the lid and leave to fry over a moderate heat until soft, about 30 minutes or so. Stir a couple of times to make sure they are cooking evenly, and if they are colouring too much or too quickly, simply slide the pan further away from the fire.

Once the onions are soft, add the garlic, smoked paprika and allspice, stirring briefly before adding the smoked oxtail and cooked beans. Pour in the chopped tomatoes, along with 500ml (2 cups) water, the brown sugar, treacle, Worcestershire sauce, mustard and bay leaves. Season with a little salt and pepper and stir well. Take a sheet of greaseproof paper and run under a cold tap. Shake dry and press onto the surface of the beans before adding the lid. This will help keep everything nice and steamy in the pot. Shut the barbecue lid and cook for another 3–4 hours until the oxtail is super-tender and falling off the bone. You may need to add a splash more water if it looks to be drying out too much.

Just before serving, sprinkle over the spring onions (scallions) and parsley.

Serves 4–6

1kg (2lb 4oz) oxtail pieces, cut
    into rings through the bone
300g (10½oz) dried cannellini
    beans
2 tbsp olive oil
1 onion, finely chopped
2 garlic cloves, crushed
2 tsp smoked paprika
1 tsp ground allspice
2 x 400g (14oz) cans chopped
    tomatoes
2 tbsp brown sugar
2 tbsp black treacle
2 tbsp Worcestershire sauce
1 tbsp English mustard
2 bay leaves
flaked sea salt and freshly ground
    black pepper

To garnish
½ bunch of spring onions
    (scallions), thinly sliced
a handful of flat-leaf parsley,
    chopped

Curry goat, grilled roti breads

Many years ago I honeymooned in Tobago where fragrant curries are a big deal; this intensely spicy dish is inspired by the food I remember eating. Strangely I have no recollection of eating a goat-based curry – there was a lot of crab, chicken and, rather memorably, a very rich frigate bird curry. Seagull is not a meat I can wholeheartedly recommend. I used bone-in neck meat, cut crossways through the bone. Once the meat hits the braising stage, the marrow will start to melt into the curry, maximizing the flavour potential. You can use bone-out neck fillets if you prefer, or indeed steaks cut from the shoulder or leg, in which case reduce the quantity a little – 600–700g (1lb 7oz–1lb 9oz) should suffice. The chickpeas here are not particularly authentic but I think them a good addition to add texture and stretch out the meat a little.

Incidentally, these rotis are also excellent with any curry or spiced dish in this chapter – try them with the smoked lamb shank vindaloo (page 97), Keralan spiced beef and aubergine (page 100) or Jerk-spiced osso buco (page 113).

Tip the coriander, cumin, fenugreek and mustard seeds, allspice berries, peppercorns and crumbled cinnamon stick into a frying pan (skillet) set over a medium heat. Toast for a couple of minutes then transfer to a spice mill, along with the turmeric, ginger and nutmeg, and grind to a powder. You can also grind in a pestle mortar. Transfer the ground spices to a small bowl and stir in the salt, sugar, thyme leaves, chopped chillies and oil to form a paste.

Put the goat in a dish so it fits in single snug layer. Spoon over the spice paste and, using your (ideally gloved) hands, work the paste really well into the meat, pushing it into all the cracks and crevices. Cover the dish and slide into the fridge to marinate and dry-brine for 24–48 hours.

When you are ready to cook, fire up your barbecue ready for gentle indirect grilling with two small fires either side (see fire set-ups on page 19). Add a couple of lumps of smoking wood to the fires. Aim for a steady air temperature of 140°C (280°F). Select a roasting tin that will fit the goat in a single layer, so you can then use it to braise the curry in once the meat has finished smoking, and set it in the base of the barbecue between the two small fires. Pour a good cup of water in the tin and set the grill bars in place. Rest the goat on the bars over the drip tray, shut the lid, and leave to smoke indirectly for 2 hours.

While the meat is smoking, begin the roti. Combine the flour, salt and sugar in a bowl then pour in the water and mix together until you have a crumbly dough. Lightly oil the worktop and tip out the dough. Knead for a few minutes until soft, smooth and elastic. Put back into the bowl, cover with a clean tea towel and set aside.

Serves 4

1 tbsp coriander seeds
1 tbsp cumin seeds
2 tsp fenugreek seeds
2 tsp mustard seeds
2 tsp allspice berries
2 tsp black peppercorns
1 cinnamon stick, crumbled
2 tbsp ground turmeric
2 tsp ground ginger
½ nutmeg, freshly grated
2 tsp flaked sea salt
2 tsp dark brown sugar
a few sprigs of thyme, leaves
    picked
1–2 Scotch bonnet chillies
    (to taste), chopped
3 tbsp olive oil
1kg (2lb 4oz) bone-in goat neck
    (cut across the bone, osso
    buco-style)
400g (14oz) can chickpeas
    (garbanzo beans), drained
    and rinsed

Continued overleaf...

Once the goat has had a couple of hours smoking, remove it to a plate. Remove the grill bars and carefully take out the drip tray, which should now contain some delicious juices from the meat. Add the chickpeas (garbanzo beans), tomatoes, coriander (cilantro), spring onions (scallions) and garlic to the juices followed by the goat, turning the meat over a few times to mix. Pour in enough water to come halfway up the meat. Cover tightly with foil and set back on the grill bars away from the fire. Leave to braise for 2–3 hours, or until the meat is fork tender and falling off the bone. About halfway though, briefly uncover and turn each piece of meat over then re-cover and keep cooking. About 30 minutes towards the end of cooking, remove the foil to allow the sauce to thicken a little. You may need to top up the fuel to maintain the temperature and, as with all these recipes, it's ok to let the temperature creep up a little here once you are at the braising stage – 170–180°C (340–350°F) wouldn't hurt at all.

While the curry is braising, continue with the roti. Scoop the dough out onto a well-oiled worktop and roll out to a 40 x 30cm (16 x12in) rectangle about 5mm (¼in) thick. Spread the ghee or softened butter all over then, starting with the longer edge, roll it up like a Swiss roll. Chop into 8 pieces.

Sprinkle plenty of flour on the worktop and take a piece of roti, turning it so the cut surface faces up. Roll out to a disc about 5mm (¼in) thick. Make sure there is plenty of flour on both sides then lift onto a clean tea towel or piece of baking paper set onto a baking sheet. Repeat with the remaining dough pieces, layering them up together between concertina folds of tea towel or paper. Slide the tray into the fridge if you can, especially if it's a hot day, to chill the dough and butter before you cook them. This will help create that all-important flakiness.

When the curry is nearly done, heat up a large frying pan on the hob and add just a little oil, wiping it over with a piece of paper towel. Once it's hot, add a roti and cook for a couple of minutes, pressing the surface with a fish slice to ensure it cooks evenly. Flip over and cook the other side. Set on a plate and cover with a clean tea towel to keep warm while you cook the rest.

Serve the curry with the warm rotis, perhaps with some cooked rice if you are extra hungry.

Pictured on page 111 (bottom).

300g (10½oz) cherry tomatoes, halved
a good handful of coriander (cilantro)
a bunch of spring onions (scallions), chopped (both white and green parts)
3–4 fat garlic cloves, crushed

For the roti
500g (4 cups) strong white bread flour
1 tsp flaked sea salt
1 tsp caster (superfine) sugar
300ml (1¼ cups) warm water
1 tbsp vegetable oil
75g (3oz) ghee or softened butter

Jerk-spiced osso buco, thyme and lime gremolata

Osso buco is the name given for veal shanks, or shin, that is cut through the bone into steaks with a chunky bit of bone (containing the tasty marrow) in the centre. Technically beef cut this way is just 'cross-cut shin' but the name has a ring to it that I like. The legs, front and rear, do a huge amount of work supporting the sheer bulk of the animal while constantly moves around grazing. The leg is made up of several muscle groups converging around the bone, with plenty of connective tissues to attach them. It's hardly surprising that this can be one of the toughest cuts to cook, making it perfect for the smoke+braise treatment. Take your time here and you will be amply rewarded. As with many slow-cooked dishes, a little freshness at the end does wonders to wake the whole thing up and this zesty gremolata sprinkle is just the ticket. This is perfect served with plenty of rice to soak up the juices.

Tip the allspice and cloves into a pestle and mortar and grind to a powder. Pour into a mini food processor and add the paprika, cinnamon, nutmeg, sugar and salt and blitz together. Add the spring onions (scallions), thyme, ginger, garlic, chillies and oil. Blitz to a paste. You can also make this in a pestle and mortar by pounding everything together by hand. Put the steaks into a dish in a snug single layer and spread the spice paste all over. Cover and slide into the fridge to marinate for 24–48 hours.

When you are ready to cook, get your grill ready for indirect cooking, piling the coals to one side. You are aiming for a temperature of around 130–140°C (260–280°F). Add a couple of lumps of smoking wood to the fire and set a roasting tin with a cupful of water on the base of the barbecue next to the fire. Choose a tin that you could fit the beef in a single layer in, and then you can use that to braise it in. Put the grill bars in place and rest the beef on the bars over the drip tray, away from the fire. Shut the lid and smoke indirectly for 2 hours.

Remove the beef to a plate and set aside. Carefully remove the grill bars and take out the drip tray (which should have a little liquid left in it along with any dripping from the meat as it smoked. Nestle the beef into the tray so it sits in a single snug layer. Tuck in the orange peel and squeeze over the juice. Pour in the beef stock and cover the pan really tightly with a layer of foil. Set back onto the barbecue away from the fire and allow to braise

Serves 4

1 tbsp allspice berries
5 cloves
1½ tbsp unsmoked paprika
2 tsp ground cinnamon
½ nutmeg, freshly grated
2 tbsp dark brown sugar
1 heaped tbsp flaked sea salt
a bunch of spring onions (scallions), chopped
3–4 sprigs of thyme, leaves picked
50g (2oz) fresh root ginger, grated
4 garlic cloves, chopped
1–2 Scotch bonnet chillies, to taste (seeds removed for less heat)
3 tbsp olive oil
1.5–1.8kg (3lb 5oz–3lb 15oz) beef shin, cut through the bone into slices (osso buco-style)
juice of 1 orange, plus 3 wide strips of pared zest
400ml (1¾ cups) beef stock

Continued overleaf...

indirectly for 2–3 hours, or until the meat is falling from the bone. At this point you can open up the vents on your barbecue to raise the temperature a little, around 150–160°C (300–320°F) would be perfect. Or, indeed, you could (as with all these smoke+braise recipes) take proceedings inside to your oven, where the same temperatures apply. Remove the foil for the last hour or so to allow the juices to concentrate and evaporate.

When the beef is nearly done, make the gremolata by mixing the thyme, garlic, lime zest and chilli in a small bowl. Once the beef has finished cooking, squeeze over the lime juice then nestle the zested and juiced lime halves in the dish with the beef. Sprinkle on the gremolata just before serving.

Pictured on page 111 (top).

For the thyme and lime gremolata

a handful of thyme, leaves picked and
    finely chopped
2 garlic cloves, finely chopped
zest and juice of 2 limes
1 red chilli (choose a mild one for colour
    or another Scotch bonnet for fire),
    finely chopped

Lamb shoulder with fennel, horseradish and milk

This recipe snuck into this chapter by a whisker as the braise part is a little borderline. The smoked lamb gets wrapped up with a glass of milk – which sounds a little weird, but so totally isn't – providing moisture that partly steams the lamb to incredible softness. Milk acids are a great meat tenderizer and, although the meat won't win any prizes for its looks, what you get is supreme succulence over gobsmacking beauty. I do tend to insert a wired temperature probe to monitor the cooking of the lamb in the later stages because the lamb gets wrapped tightly after smoking, and unwrapping to check on its progress will slow the whole cook down considerably (and perhaps risk, literally, spilling the milk).

Use a sharp knife to carefully poke plenty of deep slits into the meat. Drizzle over the olive oil and rub all over.

Toast the fennel seeds and peppercorns in a frying pan (skillet) set over a medium heat for a minute or two until fragrant. Tip into a pestle and mortar, add the salt and roughly crush. Rub this all over the lamb, along with lemon zest, working the spices into the slits. Set on a plate and refrigerate, uncovered, for 2–24 hours.

When ready to cook, fire up your barbecue ready for indirect grilling, piling the coals in a strip to one side of the barbecue. Add two lumps of smoking wood and shut down the vents of your barbecue to stabilize the temperature at 120–130°C (250–265°F).

Set the lamb on the far side of the grill, away from the fire, and smoke for 3 hours, adding top-ups of fuel as necessary.

While the lamb is smoking, measure the milk into a jug and stir through the garlic and horseradish. Set aside.

Lay 4 foil sheets in a cross shape (each about 3 times the size of your lamb) onto a baking sheet and take to your grill, along with the flavoured milk. Lift the lamb onto the centre of the foil, and crunch the sides to form walls. Pour the milk over the lamb then fold up the foil to completely enclose the milk, crimping it along the top. Insert a temperature probe through the foil deep into the centre of the meat. Leave the meat on the tray and set back onto the grill, away from the fire so it can continue cooking indirectly.

Open the vents a little to raise the temperature to 150–160°C (300–320°F) – add more fuel if needed. Cook for another 3 hours, or until the meat probe reads 94–95°C (201–203°F). Leave to rest for 30 minutes, wrapped up, which will make it more 'pull-able'.

This is great served with a punchy and peppery green salad.

Serves 4 (this is easily doubled if you want to do a whole shoulder – cooking time will increase a little, maybe another hour or two)

1kg (2lb 4oz) bone-in shoulder (½ a shoulder)
1 tbsp olive oil
2 tbsp fennel seeds
1 tbsp black peppercorns
2 tsp flaked sea salt
zest of 1 lemon
250ml (1 cup) milk
3 garlic cloves, thinly sliced
30g (1oz) freshly grated horseradish (or 2 tbsp hot horseradish from a jar)

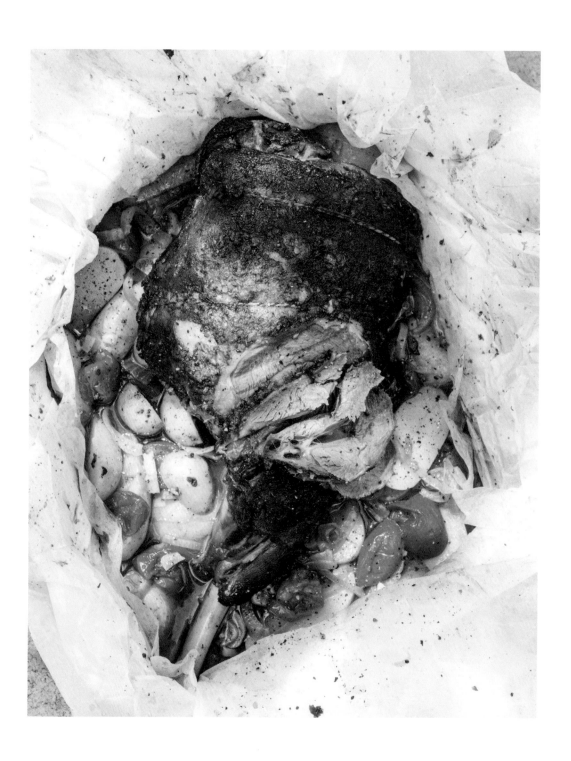

Hogget kleftiko, Greek salad

I use hogget leg for this Greek classic with a smoky twist. Hogget is a mature lamb that's between one and two years old. The legs will weigh in at over a couple of kilos or more, plenty for feeding a good crowd, and because they are older, they tend to have more succulent intramuscular fat (or marbling) through them than younger lamb. You could substitute a large lamb leg or a goat leg.

With a 3-hour smoke followed by a rather long wallow in a bath of garlicky wine, this is not a dish to be rushed in any way, shape or form. Get it on good and early and plan on a very long, very late and very joyful lunch with friends. Bliss.

Take a sharp knife and pierce lots of really deep slits all over the meat and set in a tray big enough to contain it. It needs to sit in the fridge overnight so make sure the tray fits!

In a small bowl, mix together the olive oil, 2 tablespoons flaked sea salt, oregano, cinnamon, crushed garlic and plenty of black pepper. Spoon over the hogget and rub in really well, pressing deep into the cuts you made. Slide into the fridge and leave to dry-brine and marinate for up to 48 hours.

When you are ready to cook, fire up your barbecue ready for indirect smoking, aiming for a temperature of around 140°C (280°F). Add 2–3 lumps of smoking wood to the fire. Lift the hogget from the tray onto the grill bars on the far side from the fire. Shut the lid and leave to smoke for 3 hours.

Wash the tray and line with a triple layer of large foil sheets, arranging them in a criss-cross pattern, followed by a triple layer of greaseproof paper or butcher's paper. You need the sheets to wrap up and over the meat and potatoes so be generous.

Once the hogget has almost finished smoking, tip the potato halves and sliced onions into the lined tin, scatter over the tomato and garlic slices and season with a little salt and pepper. Zest over one of the lemons and squeeze over the juice. Sit the hogget on top and zest and juice the other lemon over it. Pour the wine and olive oil over the lot. Then wrap each layer of paper and foil up and over to completely enclose it. Slide the tin back into the barbecue, again away from the fire, and cook for another good 3 hours. If you have a wired temperature probe, this is a great time to use it to give yourself x-ray eyes as to how the meat is cooking; you are aiming for a meat temperature of around 93–95°C (200–203°F). In an ideal world, the last thing you want

Serves around 8

2–2.5kg (4lb 8oz–5lb 10oz) hogget leg
4 tbsp olive oil
2 tbsp dried oregano
2 tsp ground cinnamon
1 garlic bulb, cloves peeled and crushed
1.5kg (3lb 5oz) Charlotte potatoes, sliced in half
2 red onions, sliced
300g (10½oz) tomatoes, sliced
½ garlic bulb, cloves peeled and sliced
2 lemons
400ml (1¾ cups) white wine
100ml (3½fl oz) olive oil
flaked sea salt and freshly ground black pepper

For the Greek salad
2 cucumbers, cut into chunks
10 large ripe vine tomatoes, cut into chunks
2 green peppers, sliced
a good handful of kalamata olives
2 tbsp dried oregano
200ml (generous ¾ cup) extra virgin olive oil
75ml (⅓ cup) red wine vinegar
2 x 200g (7oz) blocks of feta

Continued overleaf…

to do is unwrap the parcel and risk losing any of the lovely winey juices but if they escape just spoon them back over to serve.

Once the kleftiko has virtually finished cooking, assemble the salad. Take a couple of large shallow bowls, one for each end of the table, and scatter the cucumber, tomato, green pepper and olives between them – no need to mix. Sprinkle over most of the oregano and drizzle over most of the olive oil and all of the red wine vinegar. Top each bowl with a block of feta and sprinkle the rest of the oregano on top. Finish with a final drizzle of oil.

Venison shanks with red wine, porcini dumplings

A gorgeous dish for a chilly night, using cross-cut venison shanks and loosely based on osso buco, an Italian braise traditionally made with veal. Indeed, you could substitute veal or beef if you liked, or use whole lamb shanks. Smoking the meat adds so much complexity in terms of flavour. With a long cook, this is a serious commitment to time, but there's very little going on in terms of actual graft.

The day before you want to cook, sprinkle the salt over the venison. Place on a rack set over a tray, slide into the fridge, uncovered, and leave to dry-brine for 24 hours.

When you are ready to cook, fire up your barbecue ready for gentle indirect smoking, aiming for a temperature of around 130–140°C (260–280°F), adding a little smoking wood to the fire. Add a drip tray to the base of the barbecue and pour in a couple of cups of water to create a little steam.

Drizzle a little of the olive oil over the venison. Set the shanks onto the grill bars above the water tray, keeping them nice and snugly together – venison is a very lean meat that can dry out. Smoke indirectly for 3 hours. You may need to top up with a little fuel depending on what sort of kit you are using. Remove the venison to a plate and carefully remove and reserve the drip tray.

Set a fireproof casserole over the fire and pour in the rest of the olive oil. Add the onions, stirring to mix, and shut the lid. Cook for 20 minutes, or until the onions are softened, then add the garlic, juniper and sage and cook for a further 5 minutes.

Stir through the flour thoroughly so it mixes with the juices. Add the smoked meat to the pot, along with the wine and liquid from the drip tray, stirring well to mix. Cover with a tight-fitting lid, shut the lid of your barbecue and leave to braise for a generous 3 hours. After this time, add the drained butterbeans and briefly stir, adding a splash more water if it's looking a little dry, then re-cover a cook for another hour. It's fine to let the temperature creep up a little at this stage, 150°C (300°F) is perfect, as the meat is now protected by the liquid.

Serves 4

1kg (2lb 4oz) cross-cut venison
    shanks
1 tbsp flaked sea salt
3 tbsp olive oil
2 red onions, sliced
3 garlic cloves, crushed
1 tsp juniper berries, lightly
    crushed
2 sprigs of sage, leaves picked
    and chopped (about 1 heaped
    tbsp chopped leaves)
1 tbsp plain (all-purpose) flour
300ml (1¼ cups) red wine
400g (14oz) can butterbeans,
    drained and rinsed

For the dumplings

20g (¾oz) dried porcini, soaked
    in 200ml (generous ¾ cup)
    boiling water
200g (7oz) self-raising flour
100g (3½oz) suet
flaked sea salt and freshly ground
    black pepper

Continued overleaf...

Once the braising time is up, make the dumplings. Set a sieve (strainer) over a jug and drain the soaking mushrooms, reserving the (now cool) liquid. Finely chop the mushrooms and scoop into a mixing bowl. Add the flour and suet and season well with salt and pepper. Pour in the mushroom soaking liquid and stir well until you have a sticky dough. Using lightly floured hands, roll into about 12 walnut-sized balls, resting them on a floured plate as you go.

Drop the dumplings onto the surface of the braise, turning them gently over once or twice to coat in the liquid – this will help them go crisp and golden – and cook uncovered (but with the barbecue lid shut) for about an hour until the dumplings are cooked through.

This needs nothing more than a big bowl of buttery greens to go alongside.

Paella Valenciana with rabbit

Rabbit is the traditional meat in a Valencian paella – often with the addition of the snails that I have excluded here – but you could use jointed chicken pieces if you prefer. Rabbit is a very lean meat that is prone to drying out, which makes it the ideal candidate for braising once you have seared it.

A true paella would have been cooked over an open wood fire, and if you have a fire pit then doing it this way is very satisfying, although you can easily use a barbecue too. You need a good-sized flat pan – a paella pan is obviously ideal here, but a non-traditional large rectangular roasting tin is a good alternative. You need some space so that when the rice goes in it sits in a layer no deeper than 1cm (½in) or so.

Rabbit really benefits from the dry brining treatment because, being so lean, it is prone to drying out. Sprinkle 1 tablespoon salt all over the jointed meat and rest on a rack set over a plate. Slide into the fridge and leave, uncovered, for 24 hours.

When you are ready to cook, fire up your barbecue for direct and indirect grilling, adding a couple of lumps of smoking wood to the fire. Shut the vents down on the barbecue so the temperature is hovering around 150–160°C (300–320°F).

Drizzle a little of the olive oil onto the rabbit and sear directly over the heat for a few minutes, tuning regularly, to get some good colour all over. Remove to a plate and set aside.

Pour the rest of the oil into a large pan or tin and set it over the fire, adding the onions and peppers and a little salt and pepper. Fry over the heat for a good 20 minutes, keeping the lid shut for much of the time but stirring fairly often to make sure its cooking evenly and not burning. If it's colouring too much, slide the pan a little away from the fire. Once soft and lightly caramelized, add the tomatoes, garlic, smoked paprika, saffron and rosemary and fry for another 10 minutes or so until the tomatoes have collapsed.

Pour in the sherry and allow to evaporate a little, just 5 minutes or so, before adding the rabbit back to the pan. Pour over the stock and cover the pan with a snugly tucked piece of foil to seal it up. Slide the pan away from the fire and leave to simmer indirectly for about 45 minutes. You want to braise the rabbit pieces until the meat is really tender and beginning to fall off the bone, so test them by teasing the meat apart with a fork. If it needs a little longer, re-cover and simmer for a few more minutes.

Serves about 6

1 wild rabbit (about 800g/1lb 12oz), jointed into 6 pieces
100ml (3½fl oz) olive oil
2 onions, chopped
2 red peppers, chopped
3 large vine tomatoes, finely chopped
4 fat garlic cloves, crushed
1 tsp smoked paprika
a good pinch of saffron
a couple of sprigs of rosemary, needles picked
200ml (generous ¾ cup) dry sherry (I use Oloroso for its rich nutty flavour)
1 litre (4 cups) hot chicken stock, plus extra water if necessary
400g (14oz) can butterbeans, drained and rinsed
300g (10½oz) green beans, cut in half
350g (12oz) paella rice
flaked sea salt and freshly ground black pepper

To serve

a small handful of flat-leaf parsley, chopped
a good drizzle of extra virgin olive oil

Continued overleaf...

Remove the foil and slide the pan back over the fire. Add the butterbeans and green beans, along with the rice, giving everything a little stir to mix together, and re-cover loosely with the foil. Leave to cook directly over the fire for about 20 minutes, or until the rice is tender but with a little 'bite' to it. Do not stir the pan, you want the base to build up a delicious sticky crust of stuck on rice – this, the soccarat, is the most prized bit of the paella. You may need to add a splash of extra water if it's looking a little dry.

Sprinkle over the parsley and drizzle with plenty of extra virgin olive oil just before serving.

Chapter 5: The Barbecue BIG Guns

When it comes to barbecue there are two things any fire cooking addict wants to nail: pulled pork and smoked brisket. I could write an entire chapter, if not an entire book, on theory, technique and analysis on cooking these American low and slow smoked meat classics. There's so much information out there it can be quite overwhelming for a novice to know where to begin. And much like parenting when you've just had a newborn baby, everyone has an opinion of how to do it 'right'.

So what you get here is the basics according to me – a set of skills, or the things I find work for me, things for you to try and experiment with. I'll talk about the specifics of each cut and share my own favourite rub recipe for both pork and brisket but the way you cook them is identical. I've added a third recipe into the mix, pastrami but made with chuck (or shoulder) rather than brisket, because a) it's epic and b) you use exactly the same set of cooking skills.

What is 'smoking' meat?

In the States this kind of low and slow cooking (it's important to remember the difference between barbecue the noun and barbecue the verb, see page 5) would often be done purely with wood and in an offset smoker, were the fire is entirely separate from the meat. The meat gets gently cooked and smoked by the convection currents of hot air and smoke than pass over it. It's a total art form, an act of dedication towards the end result, which is exceptionally delicious meat. On a domestic scale we often don't, myself included, have offset smokers to hand. That is not to say you can't smoke great meat in a regular barbecue but temperature control here is everything. It will be easier to cook a brisket or pulled pork in a bit of kit where the temperature is super-controllable and steady – like a pellet smoker with an electric thermostat or a super-efficient ceramic kamado-style oven – but that doesn't mean you can't smoke meat in a regular barbecue; you just need to be prepared to babysit the fire a little more. Again, the more you use your own kit the better versed you will be in holding the temperature steady and prolonging the burn time of your fuel.

Low and slow, or hot and fast

The general method for brisket, pulled pork or pastrami is the same, and there are two common options. You can go 'low and slow' – that is at a barbecue temperature of around 120°C (250°F) or you can go 'hot and fast', using a temperature of around 150°C (300°F). Both methods work. It depends how quickly you want to eat and how long you want to hang out by the smoker. Sometimes hanging out by the smoker is the best fun; you almost always find cold beers and good company are involved.

Purists would always go low and slow, and you might be looking at 12–14, even 16 hours for a brisket, maybe 10–12 or more for pulled pork. Joints of meat are natural things, they do not always cook at the same speeds and they sometimes don't follow the textbook set of rules. If ever there was a time to reiterate 'it's done when it's done' it is now. With the hot and fast method you can knock a third or even a half off the cook times. It does yield great results, although in brisket particularly, the meat is maybe not quite as meltingly tender as if you cooked it more gently for longer. Slower also gives you a better smoke ring (see page 130).

Which method do I prefer? Neither specifically. I'm more often to be found following a middle line and aiming for a temperature of around 130–140°C (260–280°F), but I concede that 'medium and mid-length' doesn't quite have the same catchy ring to it.

Temperature, the magic numbers

A temperature probe, yet again, is supremely useful and I invariably use a wired probe for these long cooks so I can monitor what's going on without opening the lid. As long as the temperature of the meat is increasing and the temperature of the barbecue is holding steady, it's cooking.

There are two temperatures to keep an eye out for. You want to cook the meat all the way through to around 95°C (203°F) to get that all-important soft and yielding texture, but before you reach the end goal, at around 70–75°C (160–165°F), you will need to make a decision about whether to wrap or not.

The stall and the science of wrapping

Once your meat has hit an internal temperature in the low to mid-seventies (160–165°F) it will invariably stop cooking for a period of time. This period in which the temperature stubbornly refuses to rise is known as the 'stall' and it is the point where the rate of evaporative cooling on the surface of the meat is equal to the rate of energy gain it takes on from the heat source. Imagine a runner, getting hotter and hotter as they pound the pavements and their body sweating to cool the skin down. At one point the heating and the cooling are equal and opposite and the net change is zero; they cancel each other out. That is the stall.

Once you get there you have two choices. You can ride it out. Eventually, and unpredictably, at some point the energy gain side of the equation will win out and the temperature will begin to rise once more. The problem is that sometimes the stall can take hours and hours to resolve itself, or it can be relatively quick. You just don't know how a particular joint will behave.

The second option is to pull the meat out of the barbecue once it hits the stall and wrap it up tight before carrying on. A 'blanket' around the meat drastically reduces the amount of evaporation on the surface, and so the meat hops over the stall and keeps on cooking. I have encountered something like bravado regarding the stall – 'I just sit it out, I never wrap' – the inference being that wrapping is somehow cheating, but in my world getting a good meal on the table takes priority. And besides, you get a much juicier result. You'll see I use the wrapping technique in many recipes in this book, not just limited to brisket and pulled pork, as any cut from any beast (or indeed bird) can hit the stall.

You can wrap in unwaxed butcher's paper or you can wrap in foil. Butcher's paper is harder to find in the UK, but not impossible online, whereas foil is ubiquitous. I have also wrapped in unwaxed greaseproof paper too. They all work. Whatever you wrap in you want to wrap really tight (imagine you are swaddling a baby), to remove any air pockets where the meat will steam. The slow smoking the meat has undergone thus far will have created a lovely, deeply flavoured crust on the surface, known as the bark, and too much steam will soften the bark. Once you have wrapped, reinsert the probe (if you are using one) through the paper or foil and get it back on the barbecue to keep cooking.

Pros and cons over paper vs foil? Foil is quicker: you will speed up your cook by around an hour and a half or so over paper. Paper allows the meat to breathe a touch more and so your bark will stay a little more intact. There is a third option – wrap in foil to finish the cooking, then remove the foil and wrap in paper while the meat rests, which will allow the meat to breathe a little and the bark will firm up again. As always, I encourage you to experiment and draw your own conclusions.

The smoke ring

Meat that has been smoked will often have a deep pink tinge to the outer layer. This is known as the smoke ring and is evidence of a chemical reaction between the meat protein myoglobin and nitric oxide, a gas produced during combustion. Myoglobin begins to turn brown on cooking, once the meat has reached above 60°C (140°F) internal temperature, and the nitric oxide 'fixes' the myoglobin so its stays a pink colour and doesn't turn brown. The combustion of wood produces more nitric oxide than the combustion of charcoal. The smoke ring doesn't actually taste of anything in itself, so meat with a deeper smoke ring won't taste more smoky, but it does look pretty cool. You can get a deeper smoke ring by taking the cook slower, so the more time it takes to get to 60°C (140°F) the more pink colour gets fixed. You can also increase the smoke ring by cooking in a moist environment, so adding a tray of water into the barbecue, because a wet surface to the meat will attract more nitric oxide.

Preparing pastrami, brisket and pulled pork for smoking – the rub or the brine

With both pulled pork and brisket recipes that follow, I apply a dry rub 24 or even 48 hours before I want to cook. The salt in the rubs works its tenderizing magic during the dry-brining process (see page 21) and the spices 'set' onto the outside for a better bark. The pastrami is a little different because the salt in the wet brine has already done its job, but leaving it for 24 hours with the salt-free rub still also allows the spices to set.

These recipes use big pieces of meat, and would all serve more than 8 in one sitting. It's not really worth doing it for a smaller piece – small joints are much harder to nail low and slow as they are more prone to drying out. Much better to cook bigger and relish the leftovers which, incidentally, freeze really well too.

Smoked chuck pastrami

Pastrami is cured smoked beef that is traditionally made with brisket. Here I make it with chuck – a cheaper, fattier cut from the shoulder of the cow. To my mind it's easier to cook than brisket, much more juicy and less prone to drying out, but try it with brisket if you like, just following the same method.

This is not a quick recipe by any means. The meat needs curing in a spiced brine for 5–7 days, followed by a day of drying the surface with a spiced rub, followed by a very generous few hours of cooking. A project then, something to tackle when you have time and the space in your fridge to go for the long haul.

I like to serve this pastrami in a massive doorstep sandwich, as is traditional, with salad and pickled cucumber slices. I've included a recipe for a delicious sandwich spread of Gruyère, mustard and mayo that makes an excellent addition (and enough for about 4 sandwiches).

Pour 350ml (1½ cups) boiling water into a jug and stir through the salt and sugar until it has dissolved. Toast the spices in a small frying pan over a medium heat for a minute, then tip them into a pestle and mortar. Roughly crush, then add to the water along with the garlic, stirring well to mix. Hang a large food bag in a bowl and pour in the hot brine. Top up with 300ml (1¼ cups) cold water and set aside to go completely cold.

Once the brine is cold, gently lower the chuck into the bag and seal up tight, squeezing as much air out as possible as you close it. Slide the bowl into the fridge for at least 5 days, 7 would be better if you had the time. Once or twice a day (when you're opening the fridge to get the milk out or whatever) just turn and rotate the bag in the bowl to make sure all sides are getting submerged.

After brining, remove the beef to a colander and discard the brine. Run the beef under cold water to wash off the whole spices. Set the colander over a bowl to drain while you make the spice rub.

Tip the peppercorns, mustard and coriander seeds into a small frying pan (skillet) and set over a medium heat to toast for a minute or two until fragrant. Transfer to a pestle and mortar and grind coarsely. Add the brown sugar, mustard powder, paprika, garlic and olive oil and pound to a paste.

Set the beef on a rack over a tray and rub the spice paste all over. Slide into the fridge and leave for the surface to dry out, uncovered, for 24 hours.

Serves 8, with leftovers

For the brine

75g (3oz) sea salt
45g (1½oz) brown sugar
2 tsp coriander seeds
2 tsp allspice berries
2 tsp black peppercorns
2 tsp mustard seeds
1 tsp cloves
1 tsp fennel seeds
1 tsp chilli powder
4 fat garlic cloves, crushed
3kg (6½lb) beef chuck

For the rub

3 tbsp black peppercorns
2 tbsp mustard seeds
2 tbsp coriander seeds
3 tbsp dark brown sugar
2 tbsp English mustard powder
2 tbsp unsmoked paprika
3 garlic cloves
3 tbsp olive oil

To serve

170g (6oz) aged Gruyère, grated

Continued overleaf...

When you are ready to cook, set up whatever type of barbecue you are using and get it running to a steady 130–140°C (260–280°F), adding 2–3 lumps of smoking wood. Set a roasting tray of water underneath where the meat will sit. This will keep the temperature gentle and create a steamy atmosphere which will help the meat soak up the smoke.

Sit the grill bars on and rest the meat, fat side up, onto that, over the tray of water, away from the fire. If you have one, insert a meat probe deep into the centre. Shut the lid and walk away. You need do nothing more now until the meat reaches around 70–75°C (160–165°F) internal temperature, which should be in around 4–5 hours or so. Try to maintain the temperature as close to 130–140°C (260–280°F) as you can. Keep an eye on the water tray; the steam is so helpful in getting the smoke to stick so add a splash of water if you have to.

Once you've reached 70–75°C (160–165°F), remove the meat to a plate. Wrap the meat tightly in butcher's paper or foil (see page 129), set back on the grill bars in the same place, reinserting the temperature probe if you are using one, and cook indirectly until it reaches the magic number of 95°C (203°F). This may take another 3 hours or so – it will cook faster in foil than paper. As always in barbecue, we cook to temperature not time. It's impossible to be accurate with minutes and hours here, or indeed anywhere in this book.

Once you've reached temperature, remove the meat and rest, still wrapped and covered in a few clean tea towels for a good hour, maybe a touch more, before slicing.

When you are ready to make your sandwich, simply mix together the Gruyère, spring onions (scallions), dill, mayonnaise and English mustard. Spread onto thick slices of bread, top with slices of pastrami and add lettuce and pickled cucumber as you wish.

3 spring onions (scallions),
    finely chopped
a handful of dill, chopped
4 tbsp mayonnaise
2 tsp English mustard
thick slices of bread
salad leaves
pickled cucumber

Smoked brisket with black pepper and fenugreek

A perfectly cooked beef brisket is seen as the holy grail of good barbecue and certainly, when you get it right, you get intensely smoky, deeply beefy, melt-in-the-mouth food nirvana. There's no denying that it is not the easiest of cooks to master – it's an unforgiving cut and can be as tough as old boots if you get it wrong. Brisket comes from the chest of the cow, or the pectoral muscles, so these muscles are responsible for holding up the whole weight of the front of the animal. It's hardly surprising, then, that at around 600kg (1,320lb) a beast, the brisket is among one of the toughest, most connective-tissue-ridden muscles in the body. Cooking brisket is a commitment in time and money, but get it right and you will be rewarded.

A whole brisket, called a packer cut, can weigh a massive 7–8kg (15–17lb), enough to feed a lot of hungry people. Made up of two separate muscles, the pectoralis profundus, otherwise known as the point, and the pectoralis superficialis, or the flat. The point is fatter and rounder and comes with a layer of fat on top. The flat is thinner and leaner. One of the reasons a whole brisket is tricky to cook is because these two muscles are different. Given that it's quite rare, on a domestic level, that you would want to cook this much meat, I normally cook half a brisket, and the half I choose is the point. It's just a more fatty, more forgiving muscle, giving juicier results.

This is my go-to brisket rub. In Texas, fatherland of brisket, they rub in purely salt and pepper. I almost always add crushed fenugreek seeds: these are entirely untraditional, but add a deeply spicy and alluring hit nonetheless.

Trim up your brisket by cutting off any thick sections of excess fat – a 1cm (½in) layer all over the fat side is fine and will add lubrication as it renders, but any more than that won't help the smoke get into the meat.

Tip the fenugreek seeds into a spice mill and grind to a powder. Add the black peppercorns and pulse until they are coarsely ground. Pour into a bowl and stir through the salt and sugar. Sprinkle all over the brisket on both sides and around the edges, rubbing in well. Place on a rack set over a tray and slide into the fridge, uncovered, for 24–48 hours.

When you are ready to cook, set up whatever type of barbecue you are using and get it running to a steady 130–140°C (260–280°F), adding 2–3 lumps of smoking wood. Set a roasting tray of water underneath where the meat will sit. This will keep the temperature gentle and create a steamy atmosphere which will help the meat soak up the smoke (see page 130).

Sit the grill bars on and rest the meat, fat side up, onto that, over the tray of water, away from the fire. If you have one, insert a meat probe deep into the centre. Shut the lid and walk away.

Serves 8, with leftovers

3.5–4kg (7¾–9lb) point end
  brisket
2 tbsp fenugreek seeds
3 tbsp black peppercorns
4 good tbsp flaked sea salt
4 tbsp brown sugar

You need do nothing more now until the meat reaches around 70–75°C (160–165°F) internal temperature, which should be in around 4–5 hours or so. Try to maintain the temperature as close to 130–140°C (260–280°F) as you can. Add a splash of water to the tray to make sure it doesn't dry out; steam is your friend here.

Once you've reached 70–75°C (160–165°F), remove the meat to a plate. Carefully remove the pan of water and shut the lid of the barbecue to keep the heat in. If you've kept the water pan topped up you may have some delicious juices worth saving. Wrap the meat tightly in butcher's paper or foil (see page 129), set back on the grill bars in the same place, reinserting the temperature probe if you are using one. Return to the barbecue and cook indirectly until it reaches the magic number of 95°C (203°F). This may take another 3–5 hours or so – it will cook faster in foil than paper. Patience is key, there is no such thing as a 'standard brisket', some just cook more quickly than others. Have some snacks on hand, drink a beer and enjoy the process.

Once you've reached temperature, remove the meat and rest, still wrapped and covered in a few clean tea towels for a good hour, maybe a touch more. The longer you rest it the better the texture will be. If you have hungry teenagers like I do, this stage is harder than you might think.

Unwrap the brisket, saving the juices (perhaps adding to any collected in the water tray) and rest on a board. Use a sharp knife to carve into slices, dropping into the warmed juices as you go. Mac and cheese is a traditional accompaniment, or go for soft rolls and coleslaw.

Pictured overleaf (top).

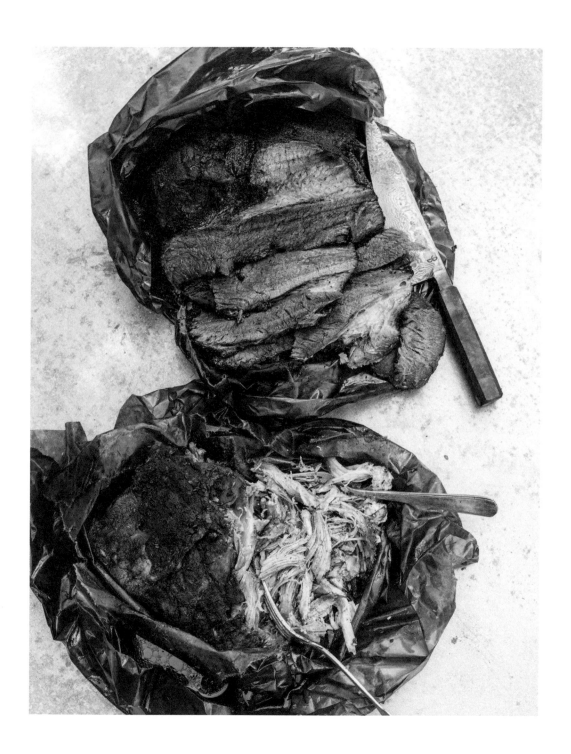

Pulled pork butt with cumin and smoked paprika

Pulled pork is made from a cut called pork butt which, perhaps confusingly, actually comes from the shoulder of a pig. These super-hard-working muscles need considerable slow, gentle cooking to tenderize until 'pull-able'. I use a bone-in pork butt here, but you could use bone-out too; it will work just as well but it may well cook a little more quickly.

Traditional pulled pork rub recipes very often call for dried garlic powder, but I don't particularly like the taste, finding it a touch artificial somehow, so I always go for fresh crushed garlic in my rubs. This is my pulled pork recipe, using the spices that I like. The thing is, you can rub your pork in whatever works for you, there are no hard and fast rules, bar the salt and the sugar. Cook pork butt slowly enough and it will become tasty and tender no matter what you rubbed it in. You can also, of course, reach for a ready-made rub; there are plenty of great ones out there.

Take a sharp knife and carefully remove the rind on the pork, leaving on as much fat as possible on the pork itself.

To make the rub, tip the cumin seeds into a small frying pan (skillet) and set over a medium-high heat to toast for a minute or two. Transfer to a pestle and mortar and grind until quite fine. Add the sugar, salt, mustard and smoked paprika and grind together until mixed. Finally add the garlic and olive oil and mash to a paste. Spread this all over the pork, rubbing it well into the cracks and crevices. Place on a rack set over a roasting tin. This just allows air to circulate all around rather than the base sit in its own juices getting soggy. Slide into the fridge, uncovered, for 24 hours, although 48 hours wouldn't hurt if you have the time.

When you are ready to cook, set up whatever type of barbecue you are using and get it running to a steady 130–140°C (260–280°F), adding 2–3 lumps of smoking wood. Set a roasting tray of water underneath where the meat will sit. This will keep the temperature gentle, create a steamy atmosphere which will help the meat soak up the smoke (see page 130) and make a delicious gravy providing you don't let it dry out.

Sit the grill bars on and rest the meat, fat side up, onto that, over the tray of water, away from the fire. If you have one, insert a meat probe deep into the centre, but avoiding the bone as it will give an inaccurate reading. Shut the lid and walk away. You need do nothing more now until the pork reaches around 70–75°C (160–165°F) internal temperature, which should be in around 4–5 hours or so. Try to maintain the temperature as close to 130–140°C (260–280°F) as you can. Keep an eye on the water tray, you don't want to let it dry out, but neither do you want it to be swimming and thin, so add a splash of water if you have to.

Serves 8, with leftovers

3–3.5kg (6½–7¾lb) pork butt, bone in
2 tbsp cumin seeds
75g (3oz) dark brown sugar
3 tbsp flaked sea salt
2 tbsp English mustard powder
1 tbsp smoked paprika
4 garlic cloves, chopped
3 tbsp olive oil

Pictured opposite (bottom).

Continued overleaf…

Once you've reached 70–75°C (160–165°F), remove the meat to a plate. Carefully remove the pan of water, which will have miraculously transformed into a delicious gravy, and shut the lid of the barbecue to keep the heat in. Wrap the meat tightly in butcher's paper or foil, reinserting the temperature probe if you are using one. Return to the barbecue and cook indirectly until it reaches the magic number of 95°C (203°F). This may take another 3–4 hours or so – it will cook faster if you are using foil rather than paper.

Once you've reached temperature, remove the meat and rest, still wrapped and covered in a few clean tea towels for a good hour.

When you are ready to serve, place the pan of gravy over the hob and reheat. Use two forks to pull apart the pork, removing and discarding the bone and any connective tissues that haven't rendered down with cooking. Drop the shreds of pork into the warm gravy as you go, tossing to coat once it's all pulled.

Serve stuffed into buns with whatever takes your fancy. Coleslaw and barbecue sauce are definitely traditional, but my kids prefer to eat this with old-school sage and onion stuffing from a packet. And I like it with hot English mustard and apple sauce. Your call.

Chapter 6: Other Slow Cooks

The recipes that follow all use a fairly gentle indirect heat to slow-cook meat to perfection. With gentle cooking and much patience you can take the cheaper, less prime cuts and turn them into something spectacular; most of these recipes use cuts from shoulders, legs or bellies. With time, the collagen in the connective tissues softens to melting gelatine and the fat renders down to make things super-succulent. One exception here – the standing rib roast is far from a cheap cut and definitely one to save for a treat of a meal. There is a lot of intramuscular fat deep within the meat that needs time to melt and besides, with a 3kg (6½lb) joint you need plenty of time to cook it evenly through to the centre. It's a little like reverse searing a large steak (see page 43) where the aim of the game is to ensure even cooking throughout, rather than an overcooked outside and an undercooked inside.

Just as in the brisket, pulled pork and pastrami recipes in the previous chapter, here you are often asked to remove and wrap the meat once it reaches potential stalling temperature (see page 129) to keep things as juicy as possible.

Rib roast, barbecued Yorkshire puddings

A generous roasting joint, the standing rib of beef makes for a spectacular Sunday lunch. Here I serve it with grilled carrots, horseradish dressing and Yorkshire puddings cooked on the barbecue. Yes, it's very possible to barbecue a Yorkshire pudding! What you need, as with any baking, is a high convection heat, so keeping the lid down is essential, as is a good hot but indirect fire. I have to thank my chef mate Henry Eldon here who taught me his 'volume method' for making Yorkshire puddings; I have to say I've never looked back. It's foolproof.

The day before you want to cook, dry-brine the beef. Rub the salt all over and place on a rack set over a tray. Slide into the fridge and leave, uncovered, for 24 hours.

The next day, mix together the mustard and thyme with plenty of black pepper, then spoon this over the beef and rub all over.

Fire up your barbecue ready for indirect grilling, lighting two fires on either side of your barbecue and aiming for a temperature of 170–180°C (340–350°F). Add a lump or two of smoking wood to each fire for a smoky roast beef. Set an old roasting tray between the fires and add the onions, carrots, bay leaves and peppercorns. Pour in the beer and water and set the grill bars in place. Put the beef on the grill bars over the tin and insert a wired meat probe deep into the centre. If you don't have a meat probe, use a regular probe and start testing the temperature after an hour. Shut the lid and leave to cook until the internal temperature deep in the centre is around 5–8 degrees below your preferred eating temperature: 52°C (125°F) for rare, 56°C (132°F) for medium-rare, 60°C (140°F) for medium. This may take around 2 hours. The beef will get a good rest for around 30–35 minutes because you need a clear barbecue to cook the Yorkshire puddings, so be sure to get it off to allow for carryover cooking while it rests (see page 34).

Meanwhile, bring a pan of lightly salted water to the boil and add the carrots. Blanch for 5 minutes then drain well. Tip into a bowl and add the olive oil, garlic and a generous grind of black pepper. Toss to mix then cover and set aside to marinate. Mix up the dressing by stirring together the crème fraîche, horseradish, most of the dill (reserve a little to garnish) and season with a little salt and pepper. Chill until needed.

To make the Yorkshire pudding batter take three identical bowls – dessert bowls are ideal. Crack the eggs into one and take a note of the level they come up to. Spoon flour into the second bowl so it comes up to the same level as the egg, then pour milk into the

Serves 6, with leftover beef

3kg (6½lb) beef rib roast
3 tbsp flaked sea salt
3 tbsp Dijon mustard
a handful of thyme sprigs, leaves picked
2 onions, roughly sliced
2 carrots, roughly chopped
4 bay leaves
2 tsp black peppercorns
500ml (2 cups) beer and 500ml (2 cups) water
2 tbsp cornflour (cornstarch) mixed to a paste with 2 tbsp cold water
freshly ground black pepper

For the carrots

1kg (2lb 4oz) carrots, halved or quartered lengthways
2 tbsp olive oil
2 garlic cloves, crushed
150g (5½oz/¾ cup) crème fraîche
50g (2oz) hot horseradish sauce, or to taste
a handful of dill, roughly chopped
flaked sea salt and freshly ground black pepper

Continued overleaf...

third to exactly the same level. Transfer the eggs, flour and milk to a bowl, add the salt and whisk vigorously to a batter. Cover and set aside for an hour or so.

Once the beef is at temperature, lift to a large plate, cover with foil and a few clean tea towels and take inside to rest. Remove the grill bars and carefully lift out the pan with the beer water and veg. Take inside for gravy making.

Add more fuel to the barbecue, building up the temperature to around 220–240°C (430–465°F). Pour the oil between the holes in the muffin tin and set on the grill bars between the fires. Rest the marinated carrots on the grill bars over the fire, cooking for around 10 minutes until lightly charred all over. Then slide away from the heat, piling them up in a corner of your grill so that they can keep softening but not colouring any more. Shut the lid of the barbecue and leave the muffin tin with oil to finish getting really hot for another 5 minutes.

Give the Yorkshire pudding batter a final quick whisk then pour into a jug. Lift the lid and pour into the hot oil in the tin, working as fast as you can and filling the cups up to the max. Shut the lid and leave for 20 minutes without checking. Be brave! If you open the lid you will lose all the hot air and your Yorkshires won't rise.

While they are cooking, make the gravy on the hob. Place a large pan over a medium heat and set a sieve (strainer) over it. Carefully pour the stock liquid in and use the back of a wooden spoon to squeeze out as much liquid as possible. Allow the stock to come up to the boil then pour in half the cornflour (cornstarch) and water paste, whisking constantly until it's thickened. If you would like it a little thicker, add the rest of the cornflour paste and whisk though. Keep warm over a low heat.

Once the Yorkshires have had 10 minutes, start carving the beef, resting it on a warm serving platter as you go.

After 20 minutes, the Yorkshires should be ready so remove them and the carrots from the barbecue. Spread the carrots out on a serving plate, spoon over some horseradish dressing and scatter over the reserved dill. Serve the gravy in a jug.

For the Yorkshire puddings
3 eggs
plain (all-purpose) flour
 (see method)
milk (see method)
½ tsp flaked sea salt
6 tbsp vegetable oil

You also need a deep 6-hole muffin tin, preferably not nonstick

Pork shoulder roast, parsnips, celeriac and apples

This is a two-stage cook – hot and fast to get the all-important crackling going, then low and slow to cook the meat to total tenderness. I also have success flipping this and other pork joint cooks the other way round, that is, start low, end hot (see the porchetta recipe on page 150). The pork will be safe to eat at 73°C (163°F) internal temperature, but really, the longer you cook it the better. I try to aim for an internal temperature of around 90–93°C (194–199°F), so the meat is almost 'pull-able'. With good, fatty, well reared pork you don't need to worry about it drying out. And don't worry about the long cooking of the veg either. The pan is between the fires and, as heat rises, they shouldn't get too hot or burn. Just keep half an eye on them, and stir them about a little if one side looks to be cooking hotter than the other.

Ideally, the day before you want to cook your pork give it the dry-brining treatment. Sprinkle 2 tablespoons salt all over, rubbing it in well, then place it on a rack set over a tray. Slide into the fridge, uncovered, and leave for 24 hours.

When you are ready to cook, get the vegetables ready. Peel and slice the celeriac (celery root) into 4cm (1½in) chunks and cut the parsnips into halves or quarters, depending on size. Tip into a bowl, toss in a good drizzle of olive oil and add the sage, then season with a little salt and pepper.

Fire up a full chimney of charcoal (see page 17) and once ready, pour it carefully into two strips on either side of your barbecue. If you have charcoal baskets (see page 19), this a good time to use them. Open the vents of your barbecue fully, top and bottom. You are looking for a really hot, but indirect, roasting heat of about 260–280°C (500–535°F) to get that crackling going.

Set a sturdy roasting tin on the base of the barbecue, between the two fires. Tip the celeriac and parsnips into the tin and then set the grill bars in place above.

Place the pork directly onto the grill bars and shut the lid, leaving it entirely alone for 20 minutes. Take a tiny peek at 20 minutes to check it's not burning but try to avoid looking before that otherwise you'll lose the oven-like heat that accumulates with the lid closed. If all is well and it's not burning, shut the lid and keep cooking hot for another 10–20 minutes. If it is catching too much, shut the vents down early to cool the fire (see overleaf).

Serves 4–6, with some meat left over

2kg (4½lb) pork shoulder, fat deeply scored, tied with butcher's string
1 celeriac (celery root), around 800g (1lb 12oz)
500g (1lb 2oz) parsnips, peeled
olive oil, for drizzling
a handful of chopped sage
4 eating apples, quartered
flaked sea salt and freshly ground black pepper

Continued overleaf…

After the initial blast of high heat, it's time to reduce the temperature. Close the air vents right down, almost closed – this will limit the air and reduce the intensity, heat and burn of the fire. As always, learning just how far you can close the air vents without putting out the fire comes with using your own kit often. The better your charcoal (see page 10) generally the bolder you can be with shutting the vents. Ideally, insert a wired meat probe deep into the centre of the pork so you can keep an eye on the cook without opening the lid. Shut the lid, and cook the pork slowly, slowly for a good 5–6 hours, just taking a peek every now and then and taking the internal temperature to 90–93°C (194–199°F). Try and keep the barbecue temperature hovering around 140°C (280°F) if you can, adding a lump or two of fuel to each fire as and when to keep it burning fairly constantly. You may need to adjust your vents up and down to moderate the heat.

A couple of hours before the end of your cook, you want to add the apple wedges to the tin of vegetables. This will mean quickly lifting the pork to a tray to get to the veg underneath. Add the apples and give everything a good stir before setting the grill bars and pork back into place and shutting the lid once more.

Once cooked the pork will benefit from a 15–20-minute rest off the heat to make the meat even more tender, almost 'pull-able' in texture, but you can also tuck in straight away.

Pork belly burnt ends with tequila and maple syrup

Super-sticky, sweet and spicy: rich, fatty pork belly excels here and these little porcine nibbles are quite addictive. This is a three-part cook: first you smoke, then you braise, then you glaze, but it's worth every minute. These are bang on as a bar snack with a few cold beers but they are also good if you shove a handful into soft baps with a dollop of classic coleslaw, watercress and a generous smear of mustard.

If you want to make these booze-free, swap the tequila for apple juice and reduce the maple syrup by a third to a half, otherwise it will be too sweet.

Set a small pan on the hob and spoon in the fennel seeds and peppercorns. Toast for a couple of minutes before tipping into a pestle and mortar and grinding to a coarse powder. Add the sugar, smoked paprika, sea salt, garlic and olive oil and grind again until you have a paste. Spoon onto the pork, then use your hands to really work the rub all over the cubes, making sure they are well covered. Slide into the fridge and leave to marinate for 24 hours if you have time.

When you are ready to cook, line up the belly cubes on a non-coated wire rack or a perforated tray. A vegetable grilling tray (see page 25) is excellent for cooking small things that might slide through the grill.

Fire up the barbecue ready for indirect grilling, aiming for a steady temperature of around 140°C (280°F). Add a couple of chunks of smoking wood.

Slide the rack or tray directly onto the grill bars, on the far side from the fire, shut the lid and leave to smoke for 3 hours. Check once or twice, rotating the rack and turning the cubes to make sure they are cooking evenly. Depending on what you are cooking on, you may need to add a little fuel during the cook to keep the temperature steady.

After 3 hours, remove the tray and shut the lid of the barbecue to keep the heat in. Transfer the cubes to a roasting tin – you want them to fit in a single, snug layer. Pour in the tequila and maple syrup and toss about to coat. Cover tightly with foil and place back on the barbecue, cooking indirectly for another 1½ hours, after which time the cubes should be really tender. Remove the foil and cook for another 30 minutes or so, sliding the tin a little closer to the fire to reduce the liquid to a sticky glaze and stirring every now and then to coat the pork evenly.

Serves about 6 (leftovers are great for stir fries and snacking)

2 tbsp fennel seeds
2 tbsp black peppercorns
3 tbsp dark brown sugar
1–2 tbsp smoked paprika, to taste
1 tbsp flaked sea salt
3 garlic cloves
3 tbsp olive oil
1.5kg (3lb 5oz) rindless boned
    pork belly, cut into cubes
    about 4cm (1½in)
100ml (3½fl oz) tequila
100ml (3½fl oz) maple syrup

Smoked gammon hock, borlotti beans and tomatoes

Gammon hock is the lower leg of the pig, either from the front or back of the animal, and is the same cut as lamb shanks or beef shin. As well as plenty of meaty muscle, it's packed full of connective tissues that cook down to a glorious unctuous texture when given the low and slow treatment. This just the sort of easy fire cooking I love to do when it's chilly – super-low maintenance, the barbecue equivalent of one-pot cooking. You do need to cook the beans at the beginning because you want the juices from the gammon to drip onto them and flavour them up to the max. This does mean they will need reheating before serving but that's a small price to pay.

For this recipe you are cooking indirectly at a temperature of around 140°C (280°F). I cooked this in a kettle barbecue, where I set up two tiny fires, one on each side, adding a lump of smoking wood to each fire for a steady stream of smoke.

Take a roasting tin and tip in the onion, garlic, olive oil, tomatoes, borlotti beans, paprika and parsley. Season well with pepper but no salt because the gammon juices will be salty. Mix, then set the tin in your barbecue, directly underneath the grill bars between the two fires – so you need to choose something that fits – and pour in the stock. Set the grill bars over and rest the gammon, fatter end down, bone side up, over the tin. If you have one, insert a wired meat probe into the thickest part of the meat and shut the lid.

Leave to cook for around 3 hours or so, until the gammon has an internal temperature of around 70–72°C (158–161°F). Keep an eye on the liquid level in the beans, adding a splash of water if needed and every hour or so add another lump of two of charcoal to each fire to keep the temperature steady. Once the gammon has reached this temperature, pull it off, wrap it in butcher's paper (or foil, see page 129) and reinsert the probe in about the same place, piercing it through the paper or foil. Remove the tray of beans and set aside, then add the wrapped gammon back onto the grill, shutting the lid. Leave to cook for another 2–3 hours until the probe reads 93°C (199°F). Remove to a plate, take inside and leave to rest for 30 minutes.

At this point, you can set your tray of beans back on the barbecue to reheat while the meat rests. If you have lost the heat of your fire, feel free to chuck 'em in a pan and do it on the hob inside.

To serve, unwrap the gammon and remove the skin. Pull the meat from the bone, removing any gristly bits that haven't cooked down – it should be tender enough to do this with your hands and a couple of forks. Scatter the parsley over the beans and top with the pulled gammon. Serve with the rocket salad alongside.

Serves 4

1 large red onion, sliced
3 garlic cloves, sliced
2 tbsp olive oil
450g (1lb) vine tomatoes, quartered
2 x 400g (14oz) cans borlotti beans, drained
1 tsp smoked paprika
a handful of parsley, chopped
500ml (2 cups) vegetable stock
1kg (2lb 4oz) unsmoked gammon hock, skin scored through in a diamond pattern every 1cm (½in)
freshly ground black pepper

To serve

a good handful of parsley, chopped
a couple of handfuls of rocket (arugula), dressed in oil and vinegar

ROLL WITH IT...

The three rolled and stuffed joint recipes that follow were designed for cooking on a rotisserie spit – a long metal spike that threads through the centre of the meat with two clamps that hold it securely in place. The spike is then slotted into a motor where is rotates slowly over the fire. I don't generally go much for 'gadgets' in my cooking, preferring to keep things simple, but I do love rotisserie cooking. The slowly turning meat cooks evenly and bastes itself beautifully in its own juices as it spins, and the end result is super-tender.

You can absolutely cook these recipes without a rotisserie but you will need to be a little more hands on, turning and rotating the meat yourself to ensure even cooking. You may lose a little of the fillings as you turn and the meat will certainly drip more juices into the base of the barbecue so set a tray underneath to catch them.

Either way, I set the fire up the same way by laying two small strips of fire, one either side of the barbecue; the meat then rests in between, on a spike or directly on the grill bars.

Porchetta with fennel, lemon and herbs

A spectacular feasting joint to share, using lean tenderloin, wrapped in rich and fatty belly pork with a seam of fennel and herbs rolled through. In an ideal world both cuts would be the same length so they wrap together neatly – if the tenderloin is too long, trim it and tuck in the scraps. If it's too short, it should be possible to pull it and stretch it a little to make it fit.

This is best begun 24–48 hours before you want to cook, to brine and marinate the meat and dry out the skin for the best crackling. Talking of crackling, you have two options: start with a low heat and finish with a high heat (see overleaf). Or do as I do for the crackling roast pork recipe on page 143 and start high and finish low. Both work well, although a word of warning – some pork skin just seems to crackle better than others. You win some, you lose some. As is the motto with this whole book, start with the best quality meat you can afford.

Using charcoal baskets (see page 19) is a good thing as you can easily manoeuvre the lit coals with tongs – especially useful at the end of this cook when you may want to create a little more direct heat to crisp up the crackling.

Tip the fennel seeds and chilli flakes, if using, into a small frying pan (skillet) and set over a medium heat on the hob to toast for a couple of minutes. Pour into a mortar and roughly grind with a pestle. Add the salt, garlic, lemon zest and juice, herbs, olive oil and a really generous grind of black pepper. Pound together to make a paste.

Serves 6–8

3 tbsp fennel seeds
1–2 tsp chilli flakes (optional, to taste)
1 tbsp flaked sea salt

Continued overleaf...

Lay out the pork belly, scored skin side down, and lay the trimmed tenderloin down the centre, making it fit as best you can. Scoop the herb and spice mixture on top and rub all over both cuts of pork. Roll the belly up and around the tenderloin, completely enclosing it. Use string to tie it up tight at 2cm (¾in) intervals all down the length. Rest on a rack set over a tray and slide into the fridge, uncovered, for 24 hours. This will give the rind time to dry out to ensure the best crackling and also for the meat to dry-brine.

When you are ready to cook, fire up your barbecue ready for indirect and direct grilling.

If you are using a rotisserie, insert the spike through the centre of the pork, add the clamps and tighten. Slide into the motor and set the pork turning. If you are going direct on the grill bars, place it between the two fires. Shut the lid and cook fairly slowly with an indirect heat until an internal temperature of around 80°C (175°F) is reached. This should take around 3½ hours or so, depending on the heat from the fire. You will no doubt need to top up the fuel a little from time to time – aiming for an air temperature of around 150–160°C (300–320°F).

Once you've hit your target internal temperature, you need to get the fire hotter to get that skin crackling. Open up the air vents to increase the rate of combustion and add a little fuel if necessary – if your fire has died down too much, light a little more charcoal in a chimney starter (see page 17). The best crackling comes from a high (250–300°C/480–570°F) but fairly indirect heat. Think of your oven indoors, this is what you are aiming for. The crackling may take another 30 minutes or so, by which time your meat should have reached 90–93°C (194–199°F) – this is the ideal temperature for succulent pork that's on the verge of being 'pull-able'. With good-quality fatty pork you don't need to worry about it drying out as you are cooking it slowly.

Carve into thick slices – traditionally this would be stuffed unadorned into squishy buns, but it makes a pretty epic roast with all the trimmings if that's what you fancy.

4 garlic cloves, roughly chopped
zest of 2 lemons and juice of 1
4 tbsp chopped mixed fresh
    herbs – oregano, rosemary,
    thyme, sage are all good
2 tbsp olive oil
freshly ground black pepper
1.8–2kg (4–4½lb) boned pork
    belly (rind scored)
500g (1lb 2oz) pork tenderloin,
    trimmed of silver skin
    (see page 55)

Venison porchetta with sausage, prune and sage

With a boned venison saddle you get both loins attached together – with the chine (backbone) removed. The is the equivalent cut to fillet steak in a cow, or a tenderloin in a pig, so it's super-lean and tender. Due to the paucity of fat it's best cooked with added juiciness, in this case from smoky bacon, sausage meat and fruit, to keep things succulent. This was designed to be cooked on a rotisserie where it will spin rather spectacularly, but you can also cook it direct on the grill bars. It is best to begin this the day before cooking so it has time to both firm up and dry-brine in the fridge.

Sprinkle 1 tablespoon flaked sea salt over both sides of the venison and set aside while you make the filling.

Set a small frying pan (skillet) over a medium-low heat on the hob and pour in the olive oil. Add the onion and sage and cook gently for around 20 minutes, stirring frequently until softening and turning translucent. Add the garlic, stirring over the heat for a minute or two, then transfer to a bowl and set aside to cool.

Once the onion is cold, add the sausage meat and prunes and a good seasoning of salt and pepper. Use your hands to mix well together until well combined.

Make a woven bacon blanket to enclose the venison by vertically lining up 8 of the bacon slices next to each other on a flat baking sheet or chopping board. Working left to right, fold every other slice in half upwards. Lay a slice horizontally across the centre of the vertical slices. Unfold the vertical slices back over the horizontal one, then fold up the other set of vertical slices. Lay over another horizontal slice and unfold the folded ones. Repeat to form a neat interwoven blanket.

Lay the venison out flat on top of the bacon blanket, cut side up, and dot the sausage meat stuffing down the centre, pressing it into a cylinder. Bring up the sides of the venison, along with the bacon, up and over to cover the stuffing, and roll together to form a neat cylinder. This is definitely at the fiddlier end of the cooking spectrum, but your patience will be rewarded.

Use lengths of butcher's string to tie the rolled stuffed saddle at 2cm (¾in) intervals. Wrap the rolled and stuffed joint really snugly in clingfilm (plastic wrap) or butcher's paper and refrigerate overnight. This will help firm it up as well as give the salt a chance to dry-brine and tenderize the meat.

Serves 4–6

1 boned saddle of venison (about 750g–1kg/1lb 10oz–2lb 4oz)
2 tbsp olive oil
1 small onion, thinly sliced
a good handful of sage, chopped
2 garlic cloves, crushed
300g (10½oz) peppery sausages (e.g. Cumberland), skin removed
75g (3oz) prunes, diced
16 slices of smoked streaky bacon, nice and fatty
flaked sea salt and freshly ground black pepper

Continued overleaf...

Fire up your barbecue ready for indirect grilling with two strips of fire, one to each side, aiming for a temperature of around 170–180°C (340–350°F).

If you are cooking on a rotisserie, thread the spike right through the centre of the rolled joint and attach the forks at either end, lining it up so the joint is in the centre of the spike. Tighten up the nuts on the forks so the meat is really secure. Attach the spike into position and set the motor turning. If you are cooking directly on the grill bars, rest the joint in the middle of the barbecue, between the two fires, and rotate every 30 minutes so it cooks evenly.

Cook for about 1½ hours – maybe a little more, maybe a little less – until a probe inserted right into the centre where the sausage meat sits reaches 73–74°C (163–165°F).

Carve into thick slices to serve.

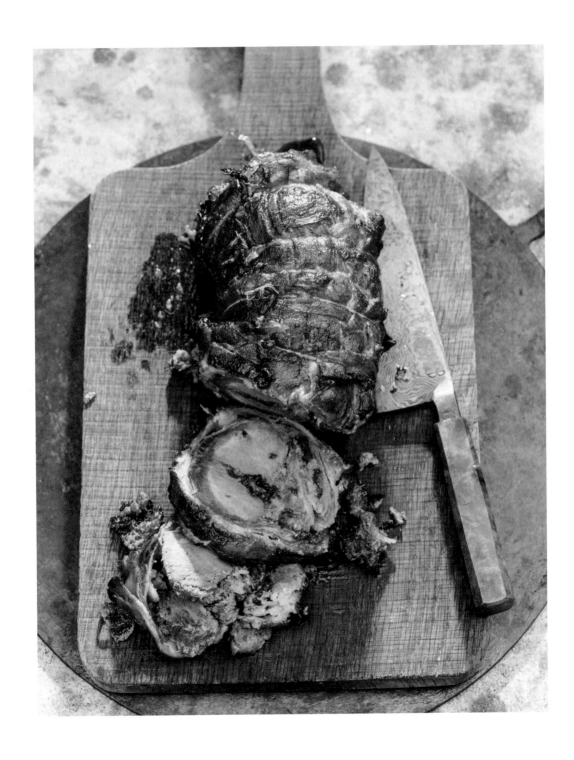

Tea-brined rolled lamb breast

In this Sri Lankan-inspired roast lamb, the tannins found in tea are used as a great meat tenderizer. Black teas (like the Earl Grey in this recipe) contain the most tannins of all. As with all brines, it's important that the liquid is completely cold before adding the raw meat.

Put the tea bags in a jug and pour over 500ml (2 cups) boiling water. Add the salt and stir until dissolved. Set aside until completely cold, then fish out the tea bags, giving them a little squeeze to extract all the flavour.

Untie the lamb if it's tied up and place in a deep bowl. Pour over the cold tea brine and top up with a litre (4 cups) of cold water. It should completely cover the lamb; if not add a splash more. Cover and slide into the fridge to brine for 24–48 hours.

Drain the lamb from the brine and discard the brine. Pat the surface dry with paper towels.

Tip the cumin, cardamom and cinnamon into a small frying pan (skillet). Set over a medium heat to toast for a couple of minutes, then grind in a spice mill or pestle and mortar. Transfer to a bowl and stir through the lime zest and juice, garlic, ginger and brown sugar to make a paste. Scoop onto the lamb and rub in all over. Turn so the meat is fat side down.

Tip the coconut into the frying pan and toast for a couple of minutes until golden all over. Sprinkle over the lamb then roll up like a Swiss roll. Use butcher's string to tie up snugly at intervals of 2cm (¾in) or so. At this stage you can slide into the fridge and leave the meat to marinate for 24 hours or so.

When you are ready to cook, fire up your barbecue ready for fairly gentle indirect grilling with two little fires to either side, aiming for an air temperature of around 150–160°C (300–320°F) inside the barbecue.

To cook on a rotisserie, insert the spike through the centre of the lamb roll, add the clamps and tighten up securely. If you are not cooking on a rotisserie, you can rest it directly on the grill bars, between the fires, but you will just need to rotate it more often so it cooks evenly. Shut the lid of the barbecue and cook until an internal temperature of 90–95°C (194–203°F) is reached. This may take around 3 hours, give or take.

Carve into slices to serve.

Serves 2–4, depending on what else you have to eat alongside

4 Earl Grey tea bags
100g (3½oz) flaked sea salt
850g (1lb 14oz) rolled lamb breast
1 tbsp cumin seeds
1 tsp cardamon pods
1 cinnamom stick, crumbled
zest and juice of 1 lime
2 garlic cloves, crushed
50g (2oz) fresh root ginger, grated
2 tbsp dark brown sugar
50g (2oz) desiccated (dried) coconut

THE GOAT STORY

Just as with veal calves (see page 68), the goats we eat are something of a by-product of the goat dairy industry. For all the goat dairy herds out there, producing the cheese, butter and milk we love, every male calf born risks being destroyed at birth as they are of no use within the dairy industry. So the more popular goat meat becomes, the less waste there is. If we enjoy eating goat's cheese, we should consider eating goat meat as an ethical and sustainable meat.

Goat shoulder with harissa, herby apricot couscous

Like the shoulders of all beasts, goat shoulders are always on the move. Therefore, in meat terms, what you have is a hard-working collection of muscles, with plenty of connective tissue attaching muscles together around the bones of the shoulder and the legs. Low, slow and indirect cooking is the only way to melting tenderness.

The day before you want to cook, rest the goat shoulder on a board and use a large sharp knife to pierce lots of deep cuts all over the meat. Spoon on the harissa and rub in really well, pushing it deep into the cuts you have made. This will help the flavours get further into the meat. Rest in a dish or roasting tray and slide into the fridge to marinate overnight.

The next day, fire up your barbecue ready for indirect cooking, adding a couple of lumps of smoking wood if you'd like smoky goat. I light two small fires to either side of the barbecue for this cook; you want to try and maintain a temperature of around 130–140°C (260–280°F). Set a drip pan on the base of the barbecue between the two fires, underneath where the goat will sit, and pour in a good 700ml (2¾ cups) water. Set the grill bars in place.

Rest the goat onto the grill bars over the tin. If you have one, insert a wired temperature probe (see page 24) into the deepest part of the shoulder, avoiding the bone as it will give a false reading. Shut the lid and cook slowly until the probe reads around 70–75°C (160–165°F). This will take 3–4 hours, so be prepared to top up with a little fuel every now and then to keep the temperature stable (see page 17).

Once the meat is at temperature, remove it to a tray, and carefully remove the drip tray of water (which will now be beautifully flavoured with meat juices), shutting the lid of the barbecue to preserve the heat inside. Wrap the meat snugly in butcher's paper or foil (see page 129) and reinsert the probe into roughly the same spot. Set back on the grill bars, again away from the fire.

Serves 6

1.7–2kg (3lb 12oz–4½lb) goat
    shoulder (I used kid goat)
4 generous tbsp harissa paste
    (I used Belazu apricot harissa)
400g (14oz) can chickpeas
    (garbanzo beans), drained and
    rinsed
3 banana shallots, sliced
2 garlic cloves, crushed
1 tbsp cumin seeds, lightly
    crushed
1 tsp chilli flakes
250g (9oz) couscous
100g (3½oz) dried apricots,
    chopped
a good handful of chopped herbs
    – parsley, coriander (cilantro),
    chives
flaked sea salt and freshly ground
    black pepper

Continued overleaf...

Then add the chickpeas (garbanzo beans), shallots, garlic, cumin and chilli flakes to the drip tray of meat juices and set on the grill bars over the direct heat. Shut the lid. Once the meat is wrapped you can open the vents a little and allow the temperature to creep up to 150°C (300°F) or so to cook it a little more quickly. You may need to add more fuel to keep the barbecue running hot enough. Leave the goat to cook until it reaches an internal temperature of around 90–95°C (194–203°F) – which may take another 3 hours or so. Keep an eye on the tray of chickpeas and shallots – you want to soften them in the meat juices – then remove it after around an hour and set aside.

Once the meat has reached temperature, remove it to a plate and set aside to rest for 30 minutes, leaving it wrapped up. This will help the meat soften and relax to a 'pull-able' texture.

Set the tray of stock and chickpeas back over the fire to heat up. Once the stock is boiling, pour the couscous in, and top up with boiling water so it comes just a couple of millimetres (¾ in) above the level of the couscous. Add apricots and herbs, stir to mix, cover with foil and leave to steam off the heat while the goat rests. If your fire has lost all its heat by now, you can set the tin on the hob inside to cook the couscous but if there's still heat available outside, I figure you may as well use it.

Unwrap the meat and shred it up with forks or a knife and fork and serve piled on top of the couscous.

Venison shoulder, creamy mustard potatoes

Venison is such a lean meat; even the hard-working shoulders don't have a lot of fat to them (unlike, say, a pork shoulder or a beef chuck) so it needs a bit of help to keep it juicy. After a good lick of smoke to flavour the meat, it gets steamed on top of a bed of potatoes and cream until it is meltingly tender. You could substitute lamb or goat shoulder but the result will be a little richer as both these meats are a touch fattier than venison.

Ideally, the day before you want to eat, dry-brine the venison by rubbing 1 tablespoon flaked sea salt all over. Place on a wire rack set over a tray and slide it into the fridge, uncovered, for up to 24 hours if you have time.

When you are ready to cook, fire up the barbecue ready for indirect cooking, aiming to stabilize the temperature at around 130–140°C (260–280°F). Add a couple of lumps of smoking wood to the fire. Set a tray of water on the barbecue base, next to the fire – this will create a steamy environment to keep the meat moist.

Pierce quite a few deep slits into the meat on both slides and poke in little bits of garlic and rosemary, using about half of what you have (save the rest for the potatoes). Drizzle over the olive oil, rubbing it all over.

Rest the meat on the grill bars, on the opposite side to the fire, above the tray of water. Shut the lid and smoke gently for 2 hours.

Meanwhile, peel and slice the potatoes and tip them into a roasting tin so they are about four layers deep. Measure the cream and stock into a jug and stir through the mustard, reserved garlic and rosemary, and season with salt and pepper. Pour over the potatoes, pushing them under the liquid as much as possible.

Remove the venison from the grill and rest it on top of the potatoes. Stick the piece of butter onto a fork and rub it all over the meat, allowing it to melt down over and onto the potatoes. Take a sheet of baking paper and run it under the tap, scrunching it up and shaking off the excess water. Open up the sheet and rest it over the meat and potatoes, tucking it in at the edges. Then cover the tin really snugly in a double layer of foil and take back to the barbecue.

Serves 4

800g–1kg (1lb 12oz–2lb 4oz)
    bone-in venison shoulder
3 garlic cloves, thinly sliced
a few sprigs of rosemary, needles
    picked
1 tbsp olive oil
1.2kg (2lb 10oz) potatoes
300ml (1¼ cups) double (heavy)
    cream
350ml (1½ cups) chicken stock
2 tbsp wholegrain mustard
50g (2oz) butter
flaked sea salt and freshly ground
    black pepper

To garnish
2 tbsp olive oil
30g (1oz) fresh breadcrumbs
a little flat-leaf parsley, chopped

Continued overleaf...

You are going to be cooking for another 3½ hours, so top up with a little fuel to keep the temperature steady at 130–140°C (260–280°F).

Rest the tin on the grill bars, again indirectly from the fire, and cook for another 1½ hours. Peel back the foil and paper, turn the venison over onto the other side, and re-cover tightly. Cook for another 1½ hours. Then remove the paper and foil and cook for a final 30 minutes, uncovered, until the potatoes and meat are both meltingly tender and the cream sauce mostly absorbed. Use two forks to pull apart the meat, removing the bone, piling it up in the centre of the potatoes.

Just before serving, set a small frying pan (skillet) over a high heat (you can use your hob inside) and add the olive oil, breadcrumbs and parsley, seasoning with salt and pepper. Fry for a few minutes until crisp then sprinkle over everything just before tucking in.

Chapter 7: Ribs of all Beasts

Ribs cooked on the barbecue are always an absolute winner. Given that they are a hard-working part of the body the meat is pretty tough and full of connective tissues, so low and slow cooking is the only way get to tenderness.

With so many different names for ribs, I admit the picture can be somewhat confusing. The main thing to say is ribs are ribs. Each animal has two sets of ribs, one either side of the body, coming off the backbone of the animal in question; it's the way the ribs are butchered that denotes the name. So with pork, the baby back ribs are cut from the top of the ribs closest to the chine bone (the butcher's term for the backbone); they are also called pork loin ribs, as the tenderloin runs alongside them. They are smaller and more curved than spare ribs which are cut from the bottom section. Spare ribs are sometimes called breast ribs, or even belly ribs. And if they are trimmed up nice and neat as a rectangular slab they become St Louis cut ribs. All clear? With beef short ribs you are essentially getting beefy spare ribs cut from the short plate, which is the belly side of the prime rib roasting joint. Short ribs either come as a rack of 4–5 bones, sometimes called a Jacob's ladder, or as individual bones with a nice thick chunk of meat on top, sometimes referred to as English-cut ribs. They can also be cut flanken-style, which is crossways through the bone, so you get a bit of steak-looking meat with a line of little bits of bone along it. Lamb also has ribs that make for good eating, less easy to find but worth it if you can, super-succulent and rich (fat is flavour, remember). Look for bone-in lamb breast when you are shopping.

The bone side of a rack of ribs, whichever beast they hail from, has a membrane attached to it, a tough layer of connective tissue that is pretty inedible no matter how you cook it. Many butchers remove it during the cutting process – but do check it's not there, you can't miss it. If it is, just nick under one end with a sharp knife, to give you a little flap to hold on to and tug away. Gripping it with a little paper towel or a pinch of rough salt will give you a little more purchase to pull.

Ribs are one of the rare occasions where a temperature probe is not that essential for monitoring the cooking progress. The bone is often too close to the meat for an accurate reading. If you make sure you stick it in a good fat bit of meat, not too close to the bone, it will be a good rough guide – anything around 90–95°C (194–203°F) is an ideal finished temperature. Even better is the 'toothpick' test – the tip of your probe is ideal – when inserted into the meat it will give instantly and feel soft and tender. If you are cooking a whole rack of ribs, the 'bend test' is another good one to go for. Pick up the whole rack in the middle with tongs – if it flops pleasingly down either side, your ribs are probably good to go.

Sri Lankan black pork spare ribs, curry BBQ sauce

This recipe uses spare ribs, sometimes known as belly or breast ribs, cut into individual rib bones with plenty of meat covering them. You are essentially dry-brining and rubbing the meat at the same time, remembering that the salt will penetrate deep, tenderizing the meat, while the spices won't go beyond a few millimetres into the surface (see page 21).

I usually make the curry BBQ sauce at the same time as rubbing the ribs. It makes more than you need for this recipe (about 3 standard jars) but it will keep in clean jars in the fridge for at least 3 months, and is delicious on all sorts of things.

Set a small frying pan (skillet) over a medium heat on the hob and add the rice, leaving it to toast for a couple minutes. Then add the coriander and cumin seeds, black peppercorns, mustard and fennel seeds, cloves and cardamom seeds. Toast for another few minutes until everything is deeply fragrant and a few shades darker. Tip into a spice mill, add the sugar and salt, and grind to a powder, or use a pestle and mortar and a bit of elbow grease. This is your black curry spice powder.

Use half the spice powder to sprinkle over the ribs, rubbing in really well all over. Place on a rack set over a tray and slide into the fridge, uncovered, for 24 hours.

To make the curry BBQ sauce, pour the oil into a heavy-based saucepan and set over a low heat. Add the onion, garlic and ginger along with the other half of the curry powder, the cinnamon stick and the chilli powder. Allow to sweat gently for a good 15–20 minutes until the onion has softened. Add the coconut cream, ketchup, vinegar, brown sugar and curry leaves. Simmer very gently for 30 minutes. Fish out the pieces of cinnamon stick and purée until smooth. Using a smoothie-type blender will give you the smoothest results, although a stick blender in the pan is fine too.

When you are ready to cook, fire up your barbecue ready for indirect cooking, closing the air vents and aiming for a low temperature of about 130–140°C (260–280°F). For this recipe I prefer to let the taste of the pork and the spices shine strong, but feel free to add a little smoking wood if you like.

Serves 4–6

2 tbsp raw basmati rice
4 tbsp coriander seeds
3 tbsp cumin seeds
2 tbsp black peppercorns
2 tbsp black mustard seeds
2 tsp fennel seeds
½ tsp cloves
seeds from 4 cardamom pods
2 tbsp dark brown sugar
2 tbsp flaked sea salt
2kg (4½lb) meaty spare ribs, cut into individual ribs

For the curry BBQ sauce

3 tbsp vegetable oil
2 onions, chopped
4 garlic cloves, chopped
50g (2oz) fresh root ginger, grated
the other half of the black curry spice powder
1 cinnamon stick, snapped into 2–3
1–2 tsp chilli powder, to taste
250ml (1 cup) coconut cream
200ml (generous ¾ cup) tomato ketchup
3 tbsp malt vinegar
100g (3½oz) dark brown sugar
4 sprigs of fresh curry leaves

Continued overleaf...

Rest the ribs directly on the grills bars as far from the fire as you can. Shut the lid and leave to cook very slowly for 5–6 hours. You may need to top up your fuel once or twice during the cook – or maybe even more – depending on what you are cooking on, the fuel you are using and your mastery of controlling the air vents. Every hour or so, turn the ribs over and shuffle them around a little in relation to where the fire is so they cook evenly.

Once the ribs are tender, you have two choices. You can either remove to a dish and serve straight away, with the BBQ sauce to dunk in as you eat. Or you can do what I usually do – and that is take a little dish of the sauce to the grill and baste it all over the ribs. Slide the ribs over a slightly higher heat and cook for a few extra minutes, basting and turning to glaze them. Serve with more sauce alongside for double sauciness.

I like to eat these ribs with an easy take on Kottu Roti, another great Sri Lankan dish. Think of it as a Sri Lankan stir-fry where you use ribboned roti bread (or in my case flour tortillas) as the noodle or rice element. Per person, take a generous handful of sliced mixed veg (carrots, leeks, cabbage, peas, peppers, anything you fancy) and fry them up in a wok with a little sesame oil, crushed garlic and grated ginger. Roll a flour tortilla up tight and slice into 5mm (¼in) discs to leave you with lots of thin ribbons when you unfurl them. Add the ribbons to the wok with a generous spoon of the curry BBQ sauce and a shake of soy sauce. Stir-fry until piping hot and serve with the ribs and more BBQ sauce.

Beef short ribs, pho-style

Not a genuine pho by any means, which takes hours of boiling bones and gelatinous beef tendons to make a rich broth and uses fast-cooked steak to finish the dish at the end... but this is a spectacular cheat of a dish. Low, slow, hands-off barbecue at its best. Beef short ribs are a quite amazing cut, equivalent to pork spare ribs but with much more meat on the bone as cows are obviously more sizeable beasts. They're full of deep, meaty flavour, but they can stay stubbornly tough if you cook them liquid free. This slow smoke+braise method is a foolproof way to tenderness.

Take a roasting tin and pour in the soy sauce, adding 250ml (1 cup) cold water. Add the brown sugar, ginger, garlic, lemongrass, star anise, cinnamon, black cardamom, peppercorns, coriander and cloves. Stir well and add the ribs, turning them over a few times to make sure they are well coated, then turn them meaty side down. Slide into the fridge to marinate overnight.

Fire up your barbecue ready for indirect grilling, aiming to stabilize the temperature at around 130–140°C (260–280°F), and add a couple of lumps of smoking wood.

Turn the ribs so they are now meaty side up, bone side down. Rest the tin on the grill bars away from the fire and shut the lid. Leave to smoke for 3 hours. Every 30–45 minutes or so, use a brush to baste a little of the cooking liquid over the ribs. Take a jug of water to the barbecue and every time you baste, add just a little. You want to keep the level of liquid the same, around 1cm (½in) deep so that the bone is submerged but the meat is not.

After 3 hours turn the ribs over so they are meaty side down, so nestled partly in the liquid – the meat will have absorbed all the smoke it's going to absorb by this time. Add a splash more water if necessary, then cover the tin tightly with foil and cook for another 3 hours or so until the meat is pull-apart tender. Depending on the type of barbecue you are using, you may need to add a little more fuel from time to time during the long, slow cook. Once you cover the ribs you can allow the temperature of the barbecue to rise a little by opening up the vents, but don't go much higher than 150°C (300°F) as the sugar in the braising liquid can make it susceptible to burning.

Once the ribs are practically done, cook your noodles until they are just getting tender but with plenty of 'chew' left in them. Drain well and run under cold water to stop them cooking.

Serves 4, generously

- 150ml (generous ½ cup) soy sauce
- 2 tbsp soft brown sugar
- 35g (1½oz) fresh root ginger, cut in matchsticks
- 4 garlic cloves, sliced
- 2 lemongrass stalks, sliced in half lengthways and cut into 5cm (2in) lengths
- 3 star anise
- 2 cinnamon sticks, snapped in half
- 2 black cardamom pods, bashed open
- 1 heaped tsp black peppercorns, roughly ground
- 1 tsp coriander seeds
- ½ tsp cloves
- 1.2kg (2lb 10oz) short ribs
- 300g (10½oz) flat wide rice noodles
- sesame oil, for drizzling
- 200g (7oz) pak choi
- ½ bunch of spring onions (scallions), sliced
- 1–3 bird's eye chillies, sliced (to taste)
- a good handful of chopped herbs – coriander (cilantro), mint, Thai basil

Tip into a bowl and drizzle in a little sesame oil, tossing them about to lightly coat and stop them clumping together.

At the same time, slice the pak choi, keeping the stalks separate to the leaves. Add the stalks to the braising liquid and re-cover, allowing them to soften for 10 minutes. Then add the leaves and cook for another 3–4 minutes, or just enough time to wilt them.

Lift the ribs from the tin and add the cooked noodles, tossing them through the liquid. Rest the ribs back on top and sprinkle over the spring onions (scallions), chillies and herbs. At this point you can shred the meat from the bones with two forks, or you can take it to the table and allow people to help themselves.

Pictured overleaf (bottom).

Cola and gochugaru flanken-cut beef ribs

Beef short ribs cut across the bone, so you have a slice of meat dotted with a row of bone discs, are called 'flanken-cut'. They are really popular in Korea where they cook them hot and fast. In my experience, though, I find they are better treated as you would any rib from any animal – that is to go for the low and slow approach to maximize tenderness. Here I use a failsafe rib cooking technique dubbed 3-2-1. Quite simply you smoke for 3 hours, cook wrapped up for 2 hours, then unwrap and baste for a further 1 hour. Works every time, for all kinds of ribs. In a nod to Korea the ribs are marinated with gochugaru, or sweet red pepper flakes, along with a couple of cans of full-fat cola, which is a marvellously sweet and sticky tenderizer, thanks to the acid content.

Lay the ribs in a single snug layer in a deep roasting tin. Pour over the cola gently then sprinkle over the garlic, gochugaru, ground pepper, salt and cinnamon. Turn the ribs over a few times to mix together then press them back down in a single layer, submerging them in the liquid as much as you can. Slide the tin into the fridge to marinate for 12–24 hours, turning the ribs a couple of times during that time.

When you are ready to cook, fire up the barbecue for indirect grilling, aiming for a temperature of around 140°C (280°F). Throw 2–3 lumps of smoking wood onto the fire and set a drip pan of water on the base of the barbecue underneath where the meat will sit. You are going in for a long slow cook, at least 6 hours, so be prepared to top up the fuel a little every now and then. With good, pure fuel you can do this by adding a lump or two of charcoal directly to the fire every now and then (see page 17).

Set the grill bars in place, rest the ribs on the opposite side to the fire and shut the lid. Reserve the marinade for basting, pouring it into a fireproof pan (no plastic or wooden handles) ready to take to the grill. Leave to smoke indirectly for 3 hours.

Remove the ribs and wrap up snugly in a large sheet of butcher's parchment or foil. Set back on the grill bars, again away from the fire, and shut the lid. Leave to cook for a further 2 hours.

Unwrap the ribs and rest back onto the grill bars, still away from the fire, and set the pan of reserved marinade over the fire to heat through. Use a silicone brush to baste the ribs all over, then shut the lid of the barbecue. Cook for a final hour, basting all over every 10 minutes or so and turning and rotating them around so they cook evenly. After an hour, insert a toothpick or the tip of your meat probe into the meat – it should feel yielding and soft. If it still shows resistance cook for a little longer.

Serves 6

2kg (4½lb) beef ribs, flanken-cut
2 x 330ml (12fl oz) cans full-fat cola
3 garlic cloves, chopped
2 tbsp gochugaru (Korean red pepper flakes)
1 tbsp black peppercorns, freshly ground
1 tbsp flaked sea salt
1 tsp ground cinnamon

Pictured opposite (top).

Baby back ribs with Vietnamese-spiced baste

These grilled baby back ribs are loosely based on the Vietnamese dish, bún thịt nướng, which are normally served with chilled noodles, but I personally prefer them hot. Also, feel free to replace the lager with apple juice, for a booze-free version – a little liquid will help them soften beautifully.

Sprinkle the salt all over the ribs and rest on a rack set over a tray. Slide into the fridge and leave to dry-brine for 24 hours.

Fire up your barbecue for indirect cooking, adding 2–3 lumps of smoking wood and aiming for around 140°C (280°F).

Rest the ribs on the grill, away from the fire, so they cook indirectly. Cook for 3 hours, checking and rotating every hour, adding a lump or two more charcoal if necessary to keep the temperature steady.

Remove the ribs to a tray and shut the lid of the barbecue so the heat doesn't escape. Take four sheets of foil, lining them up as two layers of two. Rest each rack on a double layer and bring up the sides to form walls. Pour the beer over the ribs, dividing it between the two parcels, and seal up the walls tight, keeping them seam side up so the liquid doesn't escape. Place the foil-wrapped ribs back on the barbecue, again indirectly. Cook for another 2 hours. Add a little more charcoal if needed to maintain 140°C (280°F).

Once the ribs are wrapped, pickle the carrots. Tip the grated carrot into a bowl with the salt and sugar. Briefly massage with your fingers then stir in the lime juice. Set aside.

Make the baste by adding all the ingredients to a deep jug. Blitz to a smooth paste using a stick blender. You can also make it in a small food processor or in a pestle and mortar for a slightly chunkier result.

After 2 hours remove the ribs and unwrap and discard the foil. Rest the ribs back onto the grill bars away from the heat. Cook for a final hour, basting every 10 minutes or so. Check for doneness using the 'bend test' (see page 164).

Once the ribs are done, cook the noodles and drain well. Toss in the sesame oil and toasted sesame seeds. Tip into a serving dish and serve with the mint, chilli and carrot pickle in separate bowls for people to help themselves.

Serves 4

2 racks of baby back ribs (around 1.5kg/3lb 5oz in total)
1 tbsp flaked sea salt
250ml (1 cup) lager (or use apple juice)

For the pickled carrots
2 large carrots, grated
1 tsp flaked sea salt
1 tsp caster (superfine) sugar
juice of 1 lime

For the baste
2 shallots (or 1 banana shallot), roughly chopped
3 garlic cloves, roughly chopped
25g (1oz) piece of fresh root ginger, roughly chopped
2 lemongrass stalks, roughly chopped
1–2 bird's eye chillies, roughly chopped (or sprinkle on over at the end if you prefer)
2 tbsp dark brown sugar
3 tbsp soy sauce
2 tbsp fish sauce
100ml (3½fl oz) boiling water
freshly ground black pepper

To serve
300g (10½oz) rice noodles
2 tbsp sesame oil
2 tbsp sesame seeds, toasted
a handful of mint leaves
a few chopped red chillies (bird's eye for heat, milder for colour)

Char siu pork belly

This insanely good roast pork belly recipe breaks all the rules of marinating (see page 21) as it contains quite a lot of sugar, which could burn very easily on a barbecue. The trick is to cook it indirectly, at a fairly low to moderate heat. You will still get a lot of lovely browning and sticky caramelization, which may surprise you – but remember that the marvellous Maillard reactions happen at low temperatures as well as high ones (see page 6). Traditionally maltose is the sugar of choice, which is easily found in oriental supermarkets or online, although a neutral-tasting honey is a good substitute. Beware, maltose is exceedingly thick and sticky. Use a spoon warmed in boiling water to scoop it out and into a small bowl, then give it a few seconds in a microwave to melt before using in the marinade. Pork belly, sliced into ribs, is essentially the same as spare ribs but just extra meaty and with less butchering involved, so you could substitute spare ribs if you like.

Take your pork belly and use a very sharp knife to remove the rind, cutting between the skin and fat below with gentle sweeping strokes. Cut the belly into slices, following the bones, so you get really thick, meaty ribs. At the ends the pieces may be rather more triangular than long and rib-shaped, which is just fine. Set in a shallow dish in a single snug layer.

Make the marinade by stirring together the soy, rice wine, hoisin, warmed maltose (or honey), treacle, sesame oil and tomato ketchup. Add the garlic, ginger, five-spice and white pepper and stir well to combine. Pour over the pork and toss it about to mix thoroughly. Cover the dish and set in the fridge for 24 hours if you have time, 48 hours wouldn't hurt.

When you are ready to cook, fire up your grill ready for indirect grilling, with a fire piled to one side of your barbecue. You are aiming to have a temperature of around 130–140°C (260–280°F) inside the barbecue, so shut your air vents right down to keep the temperature steady.

Rest the pork onto the grill bars, arranging it so the pieces are as far from the fire as possible. Reserve the extra marinade left in the dish. Shut the lid and cook for around 4–5 hours, maybe a little more, turning and rotating the pieces every 45 minutes or so and brushing with a little of the extra marinade as you go. You are aiming for a soft and yielding texture, so test by easing the meat from the bone. If it's resistant, cook for longer. As long as the meat is far from the fire, the cooking here is really rather hands off.

Serve hot and sticky, straight from the grill.

Serves 4–6

2kg (4½lb) bone-in pork belly
4 tbsp soy sauce
3 tbsp rice wine
3 tbsp hoisin sauce
3 tbsp maltose, warmed, or runny honey
1 tbsp black treacle (or molasses)
1 tbsp sesame oil
1 tbsp tomato ketchup
3 garlic cloves, crushed
25g (1oz) fresh root ginger, grated
1½ tsp Chinese five-spice
1 tsp white pepper, ideally freshly ground

Smoked lamb ribs, spiced honey baste

Yet another 3-2-1 ratio smoke-wrap-baste rib cook, this time using harder-to-find lamb ribs. The cooking times will be a little reduced because they are slimmer beasts than pigs. You might be looking at a one and a half hours' smoke, an hour wrap and a 30 minute baste but as usual in BBQ, it's done when it's done.

Dry-brine the lamb 24 hours before you want to cook. Sprinkle the salt all over and rub in well. Place on a rack set over a tray and slide into the fridge, uncovered, for 24 hours.

When you are ready to cook, fire up your barbecue ready for indirect cooking, aiming for an internal air temperature of around 130–140°C (260–280°F). Add 2–3 lumps of smoking wood to the fire.

Rest the ribs on the grill bars far away from the fire. Shut the lid and leave to smoke gently for 1½ hours.

Take two large sheets of foil and lay them together as a double layer. Remove the rack of ribs from the grill and lay them on the foil, drawing up the sides to create a wall. Pour in the apple juice and seal up tight, keeping the seam on top. Rest back on the grill bars, again away from the fire, shut the lid and cook for another hour.

While the wrapped ribs are cooking, make the baste for the final stage. Set a small saucepan on the hob and add the coriander seeds and peppercorns. Toast for a minute or so then tip into a pestle and mortar and grind. Add the ginger, garlic and honey and stir to a paste. Pour in the apple cider vinegar and mix together to combine. Take to the barbecue along with a silicone basting brush.

Unwrap the ribs and set back onto the grill bars, again indirectly. Baste with a little of the honey and spice mixture then shut the lid. Keep cooking and basting every 5-10 minutes until the ribs are sticky and pass the tests for doneness (see page 164) – expect it to take another 30-40 minutes or so.

Serves 2 (or more as a snack)

1kg (2lb 4oz) bone-in lamb breast
1 tbsp flaked sea salt
100ml (generous ¾ cup) apple juice

For the baste
2 tbsp coriander seeds
1 tbsp black peppercorns
2 tsp ground ginger
3 garlic cloves, crushed
4 tbsp runny honey
100ml (generous ¾ cup) apple cider vinegar

Bird

Going back to the original premise of *Seared*, that is GOOD MEAT cooked over GOOD FIRE, here I deal with just chicken, duck and turkey as these are the birds we can easily buy from well farmed, responsible sources.

Chicken makes up the vast bulk of our overall meat consumption. A mild, easy and quick meat to cook, we just can't get enough of it. Which has led to huge industrialization in the farming process. If ever there was an animal that has been turned into a pure economic commodity, the humble chicken would be it. I keep chickens for their eggs, have done for years, and they are inquisitive, clever, funny little creatures that deserve treating with as much respect as a cow or sheep in a field. A plea, then, to seek out properly free-range chicken reared on farms where they have had genuine access to perform natural behaviours, eating a natural diet and living a natural lifespan. Luckily there are many small-scale farms doing just that and you'll find a list of my favourites in the back. Of course the cost is more but it's a true cost; these animals simply take more for the farmer to rear, often just because they live longer. With clever cooking – using up leftovers and all the bits of the bird not just the 'prime cuts', making stock for future meals – we can get the most value out of them. Which is just as it should be.

Ducks and turkey are the other birds we cook regularly and, similarly, that has led to these animals being reared the wrong way. Other less commonly eaten farmed birds are quail and poussin, which are baby chickens, less than 28 days old. Wild birds – pheasant, pigeon – are seasonally available and often make for good sustainable eating – but the honest truth is during the period of writing, the season was wrong and I don't deliver recipes that haven't been through the testing process.

How cooking birds is different to cooking beasts

When compared to mammals, what you get with birds are much less wildly differing parameters in muscle types, and therefore cooking times are correspondingly less wide. While the meat from cows, for example, can be cooked in anything from a few minutes for a thin steak to a whole day for a large brisket, pretty much any bird you like – even a massive 6–7kg (13–15lb) turkey – can be cooked in under 3 hours. This chapter is divided into cooking whole birds, followed by dishes that take less than an hour and dishes that take more than an hour. There is also a little section on 'surplus' cuts, the wings that are left behind when butchers joint up birds to sell legs and breasts, and the offal that would otherwise go to waste. The more 'whole animal' eating we do the better value these animals become.

As a general rule I think birds, especially chicken, are always better cooked indirectly from the fire, taking things more gently for longer. Rushing it by burning the outside and risking a raw inside is never going to bring you the best eating. As with all meat cooking, a temperature probe is exceedingly useful, in fact I think essential, to give you confidence your meat is cooked. Head back to page 24 for my thoughts on temperature probes.

Bird muscles

There are two types of muscles out there – fast twitch, used for intense periods of short motion, and slow twitch, used for sustained periods of moderate activity. Mammals have these different muscles too, but they are perhaps more easily observable in birds. The mammals we eat generally walk, that is perform sustained, steady motion, and therefore the muscles we eat are mostly of the slow twitch variety. Birds not only walk, they can also fly and swim. Slow twitch muscles are fuelled by myoglobin, a protein that stores oxygen. Myoglobin-rich slow twitch muscles are dark red. Fast twitch muscles are fuelled by glycogen, a type of sugar that fuels short sharp bursts of activity, and these muscles are paler.

Flight muscles differ in different species of birds and this is the reason chicken has white breast meat and ducks have dark breast meat. Chickens spend the vast majority of their time on two legs, walking around in a steady sustained way using the darker slow twitch muscles. They are capable of short sharp bursts of flight, using pale fast twitch muscles, so their breast meat is pale. Ducks, on the other hand, can undergo long periods of flying and therefore their breast meat is much darker due to the prevalence of slow twitch, myoglobin-fuelled muscle fibres.

Breast meat of birds is tender because it's made up of two muscles, with just a little connective tissue in between. You have the pectoralis major that pulls the wing down, the larger of the two breast muscles as this motion takes way more energy, and the pectoralis minor, which pulls the wing up. Leg meat of birds is less tender because there are more muscles with many more connective tissues attaching them to the bones. So you need to cook leg meat for longer but the differences are way less marked than they are in mammals.

Fat in birds

Birds principally store fat in a subcutaneous layer – under the skin – rather than in the intramuscular ribbons you find in beasts. Just as with mammals, accumulated fat is an age thing – the older the animal the more fat it has but as we generally eat birds pretty young (even the most mature free-range chicken is only 3 months old) they are generally a leaner meat. Duck has a thick fat layer under the skin that serves as insulation when it's swimming in cold water.

Butchery

When it comes to buying birds to eat you have two choices: buy whole or buy jointed. It is cheaper to buy whole and joint yourself, but to get 8 thighs for a whole family-sized meal you would need to buy 4 chickens. If you have freezer space it's quite a nice afternoon's work – jointing, boning, making stock with the carcasses – but the most practical way is to buy the joints you want to eat. With chicken, for me, that is always legs or thighs but never breast, which I find too lean and rather bland on its own. Duck breast makes for good eating, especially if you get the thick subcutaneous fat layer to render down and crisp up the skin.

If you want to joint a whole bird it's really pretty easy, just use a small sharp knife to cut and slice, following the natural divisions between the bones and where the muscles connect to the bones. Sturdy scissors are also helpful to cut along the backbone. With a little practice it's a job that can take mere minutes.

If you have bone-in chicken thighs it's a breeze to take the bone out. Use a small sharp knife to make an incision following the line of the bone then use it to scrape the meat from the bone all the way around, saving the bones for stock (see page 263). If you don't always have time to make stock, you can freeze the bones in a bag very successfully for a time when you do.

Chapter 8: The Whole Bird

A whole bird placed on the table for sharing is a very lovely thing indeed. Cooking a whole bird, with its uneven rugby ball shape, is always best done over a fairly indirect heat so it cooks through and stays juicy without the skin burning. And don't be surprised at how crispy skin gets even with no direct heat – after all, you roast a chicken in your oven without it ever seeing any flames – convection currents are really remarkable things (see page 12 for more on the physics of heat).

A rotisserie spit is a great bit of kit for roasting whole birds. The constant slow turning means the meat bastes itself as it cooks. If you don't have a rotisserie, cook breast side down for the first half of cooking and then turn breast side up for the second half. A tray, placed directly under the bird, will catch any drips that will add much flavour to a gravy.

Herb and orange brined chicken, cider gravy

I can honestly say I prefer dry-brining on a day-to-day basis. It uses less salt and takes up a lot less room in the fridge for starters, but the process of wet-brining looks quite impressive and without a doubt it causes the meat to suck up water and become irresistibly juicy. I do think it can, however, have a slightly 'diluting' effect on flavour so be sure to use the very best quality bird you can buy.

Pour 1 litre (4 cups) of the water into a large stock pot and set over a medium heat on the hob. Add the salt, herbs, sugar and peppercorns. Use a vegetable peeler to pare off long wide strips of peel from the orange, dropping them into the pot as you go. Put the orange in a small bowl, cover and slide into the fridge until you are ready to cook the chicken. Simmer the brine for 5 minutes, stirring until the salt and sugar have dissolved. Remove the pot from the heat and add the remaining cold water. Set aside until it's totally cold. Once cold, add the chicken, breast side down, so it's completely submerged. Slide the pot into the fridge and leave to brine for 24 hours.

Remove the chicken from its brine, holding it cavity side down over the sink so that all the liquid drains out. Quarter the reserved orange and push into the cavity. Drizzle a little oil over the chicken and season with a good grind of black pepper. If you are cooking on a rotisserie spike, insert it now, tightening up the clamps to secure the chicken in place.

When you are ready to cook, fire up your barbecue ready for indirect grilling, moderating the air vents to get an air temperature of around 180°C (350°F). I light two small fires either side of the barbecue, so the chicken can cook in between them – see page 19 for grill set-ups.

Set a roasting tin on the base of the barbecue between the two fires. Add the quartered onion and whole garlic bulb and pour in the cider. Set the grill bars in place. Rest the chicken on the grill bars directly over the tin, starting breast side down for the first half, then turning over. If you are using a rotisserie, insert the spike into the motor and set it turning. Shut the lid to trap in the convection heat and cook until the internal temperature of the chicken reaches at least 74°C (165°F) when probed in a few places. I find that the legs of roast chicken do benefit from taking it a little higher – 80–90°C (175–195°F) wouldn't hurt at all because you are cooking slowly and gently. This may take around 2½ hours, and you may need to top up the fuel to keep the temperature steady.

Serves 4–6

4 litres (7 pints) water
200g (7oz) flaked sea salt
12 sage leaves
8 bay leaves
4 sprigs of rosemary
2 tbsp dark brown sugar
2 tbsp black peppercorns
1 large orange
2kg (4½lb) chicken
a drizzle of olive oil
freshly ground black pepper

For the gravy

1 onion, quartered through the
    root (no need to peel)
1 whole garlic bulb
440ml (15fl oz) can dry (hard)
    cider
50g (2oz) butter
50g (2oz) plain (all-purpose) flour
1 tbsp Marmite

Pictured on page 183.

Once cooked, lift the chicken onto a plate and loosely cover, leaving to rest while you make the gravy.

I usually make the gravy inside at this stage rather than firing up the heat on the barbecue again, but of course you could do that if you liked. Either way, set the tin over a medium-high heat so the stock comes to the boil. Take a potato masher and squish the garlic and onion about to mash into the liquid and leave to simmer steadily for a few minutes to extract as much flavour as possible. Meanwhile, add the butter to a saucepan and set over the heat. Once it's melted, stir through the flour to form a roux. Set a sieve (strainer) over the pan and carefully pour the liquid from the roasting tin through it, squishing with the back of a wooden spoon to extract the liquid from the vegetables. Whisk the gravy over a medium heat until it thickens. Add the Marmite and pour any juice that's collected on the chicken plate, stirring to mix. Season to taste with salt and pepper.

Buttery roast chicken with two flavoured butters

Sliding butter under the skin of chicken is a good way to guarantee deliciousness. The stock tin underneath will catch all the lovely drips as it roasts. PS – Marmite is my secret flavour enhancer and I invariably add it to any gravy I make.

Dry-brining, as with most meats (indeed, quite possibly all – see page 21), is a really good idea with a whole chicken. Simply set it on a rack over a tray, removing any string trussing the legs, and rub all over with salt, including inside the cavity, then slide uncovered into the fridge for 24 hours.

When you are ready to cook, mix up your chosen butter:

For the juniper, bay and garlic butter
Crush the juniper berries as finely as possible with a pestle and mortar and tip into a bowl. Remove the central rib of the bay leaves and chop very finely and add to the bowl, along with the garlic, brown sugar and black pepper, stirring to mix. Add the softened butter and mash to a paste.

For the tarragon, lemon and garlic butter
Add the butter to a bowl and mash through the tarragon and garlic. Season with a good grind of black pepper.

Remove the chicken from the fridge and use your fingers to ease the skin away from the breast meat, starting at the cavity end. You want to release as much skin as possible without piercing the skin, so go gently and slowly as you feel your way. The rounded handle end of a silicone spatula can help as a tool to 'extend' the length of your fingers – with practice it's possible to go beyond just the breast meat and to release the skin around the thighs a little too.

When you have released as much skin as possible, take spoonfuls of the flavoured butter and slide it under the skin as far as possible, again using your fingers. Then tie the chicken – take a generous length of string, a good arm's length, and slide under the chicken just behind the wings. Pull the string over and around the wings and cross underneath the tip of the breast, pulling tight to secure the wings close to the body. Then wrap the string around the legs and cross over, pulling tight to hold the legs secure against the body. Cross the string over and underneath the tail and tie off. If you are cooking on a rotisserie, insert the spike through the centre and secure well with the

Serves 4–6, maybe with some leftovers

2kg (4½lb) chicken
2 tbsp flaked sea salt

For the juniper, bay, garlic butter
1 tbsp juniper berries
8 fresh bay leaves
2 garlic cloves, crushed
1 tsp dark brown sugar
a good grind of black pepper
125g (4½oz) butter, slightly soft

For the tarragon, lemon, garlic butter
125g (4½oz) butter, slightly soft
30g (1oz) bunch of tarragon, leaves and thinner stalks finely chopped
2 garlic cloves, crushed
freshly ground black pepper

For the stock tray
2 onions, chopped into wedges through the root (no need to peel)
2 carrots, roughly chopped
1 whole garlic bulb
a generous handful of parsley stalks
1 tbsp black peppercorns

Continued overleaf...

clamps, then rest back on the tray. If you are cooking directly on the grill bars, just rest back on the tray ready to take to the barbecue.

Add the stock ingredients to a sturdy roasting tin and take to the barbecue with a jug of water, about 500ml (2 cups) or so.

For both rotisserie and non-rotisserie roasting of the chicken, I set up my fire exactly the same way, by lighting two small fires, one either side of my kettle barbecue, aiming for a barbecue temperature of around 180°C (350°F). The chicken then sits between the two fires to cook, either directly on the grill bars or on the rotisserie spike. Below the chicken, on the base of the barbecue, I set the stock tray and pour in the jug of water to get the gravy started. It doesn't matter if I cook a summer or winter roast chicken, there are inevitably calls for gravy in our house.

Cook the chicken for a generous 2¼ hours – maybe even 2½ – using a meat probe to test for doneness. If you are cooking directly on the grill bars, start the chicken off breast down first, turning it over halfway though. Chicken is safe to eat at 74°C (165°F), but with a roasting chicken (or indeed legs, thighs or wings) I personally think it's better to take it quite a bit higher – 85°C (185°F) or even 90°C (195°F) wouldn't hurt at all. If you have a beautifully slow grown bird that is slathered in a gorgeous flavoured butter and you are cooking indirectly it's simply not going to dry it out. Also, because you have that tray underneath, catching all the tasty drips, the gravy stock is only going to get more and more epic the longer you cook for.

Once the bird is cooked, remove to a plate and loosely cover with foil. Set aside to rest while you make the gravy.

Remove the grill bars and carefully pull out the tin of stock vegetables and liquid. Set on the hob inside – or you could make it over a direct fire on the barbecue if you have enough heat left. Take a potato masher and squish down all the vegetables as much as possible to extract maximum flavour. Simmer over a medium heat for a few minutes. Set a sieve (strainer) over a saucepan and pour the contents of the tin in, pushing the liquid through with the back of a spoon. Set the pan over a medium heat and pour in the cornflour (cornstarch) and water paste, whisking until thickened. Add a little more water to thin if necessary. Stir through the Marmite and season with a little salt and pepper to taste.

For the gravy

2 tbsp cornflour (cornstarch) mixed to a paste with 2 tbsp cold water
1 tbsp Marmite

Tabil-spiced chicken, chermoula, charred leeks

A whole chicken is a fairly uneven and unwieldy shape – like a rugby ball with sticky out bits! – which means it takes a while to cook a whole one. Spatchcocking, or flattening it out and removing the backbone, is a fantastic way to create a thinner, more regular shape. The result is a quicker cooking time, more surface area for rubs to soak in and a flatter shape that means you get crispier skin. Win-win in my book.

You could rub your flat bird in pretty much anything that takes your fancy but this is a big hit in our house. Tabil is a really enticing North African spice blend and chermoula is a fresh and punchy herb dressing from the same part of the world. Put them together and you have a rather deliciously heady flavour combination going on.

If I have time, I generally get the chicken spatchcocked and rubbed in the tabil 24 hours before cooking. The salt in the rub the then acts as a dry brine, working its magic on the proteins while the spices add bags of flavour to the surface.

Set a small frying pan (skillet) over a medium heat on the hob and spoon in the coriander, cumin, peppercorns and caraway. Toast for a minute or two until they smell fragrant then tip into a pestle and mortar, crushing until coarsely ground. Add the pul biber, salt, garlic and olive oil and mix to a paste. Set aside.

Rest the chicken breast side up on a chopping board and use a large sharp knife to cut a few deep slashes through the legs and breasts to create more surface area for the rub to soak deeper into the meat. Turn the bird breast side down and use chunky kitchen scissors to cut down each side of the backbone. Remove and discard (perhaps saving it for the stock pot, see page 263).

Spoon the spice paste onto the bird and rub in all over, working the mix really well into the cuts and crevices for maximum flavour. Set in a dish and slide into the fridge for as long as you have time for, up to 24 hours.

When you are ready to cook, fire up the barbecue ready for direct and indirect cooking (see page 19).

Rest the chicken breast side up on the grill bars, away from the fire so it cooks indirectly. Cook for around 45 minutes, with the lid down, checking once or twice and rotating to make sure it's cooking evenly (the side closest to the fire will obviously cook faster) but keep it breast side up for now.

Serves 4–6

3 tbsp coriander seeds
2 tbsp cumin seeds
1 tbsp black peppercorns
1 tbsp caraway seeds
2 tbsp pul biber (red pepper flakes), plus extra to garnish
1 tbsp flaked sea salt
2 garlic cloves, crushed
3 tbsp olive oil
1.8–2kg (4–4½lb) chicken
8 slim leeks
a drizzle of olive oil

Continued overleaf...

Once the chicken is cooking, make the chermoula. Set a small frying pan over a medium heat on the hob and tip in the coriander seeds. Toast for a couple of minutes before transferring to a pestle and mortar and grinding to a coarse powder. Add the garlic and crush together, then add the lemon zest and juice, herbs and paprika and pound together. Pour in the olive oil and season with salt and pepper, mixing together well.

Slice the leeks about two thirds down the length, then turn and cut the other side to open up the leaves into quarters while keeping them attached at the root end. Wash really well under running water and shake dry. Drizzle a little oil over the leeks and season with a little salt and pepper. Take to the barbecue ready to cook.

After the chicken has had its initial cook, turn it breast side down and keep cooking indirectly, away from the fire. At the same time, rest the leeks directly over the fire and char all over for about 10 minutes before sliding them off the fire to finish cooking indirectly.

Probe the chicken in several places to assess how quickly it's cooking. Once you have a temperature of around 70°C (158°F), slide it directly over the fire to start adding some extra-deep crispiness to the skin. Cook for a further 10–15 minutes, turning regularly until you have a temperature of at least 74°C (165°F) – personally I think you can take the temperature a little higher on the thigh meat. For this final stage you can cook with the barbecue lid up so your main source of heat is coming from below – both from the radiant heat from the coals and contact heat from the grill bars. The lack of convection heat gives you time to sear the skin to super crispiness without overcooking the rest of the bird. If the skin is colouring too much before the temperature is reached, simply slide it further away from direct fire.

Lift the chicken and leeks onto a serving board and drizzle over some of the chermoula, serving the rest in a bowl alongside. Sprinkle with a little extra pul biber. Use a large sharp knife to chop the chicken into pieces.

For the chermoula
1 tbsp coriander seeds
2 garlic cloves
zest and juice of 1 lemon
a good handful of coriander (cilantro), chopped
a good handful of parsley, chopped
1 tsp smoked paprika
8 tbsp extra virgin olive oil
flaked sea salt and freshly ground black pepper

Sesame smoked chicken, ginger and garlic rice

This one-pot dish makes a great alternative Sunday lunch. A whole chicken gets gently smoked in a casserole set on top of the grill bars; you'll be amazed how much smoky goodness it soaks up even in a pot. The bonus is that all the beautiful juices collect in the bottom and are used to add bags of flavour to the rice.

Sprinkle the salt all over the chicken, rubbing in well. Place on a rack set over a tray and slide into the fridge, uncovered, to dry-brine for up to 24 hours.

When you are ready to cook, fire up your barbecue ready for indirect cooking, aiming for a temperature of around 140°C (280°F), adding 2–3 lumps of smoking wood to the lit fire.

Set a fireproof casserole on the grill bars, away from the fire, and pour in the sesame oil. Add the chicken, breast side down and shut the lid of the barbecue. Leave the chicken to smoke for 1 hour.

Sprinkle the sesame seeds into a frying pan (skillet) and set over a medium heat on the hob. Toast for 2–3 minutes until golden then tip into a small bowl and set aside.

Use tongs to lift the chicken to a plate. Add the onion to the casserole and give it a stir before putting the chicken back in, breast side up this time. Shut the lid of the barbecue and keep cooking until the chicken reaches an internal temperature of around 65°C (150°F) when probed in a few places. This might take another hour or maybe a little more.

Once again, use tongs to lift the chicken to a plate. Add the ginger, garlic and peppercorns to the casserole and stir for a couple for minutes. Tip in the drained rice and pour in the stock, stirring well. Lift the chicken on top, breast side up, adding any juices from the plate. Sprinkle the sesame seeds over the top of the chicken, never minding if a few fall into the rice, and cover the casserole with a lid or snugly tucked piece of foil. Shut the barbecue lid and cook for another 30 minutes. Take a peek at the rice, testing a few grains to seek if they are tender. If they are you're good to go; if not, re-cover and cook for another 15 minutes or so, covered and with the barbecue lid shut.

To serve, lift the chicken onto a board to carve, tipping it in towards the rice to drain in any juice. Fluff up the grains with a fork and serve with spoonfuls of rice alongside. Add the garnishes to little dishes for people to help themselves.

Serves 4–6, perhaps with some leftover chicken

2kg (4½lb) chicken
1 tbsp flaked sea salt
2 tbsp toasted sesame oil
1 heaped tbsp sesame seeds
2 onions, finely chopped
75g (3oz) fresh root ginger, grated
3 garlic cloves, crushed
1 tbsp white peppercorns, crushed
400g (14oz) jasmine rice, soaked in cold water for 1 hour and drained
350ml (1½ cups) chicken stock

To serve

Soy sauce, chilli sauce, chopped coriander (cilantro), chopped spring onions (scallions), thinly sliced cucumber

Smoked turkey, maple coffee butter mop sauce

Mop sauces are thin basting liquids that get liberally 'mopped' over your meat as it cooks, adding moisture and flavour as the meat gently smokes. Don't be alarmed by the coffee in this recipe; your turkey won't taste even remotely of coffee, it just adds a subtle depth of flavour and a glorious colour that works a treat with a little smoke.

Turkeys always seem to cook pretty quickly on the barbecue, more quickly than they would in the oven. I think the all-round heat plays a part. A large 5–7kg (11–15lb) turkey takes approximately 3 hours to barbecue at 160–170°C (320–340°F). A smaller turkey will take a little less but not loads less, perhaps 30–45 minutes. In barbecue we always cook to temperature not time, which might feel tricky for planning a festive feast but the good news is, once your turkey is cooked it will hold its temperature for at least 60 minutes. So better to get it done and happily resting so you can finish the rest of your feast without worrying. A turkey is cooked and safe to eat when a probe reading is 74°C (165°F) in the thickest part of the leg, although I personally think leg meat benefits from being taken a touch higher, maybe 80–85°C (175–185°F). The temperature will continue to raise a little on resting, maybe by 8–10°C, so I lift the turkey from the barbecue at around 74°C (165°F) and I know it will be cooked and super-juicy.

You can also cook a turkey crown or turkey legs in exactly the same way. Expect a quicker cooking time and always use a temperature probe to check for doneness.

Sprinkle the salt all over the untrussed turkey, rubbing it lightly all over the bird and adding a little to the cavity too. Stuff the herbs into the cavity. Rest on a rack set over a roasting tin, slide into the fridge, uncovered, and leave to dry-brine for 48 hours.

When you are ready to cook, set up your barbecue ready for cooking indirectly with two fires to either side, adding a couple of lumps of smoking wood to each fire. You are aiming for a barbecue temperature of around 160–170°C (320–340°F).

Take a large, deep roasting tin and put the giblets in, along with the onion, carrots, garlic, bay leaves and peppercorns. Rest this tin in the centre of the barbecue, between the two small fires, and pour in the water and wine, if using.

Take a small metal tin or pan, add the coffee, butter and maple syrup and take to the barbecue along with a 'mop' or silicone basting brush.

Place the grill bars back onto the barbecue and lift the turkey onto the centre, breast side down, so it rests directly over the tin with the gravy stock. Brush a little of the mop sauce over the bird

**Serves 8 generously,
with lots left over**

5–7kg (11–15lb) free-range
turkey, untrussed and giblets
removed and reserved
3–4 tbsp flaked sea salt
a generous handful of woody
herbs – thyme, rosemary, bay

For the gravy
turkey giblets
1 large onion, thickly sliced
2 carrots, halved
3 garlic cloves, unpeeled
3 bay leaves
1 tsp black peppercorns
500ml (2 cups) water
500ml (2 cups) white wine
(or replace with extra water)
2 tbsp cornflour (cornstarch),
mixed to a paste with 2 tbsp
of cold water

Continued overleaf...

and shut the lid. Leave to cook for 1 hour, checking every 20–30 minutes and brushing a little more mop sauce all over the turkey.

After an hour, flip the bird over so it's breast side up and keep cooking, again mopping with sauce every 20–30 minutes. At this point you can begin to monitor the internal temperature of the turkey, inserting a probe deep into the thigh muscle. You are looking for a reading of 74°C (165°F). You can use a wired probe if you have one. You want to try and keep the barbecue temperature fairly stable, so every time you mop and check the temperature, add a lump of charcoal to each fire to keep it topped up. The gravy stock should have enough liquid and need no attention whatsoever but if it starts to look a little dry towards the end of cooking, use a jug to pour a little water carefully through the grill bars into the tin.

Once the turkey has reached temperature, lift it from the barbecue onto a clean roasting tray or large platter. Cover it with a generous sheet of baking paper followed by a few clean tea towels. Take it into the kitchen to rest for 45–60 minutes before carving.

You can make the gravy on the barbecue, or on the hob in the kitchen. Either way, set a sieve (strainer) over a large saucepan and carefully pour the stock from the tin into it, mashing a little with a wooden spoon to extract as much flavour as possible. Rest the saucepan over your chosen heat source and pour in the cornflour (cornstarch) and water paste, whisking over the heat until it's thickened. Add a splash of water to thin it to your preferred consistency. Your gravy should be really flavoursome and need nothing more added. If you prefer a thick gravy, be generous with the cornflour.

For the mop sauce

400ml (1¾ cups) strong fresh coffee

150g (5½oz) unsalted butter, melted

5 tbsp maple syrup

Smoked whole duck, duck fat potatoes

Such a simple recipe this, but delicious nonetheless. Just a good duck, some salt and a hit of beautiful, sweet smoke. Oh, and some insanely crunchy duck fat roasties to go with it. Serve with a big fresh green salad in summer or a bowl of buttery greens in winter and you have a Sunday lunch of dreams. I like to add a dollop of peppery horseradish sauce too.

I think duck is a meat that appreciates a long dry brine, so if you have 48 hours beforehand, go for it. Simply rub the duck all over, inside and out, with the salt and place on a rack set over a tray. Slide into the fridge and leave to dry-brine, uncovered, for 24–48 hours.

Once you are ready to cook, set a large saucepan of lightly salted water on the hob and add the potatoes. Bring to the boil and simmer for 10 minutes until just starting to soften. Drain well and tip into a roasting tin – one that fits into the base of your barbecue in between the fires. Drizzle over the oil and toss to mix.

Fire up your barbecue ready for indirect grilling, with two small fires either side (see page 19 for grill set-ups), aiming for an air temperature of around 140°C (280°F). Add 2–3 generous lumps of smoking wood to the fire – cherry wood is lovely here, not for the taste particularly but for the colour it gives the skin and the sweet smell that wafts out of your barbecue.

Set the tin of potatoes on the base of the barbecue between the two fires and put the grill bars in place. Sit the duck on the grill bars over the tin of potatoes so the fat drips down onto them. Ideally insert a wired probe deep into the breast meat so it can smoke undisturbed – every time you lift the lid to check it you will lose all your sweet smoke, so minimizing that is a good thing. Shut the lid and cook until the meat reaches an internal temperature of around 70°C (158°F) – this may take 2–2½ hours or even a little more. You may need to add a little fuel from time to time to keep your temperature steady. The potatoes should be quite happy if your fires are nice and gentle, but you may need to give them a stir once or twice.

Serves 4–6, perhaps with a little leftover duck

2kg (4½lb) whole duck
2 tbsp flaked sea salt
1.5kg (3lb 5oz) potatoes, peeled and cut into large chunks
2 tbsp oil

Continued overleaf...

Remove the duck to a tray and take out the probe if you are using one. Wrap tightly in foil or butcher's paper then reinsert the probe. Put the wrapped duck back on the grill bars between the fires and keep cooking until the internal temperature reaches around 93–94°C (200°F). Leave the potatoes where they are, they should be quite happy. Remove the duck to a plate – keep wrapped, covered with a few clean tea towels, and leave to rest while you crisp up the potatoes. A long rest will soften the meat's texture so it's almost 'pull-able'.

Remove the grill bars and extract the tin of potatoes. Load up your fire a little to get it a little hotter. Give the potatoes a toss about, then set the tin directly over the fire. If you have charcoal baskets this is a good time to pull them together to create one hotter fire. Shut the lid and cook for about 30 minutes until crispy, stirring from time to time so they cook evenly.

Unwrap the duck and carve into thick slices, piling onto a warm serving plate as you go. Pour over any juices that have collected during resting and serve with the potatoes alongside.

Chapter 9: Fast Bird – under an hour

All these recipes will take you an hour or less to cook. Chicken thigh fillets are one of my fave chicken cuts – relatively quick to cook, a large surface area to soak up lots of flavour and so much juicier than breast meat. Although the cook time is quicker it still pays not to rush – I generally cook chicken indirectly for at least three quarters of the cooking time, only sliding closer to the fire once the internal temperature reaches 60–65°C (140–150°F) for a final burst of heat to kick-start some Maillard-tastiness – I guess it's the chicken equivalent of a reverse sear steak.

As well as being quicker to cook, smaller jointed pieces of meat have the great benefit of more surface area. This means you, the cook, can get more going on in the taste department. Remember that flavours from the spices, herbs and other ingredients in rubs or marinades should only ever be considered a surface treatment. So, it stands to reason that more surface area equals more flavour. The tenderizing actions from acidic or lactic marinades can also get to work more quickly (see page 22), as there is more space for them to work their way deep into.

Spiced yogurt chicken skewers

Yogurt is a fabulous meat tenderizer, the lactic acids gently breaking down the protein bonds that bind muscle fibres together. It also provides a little fat that's a great carrier for helping fat-soluble spices adhere to the surface of the meat. See page 21 for more on marinades.

Set a small frying pan (skillet) over a medium heat on the hob and add the cumin seeds, peppercorns, cardamom pods, crumbled cinnamon and cloves. Toast for a minute or so then tip into a spice mill and blend to a powder (you can also use a pestle and mortar for a slightly coarser grind).

Tip the cashews into the frying pan and toast for a minute or two, then add to the ground spices, along with the turmeric and nutmeg. Grind to a powder then transfer to a bowl.

Add the chicken, yogurt, lemon juice, ginger, garlic, chillies and salt, stirring well to mix. Thread the chicken onto metal skewers, trying not to pack it super-tight, and line up on a tray or plate. Cover the bowl and refrigerate for up to 24 hours.

When you are ready to cook, fire up your barbecue with the charcoal on one side only, so you have control of the cooking temperature (see page 19).

Set the skewers onto the grill bars, slightly offset to the fire so they cook over a medium heat. Cook until the internal temperature reaches 74°C (165°F), turning regularly. This will take about 20 minutes or so depending on the heat of the fire.

Put the butter in a small fireproof frying pan and set on the grill bars away from the fire to melt. Towards the end of cooking, brush the butter all over the chicken, moving the skewers a little closer to the fire for the last few minutes to crisp them up.

Once they are cooked, make a quick salad by tossing together the tomatoes, red onion, coriander (cilantro) and lemon juice. Serve alongside the kebabs with a little extra scatter of mint.

Pictured opposite (top).

Makes 6 skewers

1 tbsp cumin seeds
1 tsp black peppercorns
6 cardamom pods
½ cinnamon stick, crumbled
4 cloves
35g (1½oz) cashews
½ tsp ground turmeric
a pinch of freshly grated nutmeg
800g (1lb 12oz) chicken thighs, diced into 3–4cm (1¼–1½in) pieces (from approx. 1.2kg/2lb 10oz bone-in thighs)
150g (5½oz/¾ cup) Greek yogurt
juice of 1 lemon
50g (2oz) fresh root ginger, grated
3 garlic cloves, crushed
2–4 green chillies, finely chopped (to taste)
1 tsp flaked sea salt
50g (2oz) butter
a few sprigs of mint, leaves chopped, to serve

For the salad
200g (7oz) cherry tomatoes, halved
1 small red onion, sliced
a little chopped coriander (cilantro)
juice of ½ lemon

Turmeric and black pepper chicken skewers

These simple skewers take no time at all to assemble, but a full 24 hours in the marinade is good, so begin them the day before you want to cook. Fresh turmeric has quite phenomenal tenderizing powers, thanks to its proteolytic enzymes. These enzymes break down proteins, essentially beginning the digestion process for you, so the meat becomes super-tender.

Tip the chicken into a bowl and add the turmeric, garlic, peppercorns, honey and salt. Mix together really thoroughly – using gloves if you want to avoid getting rather yellow hands. Thread onto skewers, line up on a plate or tray, cover and refrigerate for up to 24 hours.

Just before you are ready to cook the chicken, make the salad. Slice the cucumber in half lengthways. Use a teaspoon to scoop out the seeds in the middle – they can make the salad rather watery – then slice into half-moon pieces around 5mm (¼in) thick and tip into a bowl. Cut the carrots in half lengthways then slice into wafer thin semicircles, adding to the cucumber as you go. Stir through the lime zest and juice, fish sauce, mint, chilli and sugar. Spoon into a serving dish and scatter over the peanuts.

Fire up your barbecue ready for direct and indirect grilling, piling the lit coals onto one side of the barbecue (see page 19 for fire set-ups).

Drizzle a little oil over the skewers and rest them slightly away from the fire so they cook over a medium heat. Cook for about 25–30 minutes, or until the internal temperature is 74°C (165°F), rotating and turning frequently so they cook evenly. When grilling chicken, a slightly gentler heat is always better than hot and fast. Once the skewers are cooked you can always move them a little closer to the fire for a little last-minute extra crisping, but there's no going back from the dreaded burnt edges and raw in the middle if you cook them too quickly.

Serve the skewers with the salad alongside.

Pictured on previous page (bottom).

Makes 6 skewers, serving 4–6

800g (1lb 12oz) chicken thigh
    fillets, diced into 3–4cm
    (1¼–1½in) pieces
100g (3½oz) fresh turmeric,
    grated
2 garlic cloves, crushed
1–2 tbsp black peppercorns,
    crushed
1 tbsp runny honey
1 tsp flaked sea salt
a drizzle of vegetable oil

For the salad
1 large cucumber
2 carrots
zest and juice of 1 lime
1 tbsp fish sauce
a good handful of mint, chopped
1–2 bird's eye chillies, finely
    chopped, to taste
2 tsp caster (superfine) sugar
a handful of salted roast peanuts,
    roughly chopped

You also need 6 metal skewers

Smoked turkey steaks, peppercorn sauce, potatoes

The astute among you will note there is not a single chicken breast recipe in this book; when it comes to cooking chicken portions, thighs and legs win the day hands down. Turkeys, however, do have rather sizeable breasts (sorry, not sorry) and given that most people don't want to cook a whole one on any other day than Christmas or Thanksgiving, it seems prudent to devise something tasty to cook with them.

Like chicken breast, it can be a little on the dull side, with a tendency to dry out. The dry-brining process is your friend here (see page 21) but as the steaks are thin you can get away with doing it for a few hours rather than a day or two. Ideally, aim for a few hours. The other thing that blings them up is an ample slug of both cream and booze. Winner, winner turkey dinner.

If your turkey steaks are thicker than 1cm (½in) or so, you can thin them a little. Take 2 sheets of baking paper and lay the meat one piece at a time between them. Bash them fairly gently with a rolling pin to squish them out more thinly.

A few hours before you want to eat, sprinkle 2 teaspoons salt over the steaks. Rest them on a rack set over a tray and slide into the fridge to dry-brine.

When you are ready to cook, fire up your grill for low, indirect cooking. You are aiming for a temperature of around 120–130°C (250–265°F), so tap your air vents down quite shut. Light a little fire (no more than half a chimney) to one side of the grill, adding a lump of smoking wood to the fire.

Drizzle just a little oil over the turkey steaks. Scatter the potato cubes in a roasting tin and drizzle over a generous couple of tablespoons of oil. Season with a little salt and pepper and cover the tin with foil.

Rest the turkey on the grill bars far away from the fire so it can smoke gently and indirectly. At the same time, set the covered tin of potatoes directly over the fire. Begin the sauce by pouring 1 tablespoon olive oil into a small fireproof pan and add the shallot. Set the pan on the grill bars, in between the turkey and the potatoes so it's halfway between direct and indirect. Shut the lid and leave to cook everything for 30 minutes, stirring the shallots a couple of times so they cook evenly.

Serves 2, easily doubled

400g (14oz) turkey breast steaks
4 tbsp olive oil
500g (1lb 2oz) new potatoes, diced into 2cm (¾in) cubes
1 banana shallot, finely chopped
2 garlic cloves, crushed
1 tbsp black peppercorns, crushed
100ml (3½fl oz) Marsala
150g (5½oz/¾ cup) crème fraîche
flaked sea salt and freshly ground black pepper

To serve

2 little gem lettuces, leaves separated and washed
a generous sprinkle of red wine vinegar
a good glug of extra virgin olive oil
a few chives, snipped

Continued overleaf...

After 30 minutes, add the garlic and peppercorns to the pan of shallots and stir briefly before pouring in the Marsala. Leave to simmer and reduce the alcohol for 15 minutes or so before spooning in the crème fraîche. At the same time, remove the foil from the potatoes and keep cooking over a high direct heat for another 15 minutes or so, stirring every now and then so they start to crisp up in parts and stay soft and squishy in others.

Once the potatoes and sauce are ready, slide both to the far side of the barbecue off the heat to keep warm. Move the smoked turkey directly over the heat and sear quickly on both sides for a few minutes to get some colour (remember, colour = tasty Maillard reactions, see page 6). Slice up the turkey across the grain and drop into the sauce, tossing it about to coat.

To serve, divide the lettuce between a couple of plates. Sprinkle with the vinegar and drizzle over the oil, to taste. Scatter over the potatoes and top with the turkey and sauce. Sprinkle over the chives and tuck in straight away.

Pistachio and apricot stuffed chicken legs, fennel slaw

Here, chicken legs get part-boned, just the thigh portion, so you can fill it with a tasty stuffing. The stuffing does make turning them a little delicate – if you have a fish cage, lining them up in it will keep them a bit more secure. If not, just be extra generous with the cocktail sticks to pin them shut.

Toast the pistachios in a small frying pan (skillet) for a couple of minutes over a medium heat. Tip onto a chopping board and finely chop, then set aside. Tip the cumin, coriander and chilli flakes, if using, into the pan and toast for a minute. Tip into a pestle and mortar and roughly crush then add to a bowl with the nuts.

Pour the olive oil into the frying pan and set back over a low heat. Add the onion and sweat gently for a good 15–20 minutes until well softened. Add the garlic and stir briefly over the heat before tipping into the bowl with the pistachios. Add the chopped apricots and herbs and season well with salt and pepper. Set aside to go cold while you bone out the chicken legs.

Rest a leg, skin side down on a chopping board. Take a small sharp knife and make an incision down the thigh bone to the joint where the thigh joins the drumstick. Use the tip of the knife to scrape the meat away from the bone, working from the thigh end towards the joint. Cut through the joint; it should be fairly easy if your knife is sharp and you are working between the two bones. Discard the thigh bone (consider freezing it for stock at a later date, see page 263) but leave the drumstick bone in place.

Take the knife and cut a pocket into the deepest part of the thigh muscle to open it out a little – this will allow you to get a little more stuffing inside. Repeat with the other legs. Spoon the filling into the thigh then wrap the meat back around the filling. Use plenty of cocktail sticks to pin everything really snugly together.

Fire up your barbecue ready for indirect grilling.

If using a fish cage, line the legs up together, skin side down, and close the cage. If you don't have one it's fine; it just makes turning easier. Either way, lay the chicken onto the grill bars away from the fire and cook indirectly, skin side down, for about 40 minutes. Rotate the legs once or twice to make sure they are cooking evenly but leave skin side down. Use a meat probe to check for doneness – chicken is technically safe at 74°C (165°F), but I think legs benefit from being taken beyond this – 85°C (185°F) or so.

Toss the salad ingredients together and serve alongside the cooked chicken.

Serves 4

50g (2oz) shelled pistachios
2 tsp cumin seeds
2 tsp coriander seeds
a pinch of chilli flakes (optional)
1 tbsp olive oil
1 red onion, chopped
1 garlic clove, crushed
50g (2oz) dried apricots, finely chopped
a few sprigs of flat-leaf parsley, chopped
a few sprigs of dill, chopped
4 chicken legs
flaked sea salt and freshly ground black pepper

For the salad

1 small fennel bulb, about 200g (7oz), thinly sliced
2 heads of red chicory (endive), thinly sliced
100g (3½oz) radishes, thinly sliced
a really generous handful of soft fresh herbs, chopped (I used dill, parsley, coriander/cilantro)
juice of 1 lemon
3 tbsp extra virgin olive oil
a pinch of sugar, to taste

You also need around 12–16 wooden cocktail sticks

Smoky chicken burgers, red slaw

Another super-tenderizing yogurt marinade. Tossing the cooked fillets in crispy breadcrumbs at the end of cooking adds a lovely bit of crunch, not dissimilar to coating and frying chicken in a pan on the hob.

Add the fennel seeds to a small frying pan (skillet) and set over a medium heat to toast for a couple of minutes. Tip into a pestle and mortar and roughly grind then add to a bowl. Spoon in the yogurt and stir through the paprika, salt, garlic and a good grind of black pepper. Cut a few deep slashes into each chicken thigh and add to the marinade. Stir really well to coat, cover and slide into the fridge to marinate for 24 hours.

You can also make the slaw the day before if you want to get ahead. Take the cut garlic clove and wipe both halves around the inside of a large bowl – this will add just a little hint of garlic; if you want more crush it up and stir through. Add the cabbage, red peppers, spring onions (scallions), coriander (cilantro), yogurt, mayonnaise and vinegar. Season with a little salt and pepper and toss together. Cover and slide into the fridge. Stir again just before serving.

When you are ready to cook, fire up your barbecue ready for indirect and direct grilling, aiming for a fairly high heat of around 200°C (400°F).

Sprinkle the breadcrumbs into a fireproof roasting tin and drizzle over the olive oil. Season with a little salt and pepper. Set over the fire to toast for a few minutes until golden and crispy. Remove and set aside.

Rest the chicken on the grill bars away from the fire so it can cook gently and indirectly. Turn over a few times, moving it around so all the pieces cook evenly. Once the internal temperature reaches 70°C (158°F), remove to a plate. This may take 30–45 minutes or so, depending on the size of the thighs and the heat from the fire. Brush all over with the sweet chilli sauce then add to the tin of crispy breadcrumbs, tossing around to coat. Set the tin back on the grill bars, again away from the fire, and keep cooking for a few more minutes until the chicken reaches 74°C (165°F).

Lightly toast the buns, then add some lettuce and pile in the chicken and a big dollop of slaw. Add sauces of your choosing and tuck in.

Serves 6

1 tbsp fennel seeds
100g (5½oz/¾ cup) Greek yogurt
2 tsp smoked paprika
2 tsp flaked sea salt
2 garlic cloves, crushed
800g (1lb 12oz) chicken thigh
    fillets (from approx. 1.2kg/2lb
    10oz bone-in thighs)
75g (3oz) fresh breadcrumbs
2 tbsp olive oil
3 tbsp sweet chilli sauce
freshly ground black pepper

For the slaw

1 garlic clove, cut in half
500g (1lb 2oz) red cabbage, finely
    shredded
2 red peppers, thinly sliced
½ bunch of spring onions
    (scallions), thinly sliced
a good handful of coriander
    (cilantro), chopped
3 tbsp Greek yogurt
3 tbsp mayonnaise
1 tbsp red wine vinegar
flaked sea salt and freshly ground
    black pepper

To serve

6 brioche buns, halved
lettuce, mayo, sweet chilli or hot
    chilli sauce

Buttermilk chicken, charred broccoli, mozzarella

Buttermilk does a brilliant job of tenderizing meats, in a similar way to yogurt, as the lactic acid and enzymes in it begin to break down the protein structures of the meat over time. For it to work best, a good long soak is needed – 24 hours ideally – so the gentle acids can work their magic.

Cut a few deep slashes into each chicken thigh to allow the marinade to penetrate further into the meat and put into a shallow dish in a single layer.

Mix together the buttermilk, garlic, mustard, sugar and a good seasoning of salt and pepper. Pour over the chicken and toss the thighs about a few times to coat well. Cover and slide into the fridge for up to 24 hours.

When you are ready to cook, fire up the barbecue ready for direct and indirect grilling, adding a lump of smoking wood if you fancy smoky chicken.

Arrange the chicken thighs on the grill bars away from the fire and cook indirectly for a good 30 minutes or so until the internal temperature is around 60–65°C (140–150°F), turning over and rotating fairly frequently. Then move it just a little closer to the fire, but not directly over it, and cook until the internal temperature is 74°C (165°F).

While the chicken is cooking, blanch the broccoli florets in a big pan of boiling water for a couple of minutes. Drain well and toss with the olive oil and some salt and pepper.

When the chicken is nearly done, grill the tomatoes and blanched broccoli for a good 10 minutes directly over the fire, turning a few times to get some good colour on all sides.

Pile the chicken, broccoli and tomatoes into a sturdy roasting tin. Add the basil and gently toss to mix. Sprinkle over the Parmesan, breadcrumbs and pine nuts. Top with mozzarella and drizzle over a little olive oil and some salt and pepper. Put the tin directly over the fire for 15 minutes to melt the cheese.

Serve with crusty bread or cooked pasta, and maybe some extra mustard for kicks.

Serves 4–6

800g (1lb 12oz) chicken thighs fillets (from approx. 1.2kg/2lb 10oz bone-in thighs)
300ml (1¼ cups) buttermilk
3 garlic cloves, crushed
2 tbsp Dijon mustard
2 tsp brown sugar
1 head of broccoli, cut into florets
1 tbsp olive oil, plus extra for drizzling
250g (9oz) cherry vine tomatoes
a generous bunch of basil, roughly chopped
50g (2oz) grated Parmesan
50g (2oz) fresh breadcrumbs
50g (2oz) pine nuts
250g (9oz) mozzarella, torn
flaked sea salt and freshly ground black pepper

Spiced duck salad with grapefruit and pecans

Duck breasts have a considerable layer of fat under the skin, which means they have a tendency to cause the fire to flare up if you cook over too direct a heat. In this recipe the honey in the marinade also makes things prone to catching. If you get a big old flare-up the simplest thing to do is remove the food to a plate, allow the fire to calm down – perhaps brushing the grill bars clean with a wire brush – before carrying on.

Cut slashes at 2cm (¾in) intervals through the skin of the duck and deep into the meat. Add to a dish in a snug, single layer.

Toast the crumbled cinnamon, star anise and chilli flakes in a small frying pan (skillet) for a few minutes over a medium heat, then tip into a spice mill and grind to a powder. You can also use a pestle and mortar. Transfer to a small bowl and stir through the salt, olive oil and honey to make a paste. Rub this into the duck breasts, pushing deep into the slashes for maximum flavour. Cover and slide into the fridge to marinate, ideally for 24 hours.

Put the onion and salt in a bowl. Massage a little, then stir through the balsamic vinegar. Cover and refrigerate overnight.

The next day, use a small sharp knife to slice off the top and bottom of the grapefruit, then pare away the skin, removing as much white pith as you can. Set a sieve (strainer) over a bowl and segment the grapefruit over it – slicing either side of the membrane to release each segment into the sieve and allowing the juice to fall through into the bowl. Squeeze the leftover membranes over the sieve to extract as much juice as possible. Set the segments aside. Whisk the mustard and garlic through the juice then drizzle in the oil, whisking to form a dressing. Season to taste with salt and pepper.

Fire up your barbecue for direct and indirect grilling. Sear the duck breasts just to the side of the fire, turning them almost constantly for maximum Maillard reactions (look to page 44 on steak cooking). They will flame up a little as the fat renders – just keep them moving. Once browned and crispy, slide them away from the heat and shut the lid. Leave it to finish cooking indirectly – taking the internal temperature to 52°C (125°F) for rare, 60°C (140°F) for medium, or 74°C (165°F) for well done.

Assemble the salad. Toss the watercress, grapefruit segments and dressing together on a platter. Sprinkle over the pecans, coriander (cilantro) and pickled onions. Carve the duck into thick slices across the grain (see page 33) and rest on top of the salad.

Serves 4–8, depending on what else you are eating

4 duck breasts
1 cinnamon stick, crumbled
3 star anise
1–2 tsp chipotle chilli flakes
1 tbsp flaked sea salt
2 tbsp olive oil
2 tbsp honey
2 pink or red grapefruit
2 x 80g (3oz) bags of watercress
75g (3oz) pecans, toasted and
    roughly chopped
a good handful of coriander
    (cilantro), chopped

For the pickled onions
1 large red onion, thinly sliced
½ tsp flaked salt
2 tbsp balsamic vinegar

For the dressing
juice from the grapefruit (see
    method)
1 tbsp English mustard
1 garlic clove, crushed
4 tbsp extra virgin olive oil
flaked sea salt and freshly ground
    black pepper

TWO MINCED BIRD RECIPES

Mincing up meat is a great way of taking tougher, longer-cooking cuts – invariably legs – and making them quicker to cook. You can sometimes buy properly reared free-range minced turkey (and chicken too occasionally) but I have never seen minced duck meat. So for the duck polpette recipe you will need a meat mincer, but once you get addicted to making your own mince with the best meat you can find, buying in ready-made mince will naturally become less attractive.

Turkey meatball skewers, fennel and bean stew

These minced turkey meatballs benefit from a little chill in the fridge to set them firmly onto the skewers – an hour or two should do it.

Tip the fennel seeds in to a small frying pan (skillet) and set over a medium heat on the hob to toast for a couple of minutes. Transfer to a pestle and mortar and grind, then tip into a bowl. Add the turkey mince (ground turkey), paprika, garlic, salt and a good grind of pepper. Use clean hands to mix together really well, working the meat together for a couple of minutes (this will make it sticky and help it stick to the skewers). Divide into golf ball-sized pieces and roll firmly between the palms of your hands, setting onto a tray as you go.

When you have shaped all the meatballs, thread them onto skewers alternating with the discs of courgette (zucchini). Once everything is skewered up, use your palms to shape the meatballs a little so they are the same diameter as the courgettes. Line up on a baking sheet and slide into the fridge to chill for an hour or two. Longer (up to 24 hours) wouldn't hurt if you want to get ahead.

When you are ready to cook, fire up your barbecue ready for direct and indirect grilling.

Drizzle a couple of tablespoons of olive oil over the fennel wedges and season with a little salt and pepper. Grill over a direct heat for a few minutes on each side until lightly charred. If you have a vegetable grilling tray (see page 25) this will help prevent the wedges falling through the grill bars. Once charred, remove to a plate and set a large, deep fireproof frying pan or roasting tin onto the grill bars over the fire and pour in another

Serves 4–6

2 tbsp fennel seeds
500g (1lb 2oz) turkey mince
    (ground turkey)
1–2 tsp smoked paprika, to taste
1 fat garlic clove, crushed
1 tsp salt
1 courgette (zucchini), sliced into
    1cm (½in) discs
olive oil, for drizzling
freshly ground black pepper

For the grilled fennel

2 fennel bulbs, about 500g
    (1lb 2oz), cut into thin wedges
    through the root
4 tbsp olive oil
1 red onion, sliced
2 garlic cloves, crushed
1 tsp chilli flakes (optional)
250ml (1 cup) cold water
2 x 400g (14oz) cans borlotti
    beans, drained and rinsed
juice of 2 lemons
100g (3½oz) butter, diced
a good handful of dill, chopped

You also need 4–6 metal skewers

Continued overleaf...

couple of tablespoons of olive oil. Add the onion, stirring briefly before shutting the lid and frying until softening and lightly golden, around 15 minutes or so depending on how hot your coals are. If they are catching too quickly, simply slide the pan further away from the coals.

Add the charred fennel wedges and the garlic and chilli flakes, if using, and fry for a minute or two before pouring in the water. Stir briefly then cover with a lid or piece of foil and shut the lid of the barbecue. Simmer for 10 minutes or so, just until the fennel is softening but still a little al dente. Remove the lid or foil and stir though the beans, lemon juice, butter and most of dill (save a little for garnish). Slide the pan away from the heat so it can simmer gently over the indirect fire while you cook the skewers.

Drizzle a little oil over the skewers and set onto the grill bars directly over the fire. Grill, turning regularly, until a probe inserted deep into one of the meatballs reads 73°C (163°F), around 15 minutes or so. Cooking with the lid down when you are not turning the skewers will increase the efficiency of the fire because convection heat comes into play (see page 12 on the physics of fire).

Rest the cooked skewers over the pan of fennel and beans and scatter over the reserved dill just before serving.

Duck polpette, tomatoes and pappardelle

These delicious duck meatballs are a real lesson in fire management as duck mince is pretty fatty – cook them too hot and they are prone to flare-ups, cook them too cool and they are prone to sticking to the grill bars. It's never been more essential to master direct and indirect cooking (see page 13) so you have wriggle room to continually manoeuvre the balls around the fire. With experience you can cook the lot at once, but to begin with I advise just starting with a few meatballs at a time directly over the fire so you can concentrate on them.

Because you have freshly minced the duck yourself (and hopefully bought it from a good free-range farm) you can eat these a touch pink in the centre if you like. With a temperature probe, you are looking for 60°C (140°F) for medium, 73°C (165°F) for well done.

Use a small sharp paring knife to bone out the duck legs (see page 208) on simple butchery of poultry). Reserve the bones for making stock (see page 263). Dice the meat, including the skin and fat, into 5–6cm (2–2½in) pieces, nipping out and removing any tendons as they won't mince down very well. Spread out the pieces on a baking sheet and slide into the freezer for an hour to partly freeze (see page 78 for more on making mince and sausages safely).

Put the breadcrumbs into a bowl, pour over the milk and set aside to soak while you mince the duck.

Set up your mincer with a medium cutting blade and process the semi-frozen meat. Add the duck mince (ground duck) to the soaked breadcrumbs, along with the pecorino, egg, garlic and oregano. Season generously with salt and pepper and use your hands to really mix everything together thoroughly. Roll into walnut-sized meatballs, setting on a plate as you go. At this point you can cook straight away, or if you can, refrigerate the meatballs for a few hours to intensify the flavours.

When you are ready to cook, fire up your barbecue ready for indirect and direct grilling. Once hot, give the grill bars a really good scrub with a wire brush – meatballs are prone to sticking and a clean grill will help.

Set a large, deep fireproof frying pan (skillet) onto the grill bars in the centre of the barbecue so it's half over the fire and half away the fire. Pour in the olive oil, add the onion and shut the barbecue lid. Cook over a moderate heat for 20 minutes, stirring a few times to mix as one side of the pan will be hotter than the other, until starting to soften and caramelize a little. Slide the pan directly over the fire and add the tomatoes, garlic, oregano

Serves 4–6

4 skin-on duck legs, (yielding about 700g/1lb 9oz mince)
75g (3oz) fresh breadcrumbs
3 tbsp milk
50g (2oz) pecorino, grated
1 egg
1 garlic clove, crushed
1 tbsp chopped fresh oregano
400g (14oz) dried pappardelle
flaked sea salt and freshly ground black pepper

For the sauce

3 tbsp olive oil
1 red onion, sliced
400g (14oz) vine tomatoes, chopped
2 garlic cloves, thinly sliced
a few sprigs of fresh oregano, leaves picked
1 tsp sugar
200ml (generous ¾ cup) white wine

To serve

plenty of extra virgin olive oil
a handful of grated pecorino
a little flat-leaf parsley, chopped

Continued overleaf...

leaves and sugar and leave to cook for a few
minutes until the tomatoes start to collapse.
Pour in the wine, season with a little salt and
pepper and cook over a fairly high heat to burn
off the alcohol. Slide to the far side of the fire to
simmer away while you concentrate on grilling
the meatballs.

Begin by laying a handful of meatballs directly
over the fire, leaving them to sear for a minute or
two before teasing up off the grill surface with a
metal spatula. They may stick a little; if so, leave
for another few seconds before trying again. Turn
and sear on the other side, again directly over the
fire. The duck fat will cause the fire to flare up, so
take care, and if it's all getting a bit wild, quickly
slide them further from the fire. Once they have
a nice bit of colour, move them away from the
fire and add a few more directly over the fire
to sear. Repeat until they are all browned, then
move them all away from the fire to keep cooking
more gently, shutting the lid. Take the internal
temperature of the meatballs to 60°C (140°F) for
medium to 73°C (165°F) for well done.

While the meatballs and sauce are both
finishing cooking over an indirect heat, cook the
pappardelle according to the packet instructions.
I invariably do this on my hob indoors (shock,
horror!) but you could, in theory, do it over a
direct heat on your grill if your barbecue was
expansive enough for a big saucepan. Drain well
and toss in just a splash of olive oil to stop the
strands sticking together.

When you are ready to serve, toss the meatballs
and pappardelle through the sauce. Finish with
a really generous drizzle of your best olive oil, a
good grating of pecorino and a sprinkle of parsley.

Chapter 10: Slow Bird – over an hour

I think the trick to cooking good chicken, and indeed other birds, on the barbecue is to always cook the thighs and larger joints completely indirectly, away from the fire, only moving them closer to the direct fire at the very end to add a little crispness if necessary (although it very often isn't – your conventional oven crisps chicken perfectly well with no flames, right?). This way you are guaranteed maximum juiciness with no fear of drying out the meat, or dealing with the dreaded 'burnt on the outside but raw in the middle' scenario.

The smoke+braise tactic deployed in BEAST pops up more than once in this chapter, but as a general rule (for the reasons outlined on page 180), the meat from birds will always cook more quickly. I really do think you get the best of both worlds with this double cooking strategy; smoky 'barbecue' flavours combined with succulent, saucy meat.

Grilled Malay chicken curry

Chicken legs get the Smoke+Braise treatment (see page 96) in this Malaysian-spiced curry. As with all similar braising recipes in this book, obviously once the lid is on the casserole there is no actual benefit to cooking on the barbecue – no more smoky flavour will get into your food. So you can do the braising stage over a low simmer on your hob or in your indoor oven if you prefer, but if you have heat left in your charcoal after smoking the chicken it makes sense to use it.

You can make the curry paste in a mini food processor or in a deep jug with a stick blender. Either way you want to blitz together the shallots, garlic, lemongrass, shrimp paste, turmeric and lime juice into a paste.

Tip the coriander and fennel seeds, cinnamon, star anise, cloves and chilli flakes into a small frying pan (skillet) and set over a medium heat to toast for a minute or two. Transfer to a pestle and mortar or spice mill and grind to a powder. Add to the paste, along with the salt and sugar and blitz once more until smooth.

Take the chicken legs and cut a few deep slashes into them to help the marinade penetrate deeper into the meat. Lay the chicken in a single layer in a dish and spoon over half the curry paste, rubbing it all over, including into the cuts you made. Cover the dish and slide into the fridge to marinate for up to 24 hours if you have time – the longer the better.

When you are ready to cook, fire up the grill ready for indirect grilling. I like to cook this with two small strips of fire either side of my kettle barbecue. Add a lump of smoking wood to each fire. Shut the vents down quite low – you are aiming for a grill temperature of about 150°C (300°F).

While the barbecue is getting hot, pour the vegetable oil into a heavy fireproof casserole that will fit in the base of your barbecue, between the two fires. Set over a medium-high heat on the hob (I know! But it's just easier to do this inside while the grill is firing up) and add the other half of the spice paste. Stir-fry for a few minutes, just long enough that you can smell the fragrance wafting up beautifully. Add the coconut milk, potatoes and tomatoes and give it a good stir, then take off the heat. Take to the barbecue, along with the marinated chicken legs.

Serves 4

4 banana shallots, roughly chopped
3 garlic cloves, roughly chopped
2 lemongrass stalks, roughly chopped
10g (⅓oz) shrimp paste (try online, Asian supermarkets, or use 2–3 tbsp fish sauce)
30g (1oz) fresh turmeric, roughly chopped
juice of 2 limes
1 tbsp coriander seeds
2 tsp fennel seeds
3cm (1in) cinnamon stick, crumbled
1 star anise
5 cloves
1–2 tsp chilli flakes, to taste
1 tsp flaked sea salt
1 heaped tsp brown sugar
4 chicken legs
1 tbsp vegetable oil
400ml (14fl oz) can coconut milk
500g (1lb 2oz) potatoes, cut into large chunks
350g (12oz) tomatoes, chopped
3 sprigs of curry leaves

Pictured on page 223.

Sit the casserole between the two fires directly on the base of the barbecue. Set the grill bars on top and put the chicken legs, skin side up, on the grill bars over the casserole dish so any drips go down and flavour the curry sauce. Shut the lid and smoke the chicken for a generous hour, turning over halfway through.

Once the chicken has finished smoking, lift it from the grill to a plate. Remove the grill bars and lift the casserole out, then put the grills bars back in and set the casserole back on top, in the centre off the direct heat. Add the chicken to the sauce, pushing it under as much as you can, and sprinkle in the curry leaves. Cover with a tight-fitting lid and shut the barbecue lid. Leave to braise for another 1½–2 hours until the chicken is super-tender and falling off the bone and the potatoes are cooked through. You want to keep the temperature hovering around 150°C (300°F), so add more fuel if you need to. It's not absolutely critical though; a little more heat, it will cook more quickly; a little less it will take longer.

Serve bubbling hot with lots of steamed rice.

Chicken shawarma flatbreads with toum

This kebab-of-dreams is designed to feed a hearty crowd. Traditionally a shawarma is cooked on a vertical spit, which the majority of us won't have in a domestic situation. So here it's designed as a giant kebab cooked on a rotisserie spit. You could also cook it directly on the grill bars, away from the fire so it cooks gently and indirectly from the fire and rotating often.

The toum, an intensely garlicky sauce, can be a slightly tricky candidate. If you add the oil too fast it can end up on the thin side, but it will still taste totally delicious drizzled over the chicken. It keeps for up to a month in the fridge and leftovers are fantastic used in place of fresh garlic in pasta sauces or any general cooking.

I used whole filleted legs for this recipe, giving me a nice fat shawarma. You could use thigh fillets instead, but the overall circumference will be less, resulting in a reduced cooking time.

Set a small frying pan (skillet) over a medium heat and tip in the cumin and coriander seeds, peppercorns, cloves, cinnamon stick and cardamom pods. Toast for a minute or two until you can smell the fragrance wafting up from the pan, then transfer to a spice mill. Add the paprika and nutmeg and grind to a powder.

Add the chicken to a bowl along with the olive oil, lemon juice and salt. Sprinkle over the spice mix and stir well to mix. Cover and slide into the fridge to marinate for a good few hours, 24 would be ideal.

You can also make the toum ahead of time – it will keep (covered) in the fridge for up to a month. Peel the garlic cloves and slice in half, removing any green central stem as it can add a little bitterness to the sauce. Put the garlic into a food processor and whizz until very finely chopped, stopping the motor and scraping down the sides if necessary. Add the salt and lemon juice and process until creamy. With the motor running, very gradually drizzle in the oil, literally a few drops at a time at first so it begins to emulsify. If you add the oil too fast it can split or not thicken. Once you've added about a quarter of the oil, add a tablespoon of iced water, then continue adding more oil. Keep alternating drizzling oil with tablespoons of water until the sauce thickens. Spoon into a bowl, cover and refrigerate.

Serves 8

For the shawarma
3 tbsp cumin seeds
2 tbsp coriander seeds
2 tbsp black peppercorns, to taste
2 tsp cloves
1 cinnamon stick
1 tsp cardamom pods
2 tbsp paprika (unsmoked)
½ nutmeg, grated
2kg (4lb 7oz) chicken thigh or leg
    fillets (skin on or off)
3 tbsp olive oil
juice of 1 lemon
1 heaped tbsp flaked sea salt
1 onion, thinly sliced

For the toum
1 large garlic bulb (nice fat, firm
    cloves)
1 tsp flaked sea salt
juice of 1 fat lemon
400ml (1¾ cups) neutral oil
    (grapeseed, groundnut,
    vegetable)
4 tbsp iced water

Continued overleaf...

When you are ready to cook, assemble the shawarma by laying the chicken fillets out one on top of the other, adding a scattering of thinly sliced onion between each layer, until you have a neat vertical stack. Tuck in any little loose bits as best you can. Take your metal skewers and insert them at intervals around the circumference of the stack, piercing them all the way through as far as they will go. Turn the stack on its side and push the skewers further until they poke out the other side. Insert the rotisserie spike and attach the clamps to really secure the shawarma in place. If you are not using a rotisserie, use a few extra skewers to ensure the shawarma is really well held together.

Fire up your barbecue with two smallish fires on either side of where the rotisserie spike will sit so the shawarma can cook semi-indirectly. You are aiming for an air temperature inside the barbecue of around 150°C (300°F) or so. Slot the spike with the shawarma into place and set the motor running. Shut the lid of the barbecue and cook gently until the internal temperature, right in the middle of the shawarma, reaches 74°C (165°F). This may well take 2½–3 hours. Be patient: low and slow is best so that the chicken cooks all the way through to the centre without overcooking the outside. If you are not using a rotisserie, rest the shawarma directly on the grill bars between the two fires and turn regularly to ensure even cooking.

Once the shawarma is cooked through, remove it to a chopping board and carefully remove the rotisserie spike and clamps along with the metal skewers. Carve into slivers.

To serve, sprinkle a little salad over a wrap. Top with a handful each of chips and sliced chicken. Drizzle over toum to taste and finish with a sprinkle of herbs and chill flakes. Roll up tight and tuck in.

To serve, per person
a large flatbread (or pitta)
a handful of salad
a good handful of cooked chips
    – I don't think you can beat
    skinny oven fries here (see
    page 35 for cooking chips
    on the barbecue)
a little chopped parsley or
    coriander (cilantro)
a sprinkle of pul biber (red
    pepper flakes) or other
    chilli flakes

Pulled turkey legs, arepas and guasacaca

In an ideal world, get the turkey legs rubbed in the spices 24–48 hours before you want to cook them. The salt in the rub will begin the dry-brining process (see page 21) and the flavours will work their way into the outer surface of the meat.

Arepas are delicious, slightly chewy maize cakes from Venezuela and Colombia, made using pre-cooked white cornmeal, which sometimes goes by the name of arepa flour, and is an ingredient you'll need to seek out online or in a specialist shop. Guasacaca is the Venezuelan version of guacamole, an avocado dip that's punchier with spring onions (scallions), herbs and vinegar. If you are short of time you could serve the turkey and guasacaca in corn or flour tortillas.

Cut a few deep slashes in the turkey legs to allow the rub to penetrate deeper into the meat. Set in a dish so they fit in a single, snug layer.

Tip the chipotle flakes and cumin seeds into a small frying pan (skillet) and set over a medium heat on the hob. Toast for a couple of minutes before transferring to a pestle and mortar and grinding to a powder. Add the sugar, salt and thyme and pound together. Stir through the olive oil to make a paste and spoon over the turkey legs, rubbing in all over, making sure you get the rub deep into the cuts you made. Slide into the fridge and leave for 24–48 hours if possible.

When you are ready to cook, fire up the barbecue ready for indirect grilling, aiming for a steady temperature of around 140°C (280°F). Add a little smoking wood to the fire. Set a roasting tray on the base of the barbecue, next to the fire, and pour in a jug of water. This will create steam which will in turn attract smoke to the meat.

Rest the turkey legs on the grill bars on the opposite side to the fire. If you have one, insert a wired temperature probe deep into one of the legs and shut the lid of the barbecue. Cook for around 4–4½ hours, or until the internal temperature reaches around 93°C (199°F). Feel free to lift and wrap the legs if they hit the stall (see page 129). Depending on your fuel and temperature control, you may need to top up with fuel during this time to keep the temperature steady. Remove and wrap the legs snugly in butcher's or baking paper (if you haven't already wrapped) and cover with a few clean tea towels. Set aside to rest for 30 minutes – this will help the meat texture become 'pull-able'.

Serves 8, generously

2 large turkey legs, about
    800–850g (1lb 12oz–1lb 14oz)
    each
3 tbsp chipotle chilli flakes,
    to taste
2 tbsp cumin seeds
3 tbsp brown sugar
2 tbsp flaked sea salt
a good bunch of fresh thyme,
    leaves picked and chopped
4 tbsp olive oil
chilli sauce, to serve

For the arepas
750g (1lb 10oz) pre-cooked
    ground white cornmeal
    (arepa flour)
1 tbsp flaked sea salt
4 tbsp olive oil
850ml (3½ cups) hand-hot water
    (half cold, half boiling)
vegetable oil, for frying

Continued overleaf...

While the turkey is smoking, make the arepas dough. Put the cornmeal into a bowl and stir through the salt. Pour in the oil and water, mixing constantly until you have stiff dough. Tip onto the worktop and knead for a couple of minutes. Wrap in baking paper and set aside.

For the guasacaca, add the avocado, peppers, spring onions (scallions), garlic, herbs and vinegar to a food processor and blitz until smooth. With the motor running, gradually drizzle in the olive oil and keep blitzing until you have a smooth, creamy sauce. Season to taste with salt and pepper. Chill until needed.

Once the turkey is wrapped and resting, begin to cook the arepas. Divide the dough into 12 even-sized pieces, rolling each to a ball. Use your palm to flatten the balls out into discs, pressing out until they are about 1.5cm (½in) thick. You can cook on the hob inside if you like, or you can stoke up the fire to get it hot again. Either way, set a large frying pan over the heat and leave to get hot. Pour in a couple of tablespoons of vegetable oil. Fry the arepas, a few at a time, for around 10–12 minutes until crispy and lightly golden on both sides. Remove and keep warm on a covered plate while you cook the rest.

To serve, pull apart the turkey meat with two forks – you may need to use a knife too. Spilt the arepas down the centre (like opening up a pitta bread) and stuff a little turkey inside. Spoon in a little guasacaca, adding a drizzle of chilli sauce if you like, and tuck in.

For the guasacaca
3 large ripe avocados, peeled and stones removed
2 green peppers, deseeded and chopped
a bunch of spring onions (scallions), roughly chopped
4 garlic cloves, chopped
a good bunch of coriander (cilantro), roughly chopped
a good bunch of flat-leaf parsley, roughly chopped
4 tbsp red wine vinegar, to taste
100ml (3½fl oz) olive oil
flaked sea salt and freshly ground black pepper

Miso chicken thighs, smoked mushroom noodles

Miso (fermented soy paste) is a marvellous tenderizer, and when combined with the ginger in this marinade you get the most succulent chicken possible. Whole chicken thighs can take a good long marinade – 48 hours wouldn't hurt – so give them time if you have it. Togarashi is a delicious Japanese chilli and spice-spiked sprinkle mix – you can find it in oriental food shops, some supermarkets and online. Substitute regular chilli flakes or hot sauce of your choice.

Cut a few slashes into each chicken thigh, deep into meat. In a bowl, stir together the miso, mirin, soy, ginger and garlic. Add the chicken and toss really well to coat, working the marinade deep into the cuts. Cover and slide into the fridge for 24–48 hours.

Fire up the barbecue ready for indirect grilling, adding a couple of lumps of smoking wood to the fire, aiming for an air temperature of around 160°C (320°F).

Drizzle the sesame oil over the mushrooms and season with a little salt and pepper. Rest them stalk side up on the grill bars, away from the fire, and shut the lid. Smoke for around 30–40 minutes until soft and squishy. Remove, allow to cool a little then slice and set aside.

Rest the chicken skin side up on the grill bars, away from the fire, and leave to smoke gently for around 1 hour, or until the internal temperature of the chicken reaches 64°C (147°F). If you have space on your grill to start the chicken cooking indirectly at the same time as the mushrooms, do so.

Cook the noodles and drain, tossing though just a splash of sesame oil to stop them sticking together. Once the chicken is nearly ready, take them to the barbecue, along with a deep fireproof frying pan (skillet), the sliced smoked mushrooms and the rest of the noodle ingredients. Set the pan over the fire and add a little more sesame oil. Stir-fry the garlic, ginger and spring onions (scallions) breifly, then toss through the cooked noodles, mushrooms and coriander (cilantro). Keep tossing over the heat until hot, then slide away from the heat to keep warm.

Move the chicken a little closer towards the fire and cook for another 15-20 minutes or so, turning frequently, until the skin is crispy and the internal temperature is at least 74°C (165°F).

Divide the noodles between warmed plates and top with the chicken. Serve with the togarashi and extra soy sauce.

Serves 4–6

1kg (2lb 4oz) bone-in chicken
  thighs
3 tbsp white miso
3 tbsp mirin
3 tbsp soy sauce
50g (2oz) fresh root ginger,
  grated
2 garlic cloves, crushed

For the noodles

500g (1lb 2oz) chestnut
  mushrooms
2 tbsp sesame oil
350–450g (10½–16oz) egg
  noodles
3 garlic cloves, crushed
25g (1oz) fresh root ginger, sliced
  into matchsticks
½ bunch of spring onions
  (scallions), sliced
a handful of coriander (cilantro),
  chopped
flaked sea salt and freshly ground
  pepper

To serve

togarashi
soy sauce

Achiote chicken, lime crema

A citrussy marinade from Yucatan in Mexico featuring the glorious achiote, a brick-red paste made from the seeds of the annatto tree. Achiote comes as a solid block and you'll need to seek it out online or in a specialist shop. A lovely ingredient, it brings plenty of colour to the party and tastes earthy and slightly sweet – and perhaps a little smoky – but has no heat to it. There are a couple of other recipes in the book that use it (seek them out on page 74 and page 260).

Put the ancho chilli pieces and achiote into a heatproof jug and pour over 5 tablespoons boiling water. Stir well and set aside for 30 minutes. Add the garlic, cumin seeds, oregano, lime and orange zest and juice and a good seasoning of salt and pepper. Use a stick blender or mini processor to whizz until smooth. You could also pound it in a pestle and mortar.

Cut a few deep slashes into the chicken thighs to help the marinade penetrate deep into the meat then place in a single layer in a dish. Pour over the marinade and turn the chicken over a few times to completely coat it. Cover the dish and set in the fridge for as long as you can – 24 hours would be perfect.

When you are ready to cook, fire up your barbecue ready for direct and indirect grilling, piling the charcoal on one side of the grill and adding a lump or two of smoking wood to the fire. You are aiming to have the barbecue running around 140°C (280°F).

Lay the chicken thighs on the far side of the fire and leave to smoke for a couple of hours, turning once or twice to make sure they are cooking evenly. Use a temperature probe to check the chicken – once you have an internal temperature of around 65°C (150°F) in the deepest part of the thighs you can feel safe to move the thighs a little closer to the heat to crisp up. Keep cooking until you have an internal temperature of 74°C (165°F).

Make the lime crema by stirring together the sour cream, lime zest and juice, garlic and a little salt and pepper. Set aside.

Once the chicken is done, pile in a dish and keep warm. Add a little more fuel to the fire to get it hot. Drizzle just a little oil over the chillies and spring onions (scallions) and rest directly over the fire. Grill for a few minutes, turning regularly until lightly charred all over.

Scatter the chillies and spring onions over the chicken. Sprinkle over the coriander (cilantro) and drizzle over a little lime crema, serving the rest alongside.

Serves 4–6

For the chicken
2 dried ancho chillies, stems removed, snapped into 1cm (½in) pieces
50g (2oz) achiote paste, very finely chopped
3 garlic cloves, roughly chopped
1 tbsp cumin seeds, toasted and ground
1 tsp dried oregano
zest and juice of 1 lime
zest and juice of 1 large orange
1.2kg (2lb 10oz) skin-on bone-in chicken thighs
120g (4oz) fresh green chillies
a bunch of spring onions (scallions)
olive oil, for drizzling
flaked sea salt and freshly ground black pepper
coriander (cilantro), to garnish

For the lime crema
200g (7oz) sour cream
zest and juice of 1 lime
1 garlic clove, crushed

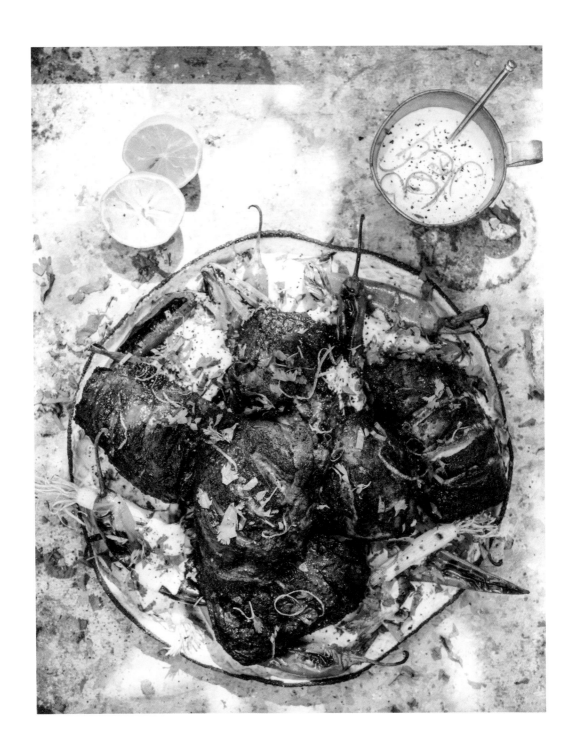

Smoked chicken, cream and whisky sauce

Another smoked and braised chicken dish, this time richly indulgent and full of cream and whisky – perfect winter barbecue food. The chicken gets a really simple rub, essentially a dry brine with extra brown sugar and black pepper that works its magic to tenderize the meat.

Ideally, apply the rub the day before you want to cook. Mix together 1 tablespoon salt, the sugar and crushed peppercorns in a small bowl. Cut a few deep slashes in each drumstick, down to the bone. Sprinkle the salt mix over them and rub in well, including into the cuts you made. Rest on a wire rack set over a tray and slide into the fridge, uncovered, for 24 hours if you have time.

Fire up your barbecue for direct and indirect cooking, adding 2–3 lumps of smoking wood, aiming for a temperature of around 140–150°C (280–300°F).

Rest the drumsticks on the grill bars, away from the fire, shut the lid and leave to smoke indirectly for an hour.

Then, set a fireproof pan or casserole onto the grill bars so it sits half on and half off the direct heat. Pour in the olive oil and add the shallots, thyme and a little salt and pepper, stirring to mix, and shut the lid of the barbecue. Leave to soften and caramelize for 30 minutes, stirring a couple of times to make sure it's cooking evenly. If colouring too quickly simply slide the pan further from the heat. Keep smoking the chicken while the shallots soften, trying to keep the lid shut as much as possible to keep the heat and smoke in.

Add the garlic and whisky to the softened shallots, sliding the pan over the heat, and allow to bubble away for a few minutes. Pour in the cream and stock, then lift in the smoked chicken, pressing it under the surface as much as possible. Slide the pan back off the heat and cover with a lid or a tightly tucked piece of foil. Shut the lid of the barbecue and simmer steadily for 1 hour. Then remove the lid or foil from the pan and keep simmering, uncovered, to reduce the sauce, for another 30–45 minutes. Keep the barbecue lid down as much as possible but every 15 minutes or so quickly turn the chicken so it stays evenly submerged.

Remove from the heat and sprinkle over the parsley just before serving. I would serve this with buttery mash and spring greens.

Serves 4

1 tbsp dark brown sugar
1 tbsp black peppercorns, crushed
8 chicken drumsticks (800–900g/1lb 12oz–2lb)
3 tbsp olive oil
4 banana shallots, chopped
a few sprigs of thyme
3 garlic cloves, crushed
100ml (3½fl oz) whisky
300ml (1¼ cups) double (heavy) cream
300ml (1¼ cups) chicken stock
a handful of flat-leaf parsley, chopped
flaked sea salt and freshly ground black pepper

Slow-roast duck leg salad

A warm salad that's a riot of colour and zingy flavours. Duck legs really take to long, slow smoking as the meat needs plenty of time to become soft and tender. As always, dry-brining is a great first step that takes seconds to do.

Sprinkle 1 tablespoon salt all over the duck legs, rubbing in well. Rest on a rack set over a tray and slide into the fridge, uncovered, to dry-brine for 24 hours.

When you are ready to cook, fire up the barbecue ready for indirect grilling with the fuel piled on one half, aiming for an air temperature of around 140°C (280°F), and adding a couple of lumps of smoking wood to the fire.

Rest the duck on the grill bars as far from the fire as you can, inserting a wired temperature probe deep into one of the legs if you have one. Shut the lid and leave to smoke gently for 2½–3 hours, or until the internal temperature reaches 90°C (195°F), topping up your fuel as and when needed. Rotate and turn the legs a couple of times to make sure they are cooking evenly.

While the duck is cooking, mix together the pomegranate molasses, garlic and a good grind of pepper to make a simple glaze for the duck. Make the dressing by whisking together the extra virgin olive oil and pomegranate molasses. Stir through the parsley and season with a little salt and pepper.

Spread the Tenderstem, chillies and lemon halves out on a tray and drizzle over a little olive oil.

Once the duck has reached temperature, brush the glaze all over and keep cooking indirectly while you grill up the veg. You may need to add a little more fuel to get the temperature up a little for grilling. Rest the lemons cut side down on the grill bars, directly over the fire, until lightly charred. Add the Tenderstem and chillies alongside and grill for a few minutes, turning regularly until lightly charred all over. As each piece is cooked, remove it to a serving platter.

Drizzle the dressing over and tuck the charred lemons in between. Top with the duck legs and scatter over the pomegranate seeds. Serve while hot.

Serves 4

4 duck legs
3 tbsp pomegranate molasses
2 garlic cloves, crushed
400g (14oz) Tenderstem broccoli
120g (4oz) mild red chillies
2 lemons, halved
2 tbsp olive oil
1 large ripe pomegranate, seeds
    picked
flaked sea salt and freshly ground
    black pepper

For the dressing
5 tbsp extra virgin olive oil
2 tbsp pomegranate molasses
30g (1oz) bunch of flat-leaf
    parsley, chopped

Chapter 11: Surplus Bird

Think of all the ready-jointed chicken and duck we buy, whether that's legs, thighs and drumsticks, or breasts – what happens to the rest of the bird? A plea here that we should adopt more of a 'beak to tail' eating philosophy and cook the 'surplus' bits for a more sustainable approach to meat eating.

WINGS

I make no apologies for including two chicken wing recipes – I quite simply think we should eat more wings. For starters, you get a higher skin-to-meat ratio and the best bit about chicken is the crispy skin, right? And wings are a cut that are in good supply because most people favour the other cuts from a jointed chicken. As always, welfare and sustainability are at the heart of this book so do seek out the best wings you can find. As a 'surplus' cut even the very best wings can be found reasonably cheaply.

The trick to cooking wings is taking it nice and slow, a generous hour and a half or more, so the meat is super-tender and the fat under the skin renders down. You can, in theory, then move them to a slightly more direct heat to finish crisping up, but I rarely find it necessary with such a languorous approach to cooking them.

Lemon and garlic wings, dukkah, labneh and crispy lentils

A slightly involved wing recipe, this Middle Eastern-inspired dish is full of contrasting textures and big flavours; I just love it. Dukkah is a nutty, spicy sprinkle and labneh is an easy, creamy homemade cheese. Start 24 hours before you want to eat – marinate the wings, cook the lentils, set the labneh straining and make the dukkah – so that the cooking part the next day is then pretty easy.

Tip the wings into a bowl and add the lemon zest and juice, crushed garlic, 2 tablespoons of the olive oil and a good grind of salt and pepper. Toss the wings about to coat them evenly, then cover and refrigerate for 24 hours.

Put the lentils in a pan and cover with cold water. Set over a high heat and bring up to the boil. Reduce the heat to a steady simmer and cook until just tender – around 20 minutes, depending on the size and age of your lentils (like barbecue, they are simply 'done when they're done'!). Drain, cool and refrigerate.

Make the labneh: stir the salt and pepper through the yogurt. Hang a clean muslin cloth (or clean tea towel) in a sieve (strainer) set over a bowl. Scoop the yogurt into the cloth, twisting the top to close. Set a saucer on top and rest something weighty on it – a small bag of rice or a tin of beans. Slide into the fridge and leave undisturbed for 24 hours so the liquid strains away.

To make the dukkah, toast the spices in a small frying pan (skillet), then tip into a pestle and mortar and roughly grind. Toast the sesame seeds and hazelnuts and add to the spices, along with the salt and pepper, and roughly grind together. You could also pulse a few times in a mini food processor but don't overdo it – you want a nice coarse texture. Tip into an airtight tub and set aside.

The next day, fire up your barbecue ready for indirect grilling, using about half a chimney of charcoal piled to one side of the barbecue. Set the chicken wings on the far side of the grill so they cook very gently for 30 minutes, shutting the lid to create an oven-like heat. After half an hour, turn over.

Once you've turned the wings, begin the onions. Pour the remaining 2 tablespoons oil into a fireproof pan and set on the barbecue, slightly off the fire so they get a medium heat. Add the butter and onions and cook for around 30 minutes, stirring a few

Serves 4–6

1.5kg (3lb 5oz) chicken wings
zest and juice of 2 lemons
5 garlic cloves, 3 crushed and
   2 sliced
4 tbsp olive oil
100g (3½oz) large green lentils
50g (2oz) butter
2 large onions, sliced
flaked sea salt and freshly ground
   black pepper

For the labneh

500g (2½ cups) Greek yogurt
½ tsp flaked salt
½ tsp freshly ground black
   pepper

For the dukkah

2 tbsp cumin seeds
2 tbsp coriander seeds
2 tbsp pul biber (red pepper
   flakes)
1 tbsp fennel seeds
50g (2oz) sesame seeds
50g (2oz) hazelnuts
1 tsp flaked sea salt
freshly ground black pepper

times, until softening and lightly caramelized. Add the cooked lentils and keep cooking for another 30 minutes or so, again stirring every now and then, where they will start to crisp up in the buttery oil.

Slide the pan of lentils further away from the fire and stir through the sliced garlic. At the same time, move the wings a little closer to the fire and cook for a final 15 minutes, turning a few times so they get a good colour. For the last few minutes sprinkle a little dukkah over the wings to give them some crunch; you will lose a little to the 'fire gods' but there is plenty. Lift the wings into the pan of crispy lentils, scooping some lentils and onions over them, sprinkle over a little more dukkah, and scatter over some of the herbs and spring onions (scallions). Slide the pan off the heat to keep warm.

Unwrap the ball of labneh and divide between two plates, using the back of a spoon to spread out, creating a few deep furrows as you go. Pour over a generous amount of extra virgin olive oil, allowing it to puddle into the dips in the labneh. Sprinkle a tablespoon or two of dukkah over each plate and arrange the raw veg around the side.

Serve the pan of lentils and wings alongside the labneh and veg, with warmed flatbreads or pitta to tear and scoop it all up with.

Pictured on page 241.

To garnish
plenty of extra virgin olive oil
a good handful of fresh herbs,
    roughly chopped – I used dill
    and flat-leaf parsley
spring onions (scallions), sliced
a selection of colourful crunchy
    fresh veg – I used sliced
    fennel, radishes, carrot
    ribbons
warm flatbreads or pitta bread,
    to serve

Smoky hot wings with buffalo sauce

A masterclass in keeping things simple, these wings are flavoured by nothing more than salt, smoke and plenty of time. Oh, and a banging little chilli sauce – buffalo sauce is a rather blissful combination of hot sauce and butter that gets basted on during cooking and served alongside as a dipping sauce as well. I used Frank's Original hot sauce, which is not actually that hot... you may want to adjust the measurements of hot sauce down a little if yours is particularly pokey.

You could also follow this wing cooking method and baste the wings in anything you like – try the curry BBQ sauce on page 165, or the coffee butter mop sauce on page 194.

Sprinkle the salt all over the chicken wings and rub in. Rest on a rack set over a tray and refrigerate for up to 24 hours, although even a couple of hours would be good.

When you are ready to cook, fire up your barbecue ready for indirect grilling, adding a lump or two of smoking wood to the fire. With this simple wing recipe, I usually light a small fire in the centre of my barbecue and cook the wings in a circle around the outside so each wing is the same distance from the fire. Rest the wings away from the fire, shut the lid and cook indirectly for 30 minutes.

Meanwhile, to make the buffalo sauce, melt the butter in a small saucepan set over a medium-low heat. Stir through the garlic for a few seconds before adding the hot sauce, vinegar, Worcestershire sauce and smoked paprika. Stir together until combined, then divide between two bowls, one for basting and the other for serving.

Once the wings have had 30 minutes, flip them over and baste with a little buffalo sauce. Shut the lid and keep cooking for another hour, basting and turning every 15 minutes or so, all the while keeping them off the direct heat so the skin renders and crisps up slowly. Serve hot from the barbecue with the extra bowl of sauce to dip into.

Serves 4–6

1.5kg (3lb 5oz) chicken wings
1 tbsp flaked sea salt

For the buffalo sauce
200g (7oz) butter
2 garlic cloves, crushed
300ml (1¼ cups) hot sauce
3 tbsp white wine vinegar
1 tbsp Worcestershire sauce
1 tbsp smoked paprika (hot for
    extra heat, or sweet for less)
1 tsp sugar

Sticky duck wings, roast plum relish

Slow-roasted until melting and sticky, duck wings are every bit as delicious as chicken wings. They do need a little more cooking than chicken to make them tender so don't rush, take it slowly and you will be rewarded.

Finding duck wings may be a little on the tricky side, but do persevere – think of all the jointed duck breasts and legs that get sold. From a sustainability point of view it makes total sense to seek out the wings as well. Many good butchers will sell them to you if you ask; I get mine from Pipers Farm. The more we ask for them the more easily available they will become.

To prepare the duck wings, take some kitchen scissors and snip through the skin on the inside joint up to the bone. Duck skin is tougher than chicken skin and this will make the eating process slightly less messy, as the two joints will pull apart more easily. Sprinkle all over with the salt and spread out on a rack set over a large tray. Slide into the fridge, uncovered, to dry-brine for 24 hours.

When you are ready to cook, fire up your barbecue ready for direct and indirect cooking, with a fire to one side, adding a little smoking wood.

Rest the brined wings on the grill bars away from the fire and leave to smoke gently for a good couple of hours. Rotate and turn every now and then so they cook evenly. You want to see the meat starting to come away from the bones, so don't rush them. Add more fuel to keep the fire topped up, aiming for an air temperature of about 150–160°C (300–320°F). Unlike most meat cookery, a temperature probe is not necessarily that helpful for wings as the bone-to-meat ratio makes it difficult to get a true reading.

Tip the plums into a large roasting tin and add the shallots, cranberry juice, star anise, cinnamon and chilli flakes. Set the tray on the grill bars over the fire, shut the lid and roast until soft and squishy, turning once or twice. Remove and set aside to cool.

Just before the wings are done, fish out and discard the whole spices from the plums. Stir in honey to taste – a little sweetness is good but keep it fairly sharp – then scoop into a serving bowl.

Mix together the honey, sriracha and soy sauce in a bowl. Brush over the cooked wings and keep turning and basting for 10–15 minutes. Keep the wings away from the direct fire – they will burn quickly because of the sugars in the glaze.

Serve the wings hot from the grill with the relish alongside.

Serve about 8 as a snack

2kg (4½lb) duck wings
1 heaped tbsp flaked sea salt

For the plum relish

1kg (2lb 4oz) plums, quartered, stone removed
5 banana shallots, thinly sliced
200ml (generous ¾ cup) cranberry juice
4 star anise
2 cinnamon sticks, snapped in half
1–2 tsp chilli flakes
2–4 tbsp honey, or to taste

For the glaze

100ml (3½fl oz) honey
100ml (3½fl oz) sriracha sauce
75ml (3fl oz) soy sauce

TWO OFFALY SNACKS

Snacks are the backbone of any good barbecue – the sacred mantra of 'it's done when it's done' means things often take longer than you hope – and here are two good'uns. First, the paté, which can be made well ahead of time. It also freezes well, so make double and have one in the bag for another day. Secondly, the chicken heart kebabs; super-tasty spicy morsels that cook in just a few minutes.

Smoked chicken liver and garlic paté with whisky

I always recommend buying organic livers. Think about the job the liver does – metabolizing waste materials from the digestive system – and it feels important that not only is the chicken's welfare box ticked but the purity of the product is too. Smoking the livers briefly before cooking really ramps up the flavours, and yes, there is an insane amount of butter. Consider it a delicious treat.

Fire up your barbecue with the coals piled to one side, adding 2–3 good lumps of smoking wood to the fire. You want the temperature to be around 180°C (350°F), so adjust your air flow vents down to keep the heat moderate.

Set the garlic cloves on the grill bars in the centre over a medium heat. Add the chicken livers to a small fireproof pan, toss in the oil and season with salt and pepper. Set next to the garlic. Add 100g (3½oz) of the butter, the shallots and chopped bay to another pan and set onto the grill bars away from the fire so they can sauté gently. Shut the lid to trap in smoke and cook for 20 minutes.

Stir the shallots and rotate the garlic so it softens evenly. Slide the pan of chicken livers directly over the fire and pour in the whisky. Give the pan a vigorous shake from side to side over the fire; this should be enough to ignite the whisky, but if it doesn't catch you can help it along with a match. Flambé the livers over a high heat for a good 5 minutes so the alcohol evaporates. If the garlic needs a little more softening you can move it closer to the fire.

When everything is cooked, take it all inside, adding the livers, shallots and juices to a food processor. Squish the flesh out of the garlic and add this too, then whizz everything until super-smooth. Scoop into a bowl and level the top, sprinkling over the crushed peppercorns. Melt the remaining butter and pour this over the paté. Chill in the fridge, preferably overnight, before eating.

Serve with toast or crackers.

Makes a bowl, serving 4–6

4 large garlic cloves, unpeeled
250g (9oz) chicken livers, preferably organic
1 tbsp olive oil
125g (4½oz) butter
2 banana shallots, finely chopped
2 bay leaves, tough central rib removed and finely chopped
4 tbsp whisky – whatever your favourite is (you can also substitute brandy if you prefer)
1 tsp mixed peppercorns, crushed
flaked sea salt and freshly ground black pepper

Devilled chicken hearts, cashew chutney

Chicken hearts do take a little time to prep to get them ready for the grill, but even free-range organic ones are cheap as chips because they are a by-product of the chicken meat industry. So, seek out good ones and enjoy the fact you are eating more sustainably in a beak-to-wing fashion. By the way, in all honesty I'm not the biggest offal fan, but chicken hearts just taste really meaty, almost beefy. And I love them.

Sambal oelek is at the heart (excuse the pun) of this super-easy recipe. It's a fiery chilli paste from Indonesia that you can find in some supermarkets, or try Asian food shops or online. Some varieties contain extras like ginger, soy and shrimp paste, which are also delicious. If you can't find any, feel free to substitute sriracha instead.

Take the chicken hearts and slice off the top, pulling away any membranes from the outside – no need to remove the fat though. Fat is flavour after all. Cut each in half and add to a bowl as you go. Stir through the olive oil, sambal oelek, ginger, garlic and season with a little salt and pepper. Cover and slide into the fridge for a couple of hours, where the salt will get to work on a quick little dry-brining. They are so small they don't need much time compared to bigger cuts.

Thread the hearts onto small skewers – about 4–5 halves per skewer. They cook so quickly this is a rare occasion where I'd say wooden skewers or even toothpicks would be ok; they shouldn't burn too much in the time they are on the grill.

When you are ready to cook, fire up the barbecue ready for direct grilling.

Tip the cashews into a small fireproof frying pan (skillet) and set over the fire to toast. You can also make this on the hob inside while the hearts are in the fridge if you prefer. Either way, once the nuts are toasted, tip onto a board and roughly chop. Add the coconut to the pan and toast for just a minute or so – keep a beady eye on it, it can catch pretty fast. As soon as it's golden, slide the pan off the heat for a moment and add the sambal oelek, lime juice and brown sugar. Return to the heat, add the chopped cashews and stir over the heat until sticky. Transfer to a serving bowl.

To cook the skewers, set on the grill bars directly over the fire and cook for a couple of minutes each side. Remove to a plate and sprinkle over the spring onions (scallions). Serve immediately with the chutney alongside.

Makes 12 little bar snack-sized skewers

500g (1lb 2oz) chicken hearts
1 tbsp olive oil
2 tbsp sambal oelek, or to taste
30g (1oz) fresh root ginger, grated
2 garlic cloves, crushed
½ bunch of spring onions (scallions), thinly sliced
flaked sea salt and freshly ground black pepper

For the chutney
75g (3oz) cashews
2 tbsp desiccated (dried) coconut
2 tbsp sambal oelek
juice of 1 lime
1 tbsp brown sugar

Chapter 12: Leftovers – the best bits!

With barbecuing I find there are very often leftovers. It's often easier to cook a larger joint of something than a smaller one as there is less chance of it drying out and besides, this way of cooking has a spirit of generosity that means we often make a little too much to eat in one sitting. Making a second delicious meal out of a handful of leftover meat is a great way of fully honouring the animal that provided you with your food.

These are just a few of my favourite things to do with any leftovers but really, this chapter could be endless... a handful of smoky meat added to a pasta sauce, chopped up into a frittata, stirred through a risotto or fried up in a pan and stuffed into a squishy bun. I could go on and on. If all else fails, just whip up some noodles. Simply take a wok and stir-fry whatever meat you have to hand with whatever chopped veg you have to hand. Pretty much anything goes – just chuck the veg in the hot wok in the order it cooks in, starting with dense things like carrots and ending with quick things like peas. Then add seasonings to taste like soy, hot sauce, sweet chilli, garlic, grated ginger... this is exactly the sort of thing I get my kids to cook for tea when I've had enough of the day.

I tend to freeze leftover meat in portions of around 250g (9oz), ready for use another day when I want some fire-cooked goodness but can't be bothered to fire up my grill. If well wrapped to prevent 'freezer burn', leftover cooked meat will keep for 3 months or so.

Pulled pork potstickers

This is one of the things I often make with leftover pulled pork, but you could use any cooked chicken, duck or beef. Dumpling wrappers are easily found in Asian supermarkets, often in the freezer section or try online.

Make the dumpling filling by adding the cavolo nero to a bowl. Sprinkle in the salt and use your hands to massage it in and soften it. Add the pork (or other meat) along with the ginger, spring onions (scallions) and a really generous grind of black pepper and mix together well.

Sprinkle the cornflour (cornstarch) over a baking sheet. Lay a few wrappers out on the worktop and have a little dish of cold water handy. Spoon a generous teaspoon of filling into the centre of each wrapper. Slide one into your hand and, using a clean finger, dab a little water around the edge of one half. Begin to pleat and fold the un-watered side up and over the filling, pressing into the wet side to stick together. It will take a little bit of practice and your first few might look a bit rough and ready but long as the filling ends up being completely enclosed, it doesn't matter too much what they look like. Once it's all sealed together, rest crimp side up on the floured baking sheet. Repeat until you have used all the filling and wrappers.

Make the dipping sauce by stirring everything together in a bowl.

To cook the potstickers, set a large frying pan (skillet) over a medium-high heat and add a good drizzle of oil. Once hot, add a few potstickers – how many you can get in will depend on the size of your pan – and fry until the bottoms are brown and crispy. Pour in 4 tablespoons water and immediately cover with a tight-fitting lid or snugly tucked piece of foil. Steam for 3 minutes, then uncover and keep cooking for another couple of minutes until the water has totally evaporated and the bottoms are crispy. Transfer to a warm serving plate and repeat until you've cooked them all.

Serve with the dipping sauce alongside.

Pictured opposite (top).

Makes about 35–38, serving 4–6, depending what else you are eating

125g (4½oz) cavolo nero, stems removed and leaves finely chopped
a good pinch of salt
250g (9oz) pulled pork, finely chopped
25g (1oz) fresh root ginger, grated
½ bunch of spring onions (scallions), finely chopped
2 tbsp cornflour (cornstarch), for dusting
450g (1lb) packet of dumpling wrappers, defrosted if frozen
vegetable oil, for frying
freshly ground black pepper

For the dipping sauce
100ml (3½fl oz) soy sauce
2 tbsp black vinegar or rice vinegar
2 tsp sesame oil
2 garlic cloves, crushed
a dash of chilli sauce, to taste (or use a sprinkle of chilli flakes)

Chicken and mushroom steamed buns, crispy fried 'seaweed'

I used leftover roast chicken for this recipe but, once again, feel free to substitute any cooked meat you like. Baozi buns are pretty filling but utterly addictive and, while these could feed more than four, my kids devour them. They freeze brilliantly well, either steamed or un-steamed so I would even consider making a double batch if I had time and was using fresh, rather than frozen, leftovers. You can cook from frozen too, making them a very handy thing to have hanging around in the freezer.

There are myriad ways to fold these baozi buns, but this is not the book (and nor am I the cook!) to teach you how. Keep it simple to start, and do as I do: that is simply scrunching them up to seal the filling inside before cooking and eating. If you get hooked on baozi-making you'll find great resources online to help you up your folding game.

To make the dough, weigh the flours into a bowl and add the sugar, baking powder, yeast and salt and stir together. Pour in the water and mix with a metal spoon until you have a shaggy dough. Tip onto a lightly oiled work surface and knead until smooth and elastic. You can also make it in a food mixer fitted with a dough hook. Either way, transfer the smooth dough to a lightly oiled bowl, cover with a clean tea towel and set aside to prove for 1–2 hours, or until it's doubled in size.

While the dough is proving, make the filling. Take a frying pan (skillet) or wok and set it over a medium-high heat. Pour in the oil and add the mushrooms and spring onions (scallions), stir-frying for a few minutes until softening. Add the ginger and garlic and fry for another couple of minutes before adding the soy, sweet chilli and oyster sauces and a generous grind of black pepper. Scoop into a bowl, stir through the chicken and set aside to cool.

Once the dough has risen, tip it onto a lightly oiled worktop and roll into a long log. Chop into 12 evenly sized pieces – you can weigh each piece if you want to be super-accurate but it's fine if they are near enough. Roll each piece into a ball and flatten to a circle with the palm of your hand: you want the dough to be around 3–4mm (⅛in) thick and approximately 12cm (5in) in diameter. Add a tablespoon of filling to the centre of the disc and draw up the sides, pinching together like a little drawstring purse. Set on an oiled baking sheet and repeat with the rest of the dough and filling, spreading the buns out over two trays so they have a little space around them. If you can, slide into the

Makes 12, serving about 4

For the dough

500g (4 cups) strong white bread flour
250g (9oz) cornflour (cornstarch)
2 tsp caster (superfine) sugar
1½ tsp baking powder
1 tsp fast-action yeast
1 tsp flaked sea salt
450ml (scant 2 cups) warm water
a drizzle of vegetable oil

For the filling

2 tbsp vegetable oil
300g (10½oz) chestnut mushrooms, finely chopped
a bunch of spring onions (scallions), thinly sliced
50g (2oz) fresh root ginger, grated
2 garlic cloves, crushed
3 tbsp soy sauce
2 tbsp sweet chilli sauce, plus extra to serve
2 tbsp oyster sauce
250g (9oz) cooked chicken, finely diced (defrosted if frozen)
freshly ground black pepper

fridge and leave to prove for another couple of hours, or 30 minutes or so on the worktop. I find a slower prove makes for slightly more flavourful bread.

Either way, once they have had a second prove, some of the seams may have opened up a little. Give them a pinch and a twist to close back up just as you cook them.

Half-fill a wok with water and set a bamboo steamer on top. Line the base of the steamer with baking paper and prick it all over a few times so the steam can get through. Add 3–4 buns to the steamer, spacing them apart, as they will grow bigger. Cover with the lid and steam for around 12–15 minutes until they are puffy. Remove to a plate and keep warm in a very low oven while you repeat with the remaining buns.

These are fantastic, I think, served with crispy 'seaweed' – not actual seaweed but very finely shredded dark green cabbage (cavolo nero is ideal) that has been deep-fried in batches until crisp. Drain on paper towel and toss together in a bowl with a generous pinch each of salt, pepper and Chinese five-spice before serving. Around 300g (10½oz) whole greens is about the right amount to start with before shredding.

Serve with chilli sauce alongside if you like.

Pictured on page 253 (bottom).

Crispy fried duck and cavolo nero with Stilton polenta

A ridiculously simple, comforting bowlful, the kind of thing to curl up on the sofa with after a long, hard day. This is an idea to run with your own way. Use any cheese you fancy – Stilton happens to be my desert-island cheese and there is invariably some tucked into a corner of the fridge. Ditto, the meat – any leftovers would work here. You want to shred up the meat quite small and fry it up hot and fast – like a stir-fry – so you get lots of delectable crispy bits. Some mushrooms fried up with the meat wouldn't go amiss if you had any that needed using up.

Begin with the polenta. Pour the stock into a saucepan and set over a high heat to bring to the boil. Once boiling, reduce to a steady simmer and pour in the polenta, stirring constantly for around 5 minutes until it thickens to a smooth paste. Stir through the butter, cheese and a generous seasoning of salt and pepper. Keep warm over a very low heat while you fry up the duck.

Pour the oil into a large, deep frying pan (skillet) or a wok and set over a high heat. Once hot, add the duck and chilli flakes, if using, and stir-fry for a few minutes until it's starting to crisp a little. Toss in the greens and garlic, adding a splash of water so they have a little steam around them to help them soften as they cook. Season with a little salt and pepper and keep on stir-frying for another few minutes until the greens are just tender, the water evaporated and the meat crispy.

To serve, spoon the polenta into deep bowls and top with the fried duck and greens. Take somewhere cosy and eat while steaming hot.

Serves 2

2 tbsp olive oil
250g (9oz) smoked duck, shredded
½ tsp chipotle chilli flakes (optional)
150g (5½oz) cavolo nero (or spring greens), shredded
1–2 garlic cloves, sliced
flaked sea salt and freshly ground black pepper

For the polenta
600ml (2½ cups) chicken or vegetable stock
150g (5½oz) quick-cook polenta
25g (1oz) butter
120–150g (4–5oz) Stilton, crumbled

Herby lamb croquettes

With just a handful of meat and a bowl of cold mashed potato, these are a great lesson in using up a few bits and bobs to create an entirely new meal. In this recipe, I used lamb shoulder left over from the recipe on page 116, but any lamb, or indeed any other cooked meat you have, would be absolutely great too. Assuming the mashed potato and meat was seasoned well, as they are leftovers, I guess in theory you shouldn't need to add any more salt and pepper, but I do find crunchy deep-fried things benefit from rather generous seasoning so I tend to add a little extra.

Gently sweat the onion in the olive oil and chilli flakes, if using, over a low heat until soft and caramelized, a good 20 minutes, perhaps a little longer. Tip into a bowl and add the mashed potato, lamb and most of the herbs, reserving a few to garnish. Stir really well to mix evenly, adding a little salt and pepper if you like.

Line up the flour, eggs and breadcrumbs in separate bowls and have a baking tray handy to put the rolled and coated croquettes on – the rolling stage gets a bit messy so it's good to be organized and set up a little production line.

Take a tablespoon of the mixture and, using wet hands, roll into a torpedo shape. Roll in the flour then dip in the egg to coat all over and roll in the breadcrumbs. Rest on the tray and repeat until you have used all the mixture. Slide the tray into the fridge to chill for 1 hour.

While the croquettes are chilling, make the sauce by adding everything to a blender and whizzing until smooth. Taste to check the seasoning, adding a little more lemon for extra sharpness. You can also do this with a stick blender in a deep jug, or indeed by hand in a bowl with a whisk if you finely chop everything first.

When you are ready to cook, heat the oil in a deep fat fryer to 180°C (350°F). Fry the croquettes a handful at a time for 4–5 minutes until deeply golden. Drain on paper towel while you cook the rest.

Serve with the sauce alongside to dip into, perhaps with a little extra sprinkle of salt for crunch.

Makes 12–14, serving about 4 as a snack

1 onion, finely chopped
1 tbsp olive oil
a pinch of chipotle chilli flakes (optional)
450g (1lb) mashed potato
200g (7oz) cooked lamb, finely chopped
a generous handful of mixed fresh soft herbs (parsley, coriander/cilantro, chives)
2 heaped tbsp plain (all-purpose) flour
2 eggs, beaten with a pinch of salt
100g (3½oz) fresh breadcrumbs
flaked sea salt and freshly ground pepper

For the tahini sauce
100g (3½oz) tahini
a loose handful of coriander (cilantro), roughly chopped
1 garlic clove, chopped
juice of ½–1 lemon, to taste
150ml (⅔ cup) water
a pinch of sugar (optional)

Cheat's beef birria queso tacos

Quite possibly the sexiest, dirtiest thing I know to do with a bowlful of leftover barbecued beef, these tacos are fabulously messy. I used leftover roast rib of beef for this but you could use any beef you like here really, from seared steak to low and slow brisket and everything in between; the important thing is to slice it across the grain for maximum tenderness. I say 'cheat's' because a true Mexican birria is made by long, slow braising of beef, but to my mind leftover barbecue that has been touched by smoke and fire is a justifiable cheat. If you want to cheat it further, grab a pack of ready-made tortillas and use those, but making tortillas from masa dough is fun and they taste great.

Make the masa dough several hours before you want to eat; it rolls better if it's had a good rest at room temperature. Measure the masa harina into a bowl and stir through the salt. Pour in the water – using hand-hot water makes the dough more pliable – and stir until completely combined. Tip onto a clean worktop and knead for a few minutes before wrapping in baking paper and setting aside at room temperature to rest.

For the birria, pour the olive oil into a deep frying pan (skillet) and set over a low heat. Add the onion, chopped achiote, cumin seeds and chilli flakes and gently fry until the onions are really soft, around 30 minutes, stirring every now and them. Add the garlic and stir briefly before adding the beef strips, orange zest and juice. Pour in a little water to just barely cover the beef and cover with a tight-fitting lid. Simmer gently for 45–50 minutes, or until the beef is really tender. Remove the lid and turn the heat up a little and continue to cook, uncovered, for another 15–20 minutes until the sauce has really reduced down and thickly coats the meat. The oil should begin to separate on the surface.

While the meat is simmering, mix together the onions, sugar and salt with your fingers in a small bowl, massaging the onions a little to soften them. Stir through the lime juice and set aside to lightly pickle.

Once the beef is ready, turn off the heat and start to cook the tacos. Heat a chapa or large frying pan over a high heat until really hot.

Makes 8, serving around 4

For the tacos
300g (10½oz) masa harina
1 heaped tsp flaked sea salt
400ml (1¾ cups) hand-hot water
    (half cold, half boiling)

For the beef birria
2 tbsp olive oil
1 onion, chopped
35g achiote paste, finely chopped
    (see page 234)
1 tbsp cumin seeds, lightly
    crushed
1–2 tsp smoked poblano chilli
    flakes (or chipotle flakes,
    which are easier to find)
3 garlic cloves, crushed
approx. 500g (1lb 2oz) cooked
    beef, sliced across the grain
    into 1cm (½in) strips
zest and juice of 1 orange
flaked sea salt and freshly ground
    black pepper

Continued overleaf…

Cut the masa dough into 8 equal-sized pieces, rolling each into a ball. If you have one, use a taco press lined with a sheet of plastic or greaseproof paper to stop the tacos sticking. Place a ball of dough into the centre and close the press to flatten out into a disc of around 3mm (⅛in) thick. You can also roll between two squares of greaseproof paper, using a rolling pin.

Lift the taco onto the hot chapa – they are a little fragile, so I find it easier to peel back one side of the plastic or greaseproof and invert it onto the chapa before peeling back and removing the second sheet. With practice you will work out your own system! Cook for a minute or two on one side then flip over and cook on the other side – they are done when you see a few little charred spots appearing. Wrap the cooked taco in a clean tea towel, where it will steam quietly to itself and stay nice and flexible. Repeat with the other balls of masa. Once you get into a rhythm you may be able to press and cook several at once, depending on the size of your chapa.

Once all the tacos are cooked, take one and dip it into the oily juices on top of the birria. Set, dipped side down, back onto the chapa. Take a good spoon of birria and dollop it onto one half of the taco. Sprinkle over some cheese, a few of the pickled onions and a little coriander (cilantro). Fold up the other half over the top so you have a half-moon shape and fry for a couple of minutes on each side until the taco is crisp and the cheese is oozing. Repeat with the other tacos – again, once you get into a rhythm here you will be able to fry a few at once.

Serve hot with plenty of napkins, taking a little care of the molten cheese as you munch.

For the pickled onions
1 red onion, thinly sliced
1 heaped tsp caster (superfine) sugar
a good pinch of salt
juice 1 lime

200g (7oz) Cheddar (or Monterey Jack if you can get it), grated
a little chopped coriander (cilantro)

Stock, the backbone of good cooking

Stocks are the ultimate way of making the most of the animal you are eating, and form the basis of many a recipe. There's so much flavour to be found in bones, carcasses and scraps. Not restricted to leftovers post cooking – raw bones from butchering and jointing meat make excellent stocks too. There is no recipe here, just a few thoughts on good stock making.

The bones
- Just add the cooked bones, skin and fat to the biggest pan you have. A big stock pot or jam pan is ideal.
- Raw poultry bones can be treated like cooked, just chuck 'em in the pan.
- Raw red meat bones benefit from a roast (or even a little smoke in a fairly hot barbecue).
- Fat is flavour, but go easy on adding in excess as it can make your stock cloudy.
- Bones freeze well so if you don't feel like making stock or only have a few bones from filleting a handful of chicken thighs, just bag up and freeze for another day. If well wrapped they should keep for 3 months.

The veg
- Always add an onion or two, quartered through the root and unpeeled – leaving the skin on will add a lovely golden colour.
- Carrot and celery are both great stock veg.
- Avoid anything starchy like potatoes.

The herbs and spices
- Add parsley in abundance, stalks and all.
- A few bay leaves are good but add other woody herbs (rosemary, sage, thyme) in moderation as they are quite strong and can be overpowering.
- I always add a tablespoon of whole black peppercorns, and if I want an Asian slant I might add a little cinnamon and star anise too, but generally I keep the spicing simple – you don't necessarily know when or in what the stock will be used.

The cooking
- Once you have everything in the pot, cover with just enough cold water to submerge the lot.
- Set over a medium heat and bring up to the boil. Once boiling reduce the heat to as low as possible, cover with a tight-fitting lid and simmer very gently for a good few hours.
- Or do as I do and turn on your oven to as low as it goes – 100°C (210°F) ideally – and slide the pot in overnight for a very gentle braise.
- The lower temperature you cook the stock, the clearer it will be.
- Once cooked, set a colander over a large bowl and pour the stock through, discarding the solids.
- Leave to go cold, then portion up into 500ml (2 cup) bags ready for freezing. You can store in the fridge too, if you're going to use within 3 days.

Index

Good Meat Suppliers

These are the UK suppliers that I know and love:

Cabrito Goat
The first UK farmer raising kid goat meat borne to dairy goats, online.
@cabritogoatmeat / cabrito.co.uk

Coombe Farm Organic
Mixed meat farm in Somerset, slow growing organic meat, online.
@coombefarmorg

Fosse Meadows
High-welfare poultry, great online store.
@fosse_meadows / fossemeadows.com

Gothelney Farm
Wonderful pork from forage-fed pigs.
@gothelneyfarmer / gothelneyfarmer.co.uk

Grassfruits
Forest-raised pork, pasture-raised chicken, small-scale and exceptional quality and provenance, online.
@grassfruits / grassfruits.farm

Hinton Harvest
Free range chicken, turkey and guinea fowl reared on a small agroforestry farm.
hintonharvest.co.uk / @hintonharvest

Meatmatters
Olly 'the beefmaster' Woolnough, I know of no better beef, online.
@meatmattersltd / meatmattersltd.co.uk

New MacDonalds Farm
Regenerative farm, pasture-reared chicken, ex-dairy cows, selling directly from the farm shop near Bath or search them up via Farmdrop.
@newmacdonaldsfarm

Peter Hannan
A total meat master supplying a lot of high end restaurants but with some online sales.
@meatpeter / hannanmeats.com

Philip Warren Butchers
Traditional Cornish butchers and farmers who sell online. Have a lot of chef fans, online and shop in Cornwall.
@philipwarrenbutchers / philipwarrenbutchers.co.uk

Pipers Farm
All sorts of excellently reared, properly free-range meat online.
@pipersfarm / pipersfarm.com

Strawberry Fields Farm
Farmer Sarah Crow produces amazing small-scale lamb, beef and pork from the farm gate in Shropshire.
@strawberryfieldsfarm

Surrey Hills Butcher
Brilliant meat with brilliant provenance, only in shop.
@surreyhillsbutchers / surreyhillsbutchers.com

Swaledale Butchers
Yorkshire-based online butchers specializing in slow-grown rare breeds.
@swaledalebutchers / swaledale.co.uk

The Native Butcher
Traditional and native breed meat boxes.
@thenativebutcher / thenativebutcher.co.uk

The New Meat project
Environmentally conscious free-range and grass-fed meat.
@thenewmeatproject / thenewmeatproject.com

Turner and George
All-round butcher, excellent ethically sourced meat, online and shops in London.
@turnerandgeorge / turnerandgeorge.co.uk

Thank You

These are some of the places that my lovely followers on Instagram have recommended they love. One day I will get around to trying them all! I have included their Instagram tags for you to have an online rummage:

@thedecentcompany, @janesfarmshop, @orieljones, @paleyfarm, @kneepwildrangemeat, @stoneleighfamilybutchers, @thebutcherye1, @waghornesbutchers, @islefwightmeat, @lakelanddexter, @always.grazing, @thehornedbeefcompany, @newlynsfarm, @thelittlefarmfridge, @homagetothebovine, @trewayfarm, @hartlyfarm, @hgwalter, @farmisonuk, @westcountrypremiumvenison, @portway_farm_shop, @jameswhelanbutchers, @higgins_butchers, @wildbynaturellp, @daylesfordfarm, @villagebutchers, @fieldandflower, @appletonbeef, @hogget_an_boar_butchery, @welshmangalitzamangalitsa, @tuckersbutchers, @mr_txuleta, @thomas.joseph.butchery, @hixsonmeatldn, @lyons_hill_farm, @artisanbutcher, @redhill_farm_freerangepork, @butcheryatbowhouse, @goldenturkeyfarmers, @sykeshousefarm, @stonebridge_cottage_farm, @perry_wood_farm, @alternativemeats, @hintonharvest, @shutelakelamb, @thestorypig, @direct.meats, @tangwholesalemeats, @lakelanddexter, @newfields_belties, @roast.mutton, @greatberwickorganics, @littlewoodsbutchers, @bulstonesprings, @naturalbranscombe, @harrietheathcoate, @heritagegraziers, @sheepdrove, @dingleydellpork, @crownandqueue, @thegoodsshedbutchery, @cornishduck, @ardgaygame, @blocknbttle, @salterandking, @phillipwarrenbutchers

To all the farmers and butchers who are slogging so hard to make the meat-producing business better for people and planet. I spoke to very many of you, and I thank and respect you hugely.

Big thanks to my favourite charcoal makers: Chops, the nicest and most hairy of fire starters, and Matt, one of the wisest owls I ever did meet, you inspire me to burn better every day. My two favourite Americans: Christian, thanks for the chats and the laughs, and Jeremy, I love your support in cross-pond translations and other matters. So many fiery thanks: Andy and Donna, two of the hardest working and lovely people in fire, Julian, for sometimes putting up with my mess, Henry, Dan, Joe, Si and Ruben for grafting with me.

The Fam: Rob, Izaac and Eve, thanks for being my everything. I love you, nuff said.

And the 'gram; #TeamFire on Instagram, all your questions and comments fire up my brain and spur me on, for which (mostly, on most days) I thank you greatly.

Huge thanks to all at Quadrille who've made this book both beautiful and useful, and to Jason Ingram, your photos never fail to bring my work to life. Martine, at Sauce Management, thanks for always being at the end of the line.

And if you are holding this book in your hands, thanks so much for your support of my work. I hope I've fired you up to get cracking. Now, go and light that fire... and make it a good 'un.

Publishing Director Sarah Lavelle
Senior Commissioning Editor Céline Hughes
Junior Commissioning Editor Harriet Webster
Copy Editor Clare Sayer
Designer Alicia House
Cover Illustration Ellie Foreman-Peck
Photographer Jason Ingram
Food Styling Genevieve Taylor
Prop Styling Jaine Bevan
Head of Production Stephen Lang
Production Controller Nikolaus Ginelli

First published in 2022 by Quadrille,
an imprint of Hardie Grant Publishing

Quadrille
52–54 Southwark Street
London SE1 1UN
quadrille.com

Cataloguing in Publication Data: a catalogue record for
this book is available from the British Library.

ISBN: 978 1 78713 745 5

Printed in China

Live-fire and BBQ expert Genevieve Taylor is the author of twelve books including *The Ultimate Wood-Fired Oven Cookbook*, *Charred* and *Foolproof BBQ*. She runs the Bristol Fire School and demonstrates live-fire cookery at food festivals all over the UK. She has presented Radio 4's *The Food Programme* and regularly contributes to the national press on all things barbecue.